Choice of Law for American Courts

Recent Titles in
Contributions in Legal Studies

Law and the Arts
Susan Tiefenbrun, editor

Contract Law and Morality
Henry Mather

The Appearance of Equality: Racial Gerrymandering, Redistricting, and the Supreme Court
Christopher M. Burke

Religion, Law, and the Land
Brian Edward Brown

The Supreme Court's Retreat from Reconstruction: A Distortion of Constitutional Jurisprudence
Frank J. Scaturro

Respecting State Courts: The Inevitability of Judicial Federalism
Michael E. Solimine and James L. Walker

Basic Principles of Property Law: A Comparative Legal and Economic Introduction
Ugo Mattei

Inherent Rights, the Written Constitution, and Popular Sovereignty: The Founders' Understanding
Thomas B. McAffee

Constitutional Structure and Purposes: Critical Commentary
Michael Conant

Constitutional Interpretation: Illusion and Reality
Jeffrey M. Shaman

Prisoners' Rights: The Supreme Court and Evolving Standards of Decency
John A. Fliter

The Four Faces of Affirmative Action: Fundamental Answers and Actions
W. Robert Gray

Choice of Law for American Courts

A Multilateralist Method

Edwin Scott Fruehwald

Contributions in Legal Studies, Number 100

GREENWOOD PRESS
Westport, Connecticut • London

Library of Congress Cataloging-in-Publication Data

Fruehwald, Edwin Scott, 1955–
Choice of law for American courts : a multilateralist method / Edwin Scott Fruehwald.
p. cm.—(Contributions in legal studies, ISSN 0147–1074 ; no. 100)
Includes bibliographical references and index.
ISBN 0–313–31753–4 (alk. paper)
1. Conflict of laws—United States—States. I. Title. II. Series.
KF417.F78 2001
340.9'0973—dc21 00–049085

British Library Cataloguing in Publication Data is available.

Library of Congress Catalog Card Number: 00–049085
ISBN: 0–313–31753–4
ISSN: 0147–1074

First published in 2001

Greenwood Press, 88 Post Road West, Westport, CT 06881
An imprint of Greenwood Publishing Group, Inc.
www.greenwood.com

Printed in the United States of America

The paper used in this book complies with the Permanent Paper Standard issued by the National Information Standards Organization (Z39.48–1984).

10 9 8 7 6 5 4 3 2 1

Copyright Acknowledgments

The author and publisher gratefully acknowledge permission for use of the following material:
Scott Fruehwald, *A Multilateralist Method of Choice of Law*, 85 KY.L.J. 347 (1996–97).
Scott Fruehwald, *Constitutional Constraints on State Choice of Law*, 24 U. DAYTON L. REV. 39 (1998).

Contents

Acknowledgments

The completion of this study brings with it the pleasure of being able to acknowledge those who aided in its writing. I would like to thank those who commented on this manuscript or my ideas on choice of law in previous articles, including Graham Lilly, George Rutherglen, Laurens Walker, John Noyes, Edward Eberle, and Lisa Kolb. I would also like to thank the staffs of the libraries of the Roger Williams University School of Law and the University of Alabama School of Law in helping me obtain materials.

Introduction

Modern choice of law lies somewhere between disarray and chaos. Even as early as 1953 William L. Prosser wrote, "The realm of the conflict of laws is a dismal swamp, filled with quacking quagmires, and inhibited by learned but eccentric professors who theorize about mysterious matters in a strange and incomprehensible jargon. The ordinary court, or lawyer, is quite lost when engulfed and entangled in it."[1] Similarly, in 1975, a federal judge declared, "The law on 'choice of law' in the various states and in the federal courts is a veritable jungle, which, if the law can be found out, leads not to a 'rule of action' but a reign of chaos."[2] More recently, Professor Perry Dane called modern conflicts, "the law's psychiatric ward."[3]

This disorder in choice of law has resulted in state courts employing four different choice of law approaches with numerous material variations.[4] In addition, some states adopt different choice of law methods for different substantive areas or even, occasionally, in the same area.[5] Conflicts scholars have added to this confusion by advocating nearly as many choice of law methods as there are conflicts scholars.

This study will argue that the dismal swamp in modern choice of law is mainly due to a shift from a multilateralist approach to choice of law to a unilateralist one. This change, which began in the 1920s, has registered in both state choice of law methods and in constitutional constraints on choice of law.[6] The result is that many jurisdictions have abandoned any attempt to choose the law of the most appropriate jurisdiction—that is, the jurisdiction with the closest ties to the litigation. Instead, courts often apply their own law, even when their jurisdiction has only a tenuous connection to the controversy.

Choice of law methods fall into three categories: (1) the unilateralist approach,

(2) the multilateralist approach, and (3) the substantive, or better rule, approach.[7] A unilateralist approach examines each law's scope (whether the lawmaker intended the law to apply to the facts or whether a state has an interest in employing its law, depending on the particular method).[8] If a law's scope encompasses the controversy, a court can adopt that law, regardless of whether another state's law has a greater claim to application. In other words, once a court has determined which states' laws might govern a case, a court can legitimately adopt any of those laws. Thus, under unilateralist approaches, courts can often properly adopt the law of more than one jurisdiction (concurrent legislative jurisdiction) because more than one lawmaker has enacted a law that applies to the situation.[9] However, unilateralist approaches usually result in the choice of forum law. For example, under governmental interest analysis, a court determines whether more than one state has an interest in having its law govern, and, if more than one state has such an interest, the court adopts forum law.[10] Use of forum law as the deciding factor is not intended to determine the most appropriate legal system; rather, it is a way of choosing between two or more (supposedly) equally legitimate state laws.

On the other hand, multilateralism tries to connect the controversy with the most appropriate legal system.[11] As Professor Gene R. Shreve has written, "To the multilateralist judge, the possible sources of chosen law are sovereigns, or jurisdictions, that make up a kind of legal community."[12] Under multilateralism, "a decision to assign a problem to one state's jurisdiction is simultaneously a decision not to assign it to the other."[13] In other words, under multilateralism, a court can properly adopt the law of only one jurisdiction in most cases (exclusive legislative jurisdiction). Furthermore, as Professor Dirk H. Bliesener has pointed out, a multilateralist method exhibits two main features: (1) "that choice of law may not reflect any unjustified preferences" and (2) that "the result of a choice-of-law decision be foreseeable by the parties to the controversy."[14]

For example, one multilateralist method chooses the law of the most appropriate jurisdiction by adopting the law of the state where the last act occurred, based on the assumption that the last act is the most important criterion in establishing the most appropriate legal system.[15] This method reflects no unjustifiable preferences since it is content and forum neutral, and, because it employs one uniform choice of law criterion, choice of law under the method is foreseeable.[16]

Finally, several choice of law scholars have advocated a substantive or better rule approach to choice of law, some adopting it as the only criterion,[17] others as one of several factors.[18] These scholars believe that choice of law should transcend state boundaries and do "justice" in each individual case,[19] on the belief "that there is a preferable result for a particular type of case (*e.g.*, plaintiffs should win products liability cases)."[20] For example, if two states' laws might be applied in a torts case—one that would bar recovery under contributory negligence and another that would allow partial recovery under comparative negligence, the court should adopt the comparative negligence rule because it is "the most just and modern."[21]

A multilateralist approach to choice of law is the best option for a group of states united under a federal government and constitution, such as the United

States.[22] Such a political structure requires that jurisdictions protect the rights of individuals in choice of law and that states respect other states' sovereignty.[23] This book will show that a multilateralist approach to choice of law can satisfy these requirements, whereas unilaterlist and substantive approaches cannot.

Scholars have also analyzed choice of law methods as consequentialist or deontological.[24] In a consequentialist system, "alternative courses of action are evaluated according to the desirability of their consequences."[25] Consequentialism focuses on policy and social goals.[26] It is most often associated with utilitarianism—the belief "that human actions and practices should be evaluated ultimately in terms of their tendencies to advance the general welfare or social good."[27] A consequentialist approach to conflicts considers a law's content and analyzes which state's law produces the better result for society at large.

On the other hand, a deontological system "is any system which does not appeal to the consequences of our actions, but which appeals to conformity with certain rules of duty."[28] Deontology emphasizes principles and personal rights.[29] It is frequently associated with Kantianism—"the view that the rational choice . . . is always the choice that respects the rights of autonomous persons freely to determine their own destinies, even if this respect is bought at the cost of a loss of happiness or well-being."[30] A deontological approach to conflicts emphasizes the litigants' preexisting rights. It downplays society's interest in the outcome, and it is often content neutral.

A multilateralist choice of law method is usually deontological because it looks for the most appropriate legal system and generally does not consider the social effects of choice of law—at least in the short term.[31] Substantive approaches are consequentialist because they emphasis social policies and goals and search for the best outcome, usually focusing on the case at hand. Unilaterlist systems can be either consequentialist or deontological, depending on what factors the method uses. However, modern unilateralist methods tend to be consequentialist because they further state policies.

Choice of law should be deontological.[32] Although conseqentialism is important in a legal system, substantive choices should be made at the substantive level, not the choice of law level. Choice of law should be both content and forum neutral.

A final way to evaluate a conflicts method is to inquire whether it employs territory—the location of events within political boundaries—or domicile—a person's connection to a state or nation—as the main connecting factor. Although most choice of law systems focus on one factor, a choice of law method should use both territory and domicile in choosing law without a preconceived notion of which is the more important. However, as the analyses of examples later in this book demonstrate, territory tends to be the most important choice of law connection in most cases.

Deciding which choice of law type (unilateralist, multilateralist, or substantive) to use and what other choice of law criteria to employ depends on normative and constitutional considerations. This book's method is based on two background criteria, which are both normative and constitutional: (1) a choice of law method must respect individual rights and (2) a choice of law method must value the horizontal structural lines that are part of our federal union and constitution—that is, state sovereignty.

Choice of law must respect individual rights on both normative and constitutional grounds. The normative aspect derives from the Kantian respect for the individual, which I mentioned above.[33] What makes humans morally relevant objects under Kantianism is "our status as free and autonomous creatures with the capacity to make choices that are rational in a special sense."[34] Thus, "[f]or an autonomous person to suppress one of his desires in order to satisfy his other desires is one thing; for a group of autonomous persons to suppress another autonomous person so that they can get their desires satisfied at his expense is something quite different."[35] Under Kantianism, people have the right to be treated as ends themselves and not as a means to an end.[36] In other words, "[a]ll rational persons have a right not to be used without their consent even for the benefit of others."[37]

Robinson v. California illustrates a Kantian approach to law.[38] In *Robinson*, a California court had convicted a person for being a drug addict. The Supreme Court ruled this conviction unconstitutional because drug addiction "is apparently an illness which may be contracted innocently or voluntarily."[39] Thus, convicting a person for being a drug addict is cruel and unusual punishment under the Eighth and Fourteenth Amendments.[40]

This holding demonstrates a Kantian respect for the individual—not using the individual as a means to an end. Because, as the Court viewed it, drug addiction is a disease, the addict does not deserve punishment (retribution). On the other hand, if the Court had adopted a utilitarian approach, it could have upheld the conviction: California could have imprisoned the defendant for the greater good—keeping an addict off the streets or providing general deterrence.

In addition to the normative requirement that choice of law respect individual rights, the due process clause of the Fourteenth Amendment limits a state's ability to impose its law on an individual because the clause protects individual liberty and regulates the relationship of the state and the individual. Chapter 3 discusses due process constraints on state choice of law in depth.

Respect for individual rights is not the only consideration in developing a choice of law system. Humans have traditionally banded together for their mutual benefit and protection, creating many kinds of governmental arrangements. In this country, we have adopted a federal union, which, as it has evolved, consists of a strong federal government with separate states that retain a great deal of autonomy. On a normative level, choice of law should respect this state autonomy.

Respect for state autonomy is required by the structural lines set forth in the United States Constitution, particularly those in the full faith and credit clause.[41] Respecting these structural lines is especially important in light of the new judicial activism that has appeared in Supreme Court and other federal decisions in recent years. As Judge Harvie Wilkinson has proclaimed, our constitutional jurisprudence is in a new period of judicial activism—one in which judges are structural referees.[42] The hallmark of this new judicial activism "is an interest in reviving the structural guarantees of dual sovereignty [vertical federalism]."[43] Judge Wilkinson has declared, "Taken as a whole, the decisions preserve Congress as an institution of broad but enumerated powers, and the states as entities having residual sovereign rights."[44]

Unlike the other two periods of judicial activism in this century,[45] the new judicial activism is substantively neutral: "The cases of the present era cannot be seen as single-mindedly promoting the interests of a particular constituency."[46] Judge Wilkinson has added that "[a]s a matter of oxen, the gored are determined by infringements upon our federal system, not by judicial disdain for enacted policies."[47] Thus, "[i]n the present period preservation of federalism values—not the maintenance of *laissez faire*—is the binding principle."[48]

Also, unlike the two earlier periods of judicial activism that "attempted to remove the subject matter of those cases from political debates altogether, . . . the present jurisprudence of federalism is purely allocative, standing for the simple proposition that the Constitution does not cast states as mere marionettes of the central government."[49] In other words, "[t]his jurisprudence removes no substantive decision from the stage of political debate."[50] Thus:

> States remain free after [*New York v. United States*][51] to reach regional solutions to hazardous waste problems, after [*United States v. Lopez*][52] to criminalize the act of bringing a firearm within a school zone, after [*Printz v. United States*][53] voluntarily to cooperate with federal law enforcement efforts, and after today's decision [*Brzonkala v. Virginia Polytechnic Institute*][54] to provide civil remedies to women who are battered or raped. No court blocks the path of legislative initiative in any of these substantive areas.[55]

The new judicial activism that Judge Wilkinson has discerned in recent cases on vertical federalism also applies to other areas where the Constitution sets structural lines, including horizontal federalism—the relation of the states. If the Court is going to give the states more authority, it also needs to protect a state's sovereignty from overreaching by other states. Choice of law affects state sovereignty. When a judge makes a choice of law decision, that judge is "polic[ing] the structural lines inherent"[56] in the Constitution's provisions concerning the relations of the states.

The Supreme Court has recently recognized the importance of the structural lines of horizontal federalism in *BMW of North America v. Gore*.[57] In this case, the Supreme Court struck down an Alabama trial court's punitive damages award on due process grounds. Part of the constitutional problem was that Alabama had calculated the award based on the defendant's conduct in other states, including states in which its conduct was legal. In doing so, Alabama had failed to recognize "the need to respect the interests of other States."[58] The Court declared, "It follows from these principles of state sovereignty and comity that a state may not impose economic sanctions on violators of laws with the intent of changing the tortfessors' lawful conduct in other States."[59]

In sum, the dismal swap that currently exists in choice of law can be drained by a choice of law method that respects individual rights and state sovereignty. I believe that a choice of law method that meets these requirements must be multilateralist and deontological. It must also look at all types of connections rather than limiting the inquiry to one factor such as domicile.

Chapter 1 of this book surveys choice of law in the twentieth century and examines the change from a uniform multilateralist system of choice of law to the use of several approaches, including unilateralist, multilateralist, and substantive systems. Chapter 2 sets forth my normative criteria for choice of law and tests existing choice of law methods against these criteria. Chapter 3 examines constitutional constraints on choice of law methods. Chapter 4 evaluates other choice of law methods. Chapter 5 presents my multilateralist choice of law method, and Chapter 6 applies the method to various choice of law problems. Finally, Chapter 7 discusses choice of law in connection with mass torts, class actions, and multidistrict litigation.

NOTES

1. William L. Prosser, *Interstate Publication*, 51 MICH. L. REV. 959, 971 (1952–53).

2. *In re* Paris Air Crash of March 3, 1974, 399 F. Supp. 732, 739 (C.D. Cal. 1975).

3. Perry Dane, *Conflict of Laws,* in A COMPANION TO PHILOSOPHY OF LAW AND LEGAL THEORY 209 (1996).

4. These methods are (1) the *First Restatement*'s vested rights approach, (2) the *Second Restatement*'s most significant relationship test, (3) Brainerd Currie's governmental interest analysis, and (4) the better rule approach. For a list of methods used by the states, *see* Symeon C. Symeonides, *Choice of Law in American Courts in 1997*, 46 AM. J. COMP. L. 233, 266 (1998). Chapter 1 discusses these approaches in detail, and it lists the states' approaches to torts and contracts at the end of the chapter.

5. *E.g.*, Melville v. American Home Assurance Co., 443 F. Supp. 1064, 1094 (E.D. Pa. 1977), *rev'd*, 584 F.2d 1306 (3d Cir. 1978) ("Thus it seems fair to conclude that Pennsylvania has not 'a' system of choice of law but two if not three competing systems, each claiming the same legal territory and leading to enormous confusion.").

6. Chapter 1 examines the history of choice of law and modern choice of law methods.

7. FRIEDRICH K. JUENGER, CHOICE OF LAW AND MULTISTATE JUSTICE 45–46 (1993). Professor Juenger presents a historical discussion of these categories in the above. *Id.* at 6–46.

8. William S. Dodge, *Extraterritoriality and Conflict of Laws Theory: An Argument for Judicial Unilateralism*, 39 HARV. INT. L.J. 101, 107 (1998); LEA BRILMAYER, CONFLICT OF LAWS 17–19 (2d ed. 1995); Gene R. Shreve, *Choice of Law and the Forgiving Constitution*, 71 IND. L.J. 271, 284 (1996); Dirk H. Bliesener, *Fairness and Choice of Law: A Critique of the Political Rights-Based Approach to the Conflict of Laws*, 42 AM. J. COMP. L. 687, 704 (1994).

9. Dodge, *supra* note 8, at 107.

10. BRAINERD CURRIE, SELECTED ESSAYS ON THE CONFLICT OF LAWS 183–84 (1963). Chapter 1 discusses governmental interest analysis in greater detail.

11. Dodge, *supra* note 8, at 107–8; Bliesener, *supra* note 8, at 705; BRILMAYER, *supra* note 8, at 18.

12. Shreve, *supra* note 8, at 282.

13. BRILMAYER, *supra* note 8, at 18.

14. Bliesener, *supra* note 8, at 708.

15. RESTATEMENT OF THE LAW OF CONFLICT OF LAWS § 332, 377 (1934); *see also* 2 JOSEPH BEALE, A TREATISE ON THE CONFLICT OF LAWS § 378.2, at 1289–90 (1935). Chapter 1 discusses this method in detail.

16. As the discussion of Beale's method in Chapter 2 observes, other aspects of his system can affect these factors.

17. *E.g.*, JUENGER, *supra* note 7; Patrick J. Borchers, *The Origins of Diversity Jurisdiction, the Rise of Legal Positivism, and a Brave New World for Erie and Klaxon*, 72 TEX. L. REV. 79 (1993).

18. ROBERT A. LEFLAR, AMERICAN CONFLICTS LAW 195 (3d ed. 1977).

19. Juenger, *supra* note 7, at 236.

20. Shreve, *supra* note 8, at 282.

21. Borchers, *supra* note 17, at 129.

22. A choice of law method that works well in an international setting may not be the best method for a group of states united under a federal government and constitution. As David Cavers has noted, "Though our nation is divided into fifty-one separate legal systems, our people act most the time as if they lived in a single one. In contrast, when people or their transactions cross national border lines, I suspect the legal significance of the action is much more likely to be observed." DAVID CAVERS, THE CHOICE-OF-PROCESS 119 (1965).

23. I develop these ideas more fully throughout this book.

24. These are not additional categories to the three categories mentioned above but rather characteristics that a choice of law method might exhibit.

25. BRILMAYER, *supra* note 8, at 225.

26. *Id.* at 229.

27. JEFFRIE G. MURPHY & JULES L. COLEMAN, PHILOSOPHY OF LAW: AN INTRODUCTION TO JURISPRUDENCE 72 (1990).

28. J. J. C. Smart & Bernard Williams, *An Outline of a System of Utilitarian Ethics* in UTILITARIANISM: FOR AND AGAINST 5 (1973).

29. BRILMAYER, *supra* note 8, at 229.

30. MURPHY & COLEMAN, *supra* note 27, at 71.

31. A notable exception is Professor Baxter's comparative impairment approach, which is examined in Chapter 1.

32. Chapter 1 develops these ideas further.

33. Modern legal scholars who adopt a Kantian attitude include John Rawls and Ronald Dworkin. *See* JOHN RAWLS, A THEORY OF JUSTICE (1971); RONALD DWORKIN, TAKING RIGHTS SERIOUSLY (1978); RONALD DWORKIN, LAW'S EMPIRE (1986).

34. MURPHY & COLEMAN, *supra* note 27, at 77.

35. *Id.* at 77; *see also* RAWLS, *supra* note 33, at 4 ("[I]n a just society the liberties of equal citizenship are taken as settled; the rights secured by justice are not subject to political bargaining or the calculus of social interests." *Id.* at 4.).

36. MURPHY & COLEMAN, *supra* note 27, at 79.

37. *Id.*; *see also* RAWLS, *supra* note 33, at 3–4.

38. 370 U.S. 660 (1962).

39. *Id.* at 667.

40. *Id.* at 666–67.

41. Chapter 3 examines these structural lines in depth.

42. Brzonkala v. Virginia Polytechnic Institute, 169 F.3d 820, 890–96 (4th Cir. 1999) (Wilkinson, J., concurring), *aff'd sub nom.* United States v. Morrison, 120 S.Ct. 1740 (2000); *see also* Scott Fruehwald, *If Men Were Angels: The New Judicial Activism in Theory and Practice*, 83 MARQ. L. REV. 435 (1999).

43. *Brzonkala*, 169 F.3d at 893.

44. *Id.*

45. The other two periods were the "Lochner" era at the beginning of the century in which courts struck down progressive legislation on substantive due process grounds ("liberty of contract") and commerce clause grounds, and the Warren Court–early Burger Court era in which the Court found "new substantive rights in the constitution and down played that document's structural mandates." *Id.* at 890–92.

46. *Id.* at 893.

47. *Id.* at 894.

48. *Id.*

49. *Id.* at 895.

50. *Id.*

51. 505 U.S. 144 (1992).

52. 514 U.S. 549 (1995).

53. 521 U.S. 898 (1997).

54. 169 F.3d at 820.

55. *Id.*

56. *Id.*

57. 517 U.S. 559 (1996). Chapter 3 analyzes this case in greater depth.

58. *Id.* at 571.

59. *Id.* at 572.

Chapter 1

Choice of Law in the Twentieth Century

Choice of law in the early twentieth century consisted of a uniform multilateralist method, most often associated with Professor Joseph Beale. In addition, Supreme Court opinions from that time virtually constitutionalized Beale's system. In the 1920s and 1930s, realist scholars harshly criticized Beale's method, and they suggested unilateralist and substantive approaches to choice of law. Similarly, in the 1930s, Justice Harlan Fiske Stone's opinions on constitutional constraints on choice of law rejected multilateralist constraints in favor of unilaterlist ones, which allowed greater experimentation in conflicts methods. In the 1950s, 1960s, and 1970s, scholars and courts advocated competing conflicts approaches, some of which were unilateralist, some multilateralist, and others substantive. These methods remain today, although younger scholars have advanced additional approaches, many of which are rights based. Meanwhile, the Supreme Court has placed few constitutional constraints on choice of law, permitting the many contemporary systems to persist, despite the great confusion mentioned in the introduction.

A. THE VESTED RIGHTS APPROACH TO CHOICE OF LAW

1. Joesph Beale's Multilateralist, Territorialist Choice of Law Method

Joseph Beale's multilateralist, territorialist choice of law method, often called "vested rights," dominated conflicts during the first third of the twentieth century.[1] Beale derived his territorialism from Justice Joseph Story, who had produced the most important nineteenth-century American treatise on choice of law. Justice Story had written that "every nation possesses an exclusive sovereignty and jurisdiction within its own territory."[2] Thus, it "would be wholly incompatible with the equality and exclusiveness of the sovereignty of any nation, that other nations should be at liberty to regulate either persons or things within its territories."[3]

Beale's method also reflected the dominant legal scholarship of his time—Classical Legal Thought.[4] Classical Legal Thought emerged after the Civil War and represented an attempt to formulate an autonomous legal culture that could deal with the enormous economic and social changes that were occurring at that time.[5] Classical Legal Thought lasted from approximately 1870 until the 1930s. Major proponents of this school included Christopher Columbus Langdell, Samuel Williston, and Beale.

Classical Legal scholars considered law a science.[6] Modern scholars have labeled their mode of thinking "conceptualistic" or "formalistic."[7] Professor G. Edward White has written,

> Obsession with ineluctable rules, principles, and axioms became characteristic of the academic disciplines of the time. By applying a curious combination of spiritualism and Darwinism, economists, natural scientists, and sociologists discovered universal absolutes that governed their fields . . . . One had only to discover these truths: political, economic, sociological, and biological theories flowed from these discoveries.
>
> Jurisprudence was likewise attracted to the universal principle. Judges began their decisions by making verbal distinctions, defining concepts in useful ways. They then pronounced their definitions as axiomatic. From then on it was a rush downward to the result: the axiom was applied to the facts of the case, and certain things "invariably" followed.[8]

Related to this syllogistic thinking was the nineteenth-century preoccupation with categories.[9] Professor White has declared that "[f]or late nineteenth-century scientists, the primary end of legal scholarship was the extraction and classification of governing principles in an area of law."[10] These thinkers used bright-line distinctions rather than differences of degree.[11] The key was to place a dispute in the correct category; once the dispute was in the correct category, the result became clear.

Also part of Classical Legal Thought was an objective approach to law.[12] Thinkers adopted objective theories to create uniformity.[13] For example, courts examined questions of contract formation not based on the parties' subjective intent, but on objective factors.[14]

Professor Thomas C. Grey has aptly described the approach taken by Harvard's influential law school dean, Christopher Columbus Langdell: "Langdell believed that through scientific methods lawyers could derive correct legal judgments from a few fundamental principles and concepts, which it was the task of scholar-scientists like himself to discover."[15]

Professor Elizabeth Mensch has demonstrated how this process worked in contracts:

> Williston's monumental treatise on contracts assumed that from the general principle of free contract one could derive the few central doctrines around which the treatise was organized—offer and acceptance, consideration, excuse, etc.—and from the logic of these central doctrines one could derive all the specific rules that made up the law of contracts. Those rules could then be applied, rigidly and formally, to *any* particular social context; in fact, failure to do so would be evidence of judicial irrationality and irresponsibility.[16]

Justice Stephen Johnson Field's opinion on personal jurisdiction in *Pennoyer v. Neff* illustrates how Classical Legal Thought worked.[17] Field started with two universal principles:

1. One of these principles is that every State possesses exclusive jurisdiction and sovereignty over persons and property within its territory.
2. The other principle of public law follows from the one mentioned; that is, that no state can exercise direct jurisdiction and authority over persons or property without its territory.[18]

From these principles, Field deduced that when jurisdiction is *in personam* that "the tribunals of one State cannot run into another State, and summon parties there domiciled to leave its territory and to respond to proceedings against them."[19] Likewise, "[p]ublication of process or notice within the state where the tribunal sits cannot create any greater obligation upon the non-resident to appear."[20] Thus, "[i]t follows from the views expressed that the personal judgement recovered in the State court of Oregon against the plaintiff herein, then a non-resident of the State, was without any validity, and did not authorize a sale of the property in controversy."[21]

Beale's vested rights approach to choice of law employed similar methodology. Because choice of law was based on territory, a state had exclusive jurisdiction within its borders, but no authority outside its boundaries.[22] The location of a single, significant factor within a jurisdiction—usually the last act in a transaction or occurrence—determined which state's law would govern.[23] For example, the law of the place of the injury governed in tort cases, while the law of the place of the making of the contract controlled in contract cases.[24]

Under Beale's vested rights theory, rights and other obligations "vest" at the applicable time and place in accordance with the governing state's law, and other jurisdictions *must* recognize the right or obligation.[25] As Justice Holmes wrote, "The theory of the foreign suit is that although the act complained of was subject to no law having force in the forum, it gave rise to an obligation, an *obbligatio*, which follows the person, and may be enforced wherever the person may be found."[26] This conception contrasts with the theory of comity, "the principle that courts of one state or jurisdiction will give effect to laws and judicial decisions of another state out of deference and mutual respect rather than out of duty,"[27] which was the basis of adopting foreign law for Justice Story.[28]

Judges applying the vested rights approach to choice of law eventually developed escape devices that permitted judges to avoid "awkward" results. One of these mechanisms was characterization. For example, a court could characterize a problem as a contracts case instead of a torts case, allowing a different state's rule to apply.[29] Similarly, vested rights, as incorporated in the *First Restatement*, permitted a court to decline to enforce these rights if such enforcement would contravene the forum's public policy.[30]

Beale gave numerous examples of how vested rights worked in practice. For instance, when a train traveling in Kansas gave off sparks and set fire to the plaintiff's barn in Oklahoma, Oklahoma law governed because the last act happened in Oklahoma.[31] Similarly, when a plaintiff was injured in Arkansas by rock blasted in a stone quarry across a state line, Arkansas law applied because that was where the plaintiff was at the time of the injury.[32] Likewise, if the place where an alleged conversion occurred did not recognize a cause of action for conversion, the plaintiff could not recover in another forum.[33]

As mentioned above, Beale's method was multilateralist—only one state's law could govern a controversy because his system used a single factor, the last act, to establish the most appropriate legal system. Thus, insofar as concerns the legal rules, the decisions in the foregoing examples should be the same regardless of where the suit was filed because the forum court would look to the jurisdiction where the right to be enforced vested.[34] Beale declared that "[i]f two laws were present at the same time and in the same place upon the same subject matter we should also have the condition of anarchy."[35]

Beale's method employed highly mechanical rules. His system did not consider policy or state interests, and it was deontological—it was not concerned with the desirability of the outcome. In addition, it sometimes allowed a state with a tenuous connection to govern a case, such as when most of a tort occurred in one state, but the last act fortuitously took place in another.[36] As will be discussed below, conflicts scholars of the next generation strongly criticized these and other aspects of vested rights.

2. The Constitutionalization of Vested Rights

Several early twentieth century Supreme Court cases suggested that vested rights was constitutionally required.[37] For example, in *New York Life Ins. Co. v. Dodge*, the Court struck down the application of a Missouri statute that precluded certain insurance policy forfeitures on the ground that the legislature lacked the power to regulate contracts executed outside the state, even though the policy insured a Missouri resident and the state licensed the company to do business there.[38]

In this case, the beneficiary of her husband's life insurance policy sued in Missouri to enforce the policy. The husband had entered into the policy in Missouri, and the policy was governed by Missouri law.[39] However, the husband had borrowed against the policy, after having paid three of four annual premiums, and he had failed to repay the loan and pay the final premium. Under New York law and the loan agreement, the policy reserve was to be used to satisfy the loan, and any obligation to the loan's beneficiary ceased.[40] However, the Missouri statute prevented forfeiture after three annual premiums had been paid.[41]

The Court adopted New York law because the loan had been made there.[42] The loan had been accepted in New York (the last act), and the documents stated that New York law governed.[43] The Court concluded that Missouri could not extend its laws to contracts executed outside that state.[44] The Court also believed that Missouri could not bring the contract under its law on the ground that it had licensed the company to do business. Speaking through Justice James Clark McReynolds, the Court declared that "[t]o hold otherwise would permit destruction of the right—often of great value—freely to borrow money upon a policy from the issuing company at its home office and would, moreover, sanction the impairment of that liberty to contract guaranteed to all by the Fourteenth Amendment."[45]

A similar case on an insurance contract made the due process basis of such decisions even clearer:

> The Mississippi statutes so construed, deprives the appellant of due process of law. A state may limit or prohibit the making of certain contracts within its own territory . . . ; but it cannot extend the effect of its laws beyond its borders so as to destroy or impair the rights of citizens of other states to make a contract not operative within its jurisdiction, and lawful where made . . . . Nor may it in an action based upon such a contract enlarge the obligations of the parties to accord with every local statutory policy solely upon the ground that one of the parties is its own citizen.[46]

The full faith and credit clause created constraints similar to those under the due process clause. In *Bradford Elec. Light Co. v. Clapper*,[47] the decedent's administrator brought an action in New Hampshire to recover for the decedent's death under the New Hampshire wrongful death act; the defendant removed the case to federal court. The administrator was a New Hampshire citizen, and the accident had occurred in New Hampshire where the decedent was making emergency repairs at an electrical substation. However, both the decedent and the electric company were Vermont citizens, they had entered into the employment contract there, and both parties had accepted the Vermont worker's compensation act as a term of their contract. The electric company argued that the Vermont worker's compensation act and the full faith and credit clause barred any claim under the New Hampshire act.[48] The district court rejected this defense, ruling that the Vermont act had no extraterritorial effect.

Because there were considerable differences between the acts (New Hampshire allowed the plaintiff to sue for damages under the common law, while Vermont did not), a conflict existed. Justice Brandeis framed the issue as "whether the existence of a right of action for Leon Clapper's death should be determined by the laws of Vermont, where both parties to the contract of employment resided and where the contract was made, or by the laws of New Hampshire where the employee was killed."[49]

Justice Louis Dembitz Brandeis concluded that the accident was governed exclusively by Vermont law. He declared that

> [t]he relation between Leon Clapper and the Company was created by the law of Vermont; and as long as that relation persisted its incidents were properly subject to regulation there. For both Clapper and the Company were at all times residents of Vermont; the Company's principle place of business was located there; the contract of employment was made there; and the employee's duties required him to go into New Hampshire only for temporary and specific purposes in response to orders given him at the Vermont office.[50]

After rejecting the argument that enforcing the Vermont act in New Hampshire was extraterritorial, Justice Brandeis held that New Hampshire must enforce Vermont's act in its courts under the full faith and credit clause. He asserted, "[T]he rights created by the Vermont Act are entitled to like protection when set up in New Hampshire by way of defense to the action brought there. If this were not so, and the employee or his representative were free to disregard the law of Vermont and his contract, the effectiveness of the Vermont Act would be greatly impaired."[51]

This result reflected the influence of vested rights. According to Beale, "it was soon agreed that, since the acceptance or rejection of the [worker's compensation] Act was in the hands of the parties at the time of hiring, if they did not at that time disaffirm the Act they entered into a consensual relation on the terms of the Act of the place of hiring; and that wherever injured, even in another state, if it was in the course of employment for which the employee was hired, the injury came within the Act."[52]

B. THE REALIST ATTACK ON VESTED RIGHTS

1. The Realist Attack on Beale's Method

Realist scholars in the 1920s and 1930s attacked both the tenets of Classical Legal Thought and Beale's vested-rights approach to choice of law, which exemplified Classical Legal Thought. As Professor Horwitz has observed, "[t]he point of the Realist critique was to emphasize that the architecture of Classical Legal Thought was neither neutral, natural, nor necessary, but was a historically contingent and socially created system of legal thought."[53]

Realist scholars viewed syllogistic reasoning as mechanical, formalistic, and conceptualistic.[54] They believed that judges should not derive legal rules from general principles, adopting Justice Holmes's aphorism "[g]eneral propositions do not decide concrete cases."[55] Rather, these thinkers drew on experience, reality, and social policy making.[56] Professor Felix Cohen declared: "Fundamentally there are only two significant questions in the field of law. One is 'How do courts decide cases of a given kind?' The other is 'How ought they to decide cases of a given kind?' "[57]

These scholars also rejected bright-line categories, in favor of balancing tests and distinctions of degree.[58] For example, a rule of reason test replaced an absolute view of restraints of trade in antitrust law.[59] Similarly, courts often used balancing tests when evaluating negligence in torts.[60]

An article by Walter Wheeler Cook, one of Beale's major critics, exemplifies Realist legal reasoning. Professor Cook declared that "[i]t may seem incredible, but it is still possible for eminent members of the bar to assert that all a court does in deciding doubtful cases is to deduce conclusions from fixed premises."[61] Cook thought that, rather than applying pure logic to a case, judges legislate; they make law.[62] Because a judge makes law, Cook believed that a judge should base his analysis on social or economic policy. Consequently, "the judge will need to know two things: (1) what social consequences or results are to be aimed at; and (2) how a decision one way or another will affect the attainment of these results."[63]

Realist scholars also attacked vested rights.[64] First, they believed that vested rights failed to reflect the law in practice.[65] Instead of following the *a priori* approach of Classical Legal Thought, they advocated observing concrete phenomena first and forming generalizations afterward.[66] Professor Yntema asserted, "[L]aw is not a theoretic but an applied science."[67]

Second, they contended that judges often chose law based on unacknowledged policy considerations, not territory,[68] and that courts should in all cases openly consider the policy behind a rule.[69] Professor Lorenzen declared that "[t]he common law has not hidden in its bosom a logical set of rules which can be derived from its notion of territoriality. Sound progress in this field of law, as in all other departments of knowledge, can be made only if the actual facts be faced, which show that the adoption of the one rule or the other depends entirely upon considerations of policy which each sovereign state must determine for itself."[70] In other words, choice of law should be consequentialist—courts should consider the desirability of the outcome when choosing law.

Third, the Realists criticized vested rights as being mechanical.[71] In particular, they objected to the rigid use of one territorial factor over another as the deciding factor in choice of law and the total disregard of nonterritorial criteria when choosing law.[72]

Fourth, they rejected the method on the ground that rights and other obligations do not automatically vest; rather, law is the prophecy of what the courts will do.[73] In other words, there is no right until a court declares that the right exists; there is no such thing as preexisting rights based on natural law.[74] Finally, they attacked the consistency of a theory that created a right that must be recognized by other states, then allowed a state to refuse to enforce that right based on policy.[75] As Professor Lorenzen asserted, "The doctrine of public policy in the Conflict of Laws ought to have been a warning that there was something a matter with the reasoning upon which the rules to which it is an exception were supposed to be based."[76]

The Realists' harsh criticisms of vested rights led Cook to abandon Beale's multilateralist approach to conflicts. In one of the key passages in the history of conflicts law, Cook wrote,

> [T]he forum, when confronted by a case involving foreign elements, always applies its own law to the case, but in doing so adopts and enforces as its own law a rule of decision found in the system of law in force in another state or country with which some or all of the foreign elements are connected, the rule so selected being in normal cases and subject to the exceptions to be noted later, the rule of decision which the given foreign state or country would apply, not to this very group of facts now before the court of the forum, but to a *similar but purely domestic group of facts involving for the foreign court no foreign element.*[77]

In other words, "a court never enforces foreign rights but only rights created by its own law."[78] The focus is now on the forum's relation to choice of law, not the relationship of the facts to the most appropriate legal system (multilateralism).

Professor Cavers, another influential conflicts scholar, similarly rejected Beale's multilateralist approach. Indeed, he rejected any "jurisdiction-selecting" rule—a rule that chooses law without considering the law's content—in favor of a substantive approach.[79] He asked, "Without taking the content of the conflicting laws into account, how could one know what would satisfy the demands of justice or the requirements of policy?"[80]

2. The Supreme Court's Rejection of Vested Rights and Multilateralist Constraints in Constitutional Law

Along with the Realist scholars' repudiation of vested rights as a choice of law system came a change in the Supreme Court's analysis of the effect of the Constitution on choice of law. In *Alaska Packers Ass'n v. Industrial Accident Comm'n*[81] and *Pacific Employer's Ass'n v. Industrial Accident Comm'n*,[82] Justice Stone declined to incorporate, as a constitutional standard, the rigid territorial rules of vested rights. Instead, he determined the bounds of constitutionality by examining whether the state whose law was being applied had "a legitimate public interest" in having its law govern.[83] As will be shown below in detail, this shift often allowed more than one state's law to be applied to a case without any priority among those competing laws, which meant that constitutional constraints on choice of law had become unilateral.

In *Alaska Packers*, the California Industrial Accident Commission had awarded worker's compensation benefits to an injured worker based on a California statute, the state where the employment contract had been executed, rather than an Alaska statute, the state where the injury had occurred.[84] The injured party was a nonresident alien (Mexican), who had entered into an employment contract in California for seasonal employment in Alaska.[85] The California employer was to transport the worker to Alaska and return him to California at the end of his employment and pay him there. The contract stipulated that the Alaska worker's compensation statute would govern.

California's statute gave the Commission "jurisdiction over all controversies arising out of injuries suffered without the territorial limits of the state in those cases where the injured employee is a resident of this state at the time of the injury and the contract of hire was made in this State."[86] The California Supreme Court had interpreted this statute as also applying to nonresidents who entered into employment contracts within the state on the ground that excluding nonresidents would be unconstitutional under the privileges and immunities clause of the United States Constitution.[87] The statute also stated that no contract shall exclude an employee from the liability it provided,[88] rendering the contractual application of the Alaska statute void if California law governed.

The petitioner contended that the California statute violated both the due process and full faith and credit clauses.[89] The petitioner began by declaring that "[i]t is an elementary principle in conflict of laws that the contract is governed by the laws with a view to which the parties make it."[90] Next the petitioner asserted that "the State has no reasonable basis for extending, and no power to extend, its compulsory worker's compensation act to *extraterritorial injuries* arising from such employment."[91] The petitioner further contended that in sustaining the award, the lower court had invalidated the parties' contract, unreasonably limiting freedom of contract under the due process clause.[92] Finally, the petitioner concluded that "[t]he fact that the agreement was made in California is not enough to justify the courts of that State in invalidating it."[93]

Justice Stone first considered whether the California statute as applied in this case violated the due process clause.[94] He declared, "But where the contract is entered into within the state, even though it is to be performed elsewhere, its terms, its obligation and its sanctions are subject, in some measure, to the legislative control of that state. The fact that the contract is to be performed elsewhere does not of itself put these incidents beyond reach of the power which a state may constitutionally exercise."[95] Justice Stone pointed out that "the liability under worker's compensation acts is not a tort. It is imposed as an incident of the employment relationship, as a cost to be borne by the business enterprise, rather than as an attempt to extend redress for the wrongful act of the employer."[96] In other words, "the power of a state to effect legal consequences is not limited to occurrences within the state if it has control over the status which gives rise to those consequences."[97]

Thus, "[o]bjections which are founded upon the Fourteenth Amendment must, therefore, be directed not to the existence of the power to impose liability for an injury outside state borders, but to the manner of its exercise as being so arbitrary or unreasonable as to amount to a denial of due process."[98] Justice Stone found that California had "a legitimate public interest" in applying its statute to the case because (1) the parties executed the employment contract in California; (2) the employee was transported to Alaska for seasonal employment and returned to California where his wages were to be paid; (3) the above conditions made it unlikely that the employee would be able to obtain compensation in Alaska; and (4) without a California remedy, the employee might not be compensated, and the employee might become a California charge.[99]

Concerning the argument that the statute was unconstitutional because it interfered with freedom of contract, Justice Stone stated, "Legislation otherwise within the scope of acknowledged state power, not unreasonably or arbitrarily exercised, cannot be condemned because it curtails the power of the individual to contract. As the state had the power to impose the liability in pursuance of state policy, it was a rational, and therefore a permissible, exercise of state power to prohibit any contract in evasion of it."[100]

In Stone's view, the constraint on choice of law under the full faith and credit clause was stricter than the one under the due process clause.[101] Because the California and Alaska statutes provided different remedies, they directly conflicted.[102] The question, then, was whether the full faith and credit clause required California to apply the Alaska statute rather than its own.

Justice Stone pointed out that "[a] rigid and literal enforcement of the full faith and credit clause, without regard to the statute of the forum, would lead to the absurd result that, wherever the conflict arises, the statute of each state must be enforced in the courts of the other, but cannot be in its own."[103] A conflict is resolved, not by mechanically applying the full faith and credit clause, "but by appraising the governmental interests of each jurisdiction, and turning the scale of decision according to their weight."[104] Thus, "[i]t follows that not every statute of another state will override a conflicting statute of the forum by virtue of the full faith and credit clause; that the statute of a state may sometimes override the conflicting statute of another, both at home and abroad; and, again, that the two conflicting statutes may each prevail over the other at home, although given no extraterritorial effect in the state of the other."[105]

Justice Stone stated that the burden of proving that Alaska had a greater interest than California in enforcing its statute under the full faith and credit clause was on the defendant.[106] Because the petitioner had not met this burden, California's use of its statute did not violate the full faith and credit clause.

A subsequent case, *Pacific Employer's*, involved almost exactly the opposite facts from *Alaska Packers*.[107] In *Pacific Employer's*, California had applied its worker's compensation statute to a situation where the injury occurred in California, but the employee was a Massachusetts resident, the employer was centered in Massachusetts, and the parties executed the employment contract there. In addition, the employee expected to return to Massachusetts after the temporary assignment in California, and the employment contract stipulated that the Massachusetts act would govern injuries within or without Massachusetts.

Because there was no due process question in this case,[108] Justice Stone examined the full faith and credit constraint on California's application of its statute. Although there are limits on a state applying its law to contracts executed in another state under the full faith and credit clause, Stone asserted that "there would seem to be little room for the exercise of that function when the statute of the forum is the expression of domestic policy, in terms declared to be exclusive in its application to persons and events within the state."[109] He added that "[a]lthough Massachusetts has an interest in safeguarding the compensation of Massachusetts employees while temporarily abroad in the course of their employment, and may adopt that policy for itself, that could hardly be thought to support an application of the full faith and credit clause which would override the constitutional authority of another state to legislate for the bodily safety and economic protection of employees within it."[110] In addition, "[i]t would be obnoxious to [California's] policy to deny persons who have been injured in this state the right to apply for compensation when to do so might require physicians and hospitals to go to another state to collect charges for medical care and treatment given to such persons."[111]

In sum, *Alaska Packers* and *Pacific Employer's* constituted a radical reorientation in the constitutional analysis of state choice of law. Instead of looking at rigid territorial factors, Justice Stone focused on legitimate public interests. If a state had a legitimate public interest in adopting its law, such a choice satisfied due process even if other states' laws could be applied. Similarly, if a state's legitimate interest outweighed other states' interests, there was no violation of full faith and credit. Finally, Justice Stone looked at the consequences of the choice of law decision; a Bealian judge would never have considered the effect of noncompensation on the defendant or the public.

Justice Stone's analysis allows for the possibility that more than one state's law may be employed in a dispute without violating the Constitution (concurrent legislative jurisdiction), a unilateralist view of constitutional constraints on choice of law. In *Alaska Packers*, he declared that "two conflicting statutes may each prevail over the other at home."[112] Moreover, one may assume that he would have upheld the adoption of Massachusetts law in *Pacific Employer's* had the case been brought in Massachusetts.

In *Watson v. Employers Liability Assurance Corp.*, the Supreme Court explicitly recognized concurrent legislative jurisdiction.[113] Louisiana, the place of the injury in *Watson*, allowed direct actions against insurance companies (a plaintiff could sue an insurer before establishing the insured's liability) even if there was a clause in the contract that forbid it; however, Massachusetts, where the policy was negotiated, issued, and delivered, upheld clauses in insurance contracts precluding direct actions. The Louisiana federal district court and the court of appeals had held that the application of the Louisiana statute to policies issued outside Louisiana was unconstitutional.[114] In reversing, the Supreme Court declared, with respect to the due process clause, that "as a consequence of the modern practice of conducting wide-spread business activities throughout the entire United States, this Court has in a series of cases held that more than one [state] may seize hold of local activities which are part of multistate transactions and may regulate [them] to protect interests of its own people, even though other phases of the same transaction might justify regulation in other states."[115]

The Court also rejected the need to balance state interests under the full faith and credit clause.[116] In *Carroll v. Lanza*, the next case of significance, the Court upheld the use of the Arkansas worker's compensation act where the employer and employee were Missouri residents and the contract was executed in Missouri, but the injury occurred in Arkansas. As Justice Felix Frankfurter's dissent noted, "[n]o rights of Arkansas residents are involved, since none of the parties is an Arkansan; the workman was removed immediately to a Missouri hospital and has, so far as appears, remained in Missouri."[117] Obviously, Arkansas's interest did not outweigh

Missouri's, and, consequently, *Carroll* is a final confirmation that balancing was no longer required under the full faith and credit clause.

In sum, the above cases rejected the early twentieth century's multilateralist view of constitutional constraints on choice of law in favor of a unilateralist one that often allowed more than one state's law to be adopted without violating the Constitution. This shift to a unilateralist conception of constitutional constraints permitted the development of the conflicts methods discussed in the next section.

C. MODERN CHOICE OF LAW SYSTEMS

The work of the realist scholars was critical rather than constructive. It was not until Brainerd Currie's governmental interest analysis that a scholar developed a system that seriously challenged Beale's approach.[118] Since Currie presented his method, several scholars have advocated other approaches, and courts have adopted many of the new systems. In addition, some courts have continued to employ Beale's method without his jurisprudence.[119]

This section examines the beginnings of modern conflicts methods in scholarly writings and cases in the 1940s and 1950s. It then discusses Professor Currie's unilateralist choice of law method and variations on his method. Finally, it analyzes the major alternatives to Currie's system—the substantive approaches of Robert Leflar and Friedrich Juenger and the most substantial relationship test of the *Second Restatement*.

1. Choice of Law Developments the 1940s and 1950s

a. Antecedents of governmental interest analysis. Continuing the policy-based orientation of the realists, a few scholars and judges in the 1940s anticipated elements of governmental interest analysis. Paul A. Freund sketched a choice of law method, which borrowed elements from Justice Stone's opinions on constitutional constraints on choice of law.[120] Professor Freund advocated an "approach to these [choice of law] problems by way of attempting to harmonize and to weigh the respective interests of the states in light of the policies sought to be subserved."[121] He suggested a two-step approach that resembles Currie's method in its first step. Concerning the first step, he stated, "The approach which emphasizes the interests involved would carry the analysis still further. If state B would not apply its domestic rule to the bi-state situation, state A will not do so, not because of uniformity but because the apparent conflict of interest has been dissolved."[122] Governmental interest analysis calls this a "false conflict."[123]

A second step is necessary when both states would apply their rule (a true conflict under governmental interest analysis).[124] Here Freund noted, "[T]he conflict is inescapable and is to be resolved by considering the competing policies more closely."[125] In addition, a court may consider whether one of the laws is "attenuated or anachronistic," or the court might choose the law of the state that imposes liability.[126]

Professor Moffatt Hancock proposed looking at state interests as one of several choice of law criteria.[127] He thought that sometimes a court can easily reconcile the states' interests; however, "[s]ometimes the policy of one state's law comes into direct conflict with that of another's."[128] For example, "[s]uppose a sheriff, standing in state X, shoots an escaping criminal who has crossed the border into state Y. The law of state X makes the shooting of escaping criminals a privileged act; the law of state Y forbids it. Here the two states' policies clash and the court of the forum will have to choose between them."[129]

A careful examination of a rule's policies and purposes will often establish whether it applies to a situation. For example, a Louisiana rule requiring that a husband bring an action for a tort against his wife did not control in a Louisiana case where the couple was domiciled in a state with a different rule. Professor Hancock wrote, "Since plaintiff and her husband lived in Mississippi, their relations with respect to their property were of little interest to Louisiana, of more interest to Mississippi."[130]

California Justice Roger Traynor was one of the key judicial innovators in twentieth-century choice of law. While most of his decisions prior to Currie's articles try to make these innovations within the confines of traditional choice of law analysis,[131] he anticipated interest analysis in his dissent in *Ohio ex. rel. Squire v. Porter*.[132] The issue was whether the Ohio or California statute of limitations applied in a case involving a 100 percent assessment against the California stockholders of an insolvent Ohio bank. The majority adopted the California statute of limitations, but looked to Ohio law to determine when the liability had been created, barring the action. The court employed the California statute of limitations because "it is well settled that the statute of limitations of the forum governs the time for the commencement of an action arising in other states."[133]

Justice Traynor looked at the policy behind the California statute in determining that it did not govern this case.[134] He thought that this statute of limitations was an integral part of the liability against stockholders under California law, not "a procedural regulation of the forum with respect to actions involving the enforcement of foreign rights and liabilities."[135] More important, he declared, "California has no policy necessitating the destruction of the substantive right of the foreign bank depositors to enforce the liability imposed upon the bank's shareholders, and no interest in riding over such rights."[136] In fact, California expressed a policy similar to Ohio's in its cause of action against shareholders.

2. Antecedents of the Second Restatement. Several writers and cases from the 1930s, 1940s, and 1950s anticipated the *Second Restatement*'s multilateralist "most significant relationship" test.[137] In his 1941 casebook, Professor Elliot E. Cheatham suggested a contacts approach to choice of law that searched for the most appropriate legal system.[138] He wrote that "[t]he court may examine into the contacts or relations which the transaction in question and the parties have with each of the states and determine which contact or groups of contacts is the most important for the purpose in hand. After making the determination, it will apply the local or internal rule of the state so pointed to or identified."[139]

In 1952, Professor Cheatham, along with Willis Reese—later principal draftsman of the *Second Restatement*—followed up on this proposal.[140] Cheatham and Reese advocated looking at nine choice of law influencing considerations, such as the needs of the interstate and international system and protection of justifiable expectations.[141] Among these factors is the application of the law of the state of dominant interest: "A choice of law decision is, therefore, of real concern to the states involved, since in net effect it determines whose policy shall prevail in the particular case. This consideration dictates that the law of the state with the dominant interest should, normally at least, be applied."[142] For example, if a Nevada husband shakes his fist at his Nevada wife while in Illinois, Nevada law controls whether the act constitutes grounds for divorce because Nevada is their domicile.[143] However, if the wife sues for damages, Illinois law will determine whether the wife has a claim because that is where the act occurred.

Similarly, the state with the majority of the essential elements of the occurrence has the strongest claim to have its law govern.[144] For instance, if two New York citizens entered into a contract, with one signing it in New York and the other by chance signing it in Illinois, New York law should govern because it is "the state most intimately concerned with the transaction."[145] However, under the *First Restatement*, a court would have applied Illinois law because that was where the contract was accepted and the right of enforcement vested. Although both the Cheatham-Reese approach and the *First Restatement* are multilateralist because they look for the law of the most appropriate legal system, they come to different conclusions because they use different criteria to find the most appropriate legal system. Professor Cheatham and Reese's criterion (and the *Second Restatement*'s "most significant relationship" test, of which the Cheatam-Reese approach is an antecedent) produces the preferable result because it does not adopt the law of a jurisdiction with a tenuous connection to the case, as the *First Restatement* did in the above example.

Similarly, Professors Fowler Vincent Harper and Charles W. Taintor thought that some cases looked at the accumulation of contact points.[146] They declared that "[m]any courts purport to find the most significant contact point, with respect to contractual transactions, at the place intended by both parties. It seems, rather, that these courts examine all the circumstances which could be supposed to have influenced the actions of the parties, and find the most intimate contact at that place which might be characterized as the center of gravity of the circumstances."[147]

Finally, Professor J. H. C. Morris was dissatisfied with the *First Restatement* rule that tort liability is governed by the law of the place of the wrong.[148] He argued that "[i]t seems extraordinarily unlikely that all these questions can be satisfactorily answered by mechanically applying the law of the place of the wrong without reference to the social factors involved, particularly if the wrongful act and the consequential harm occurred in different states, one of which has to be arbitrarily selected as the place of the wrong."[149] Consider, for example, the following hypothetical in which the defendant wants to rely on a guest statute (precluding a guest passenger in an automobile from suing the owner for the owner's negligence).[150] The accident occurred in State X, which has a guest statute, but the owner, the defendant, and the owner's insurance company are all domiciliaries of State F, which lacks such a statute. Under Beale's method, the guest statute defense would bar the action because the last act occurred in State X. However, Professor Morris argued that the more sensible approach would adopt the law of State F "since all the significant factors are F factors except the fortuitous place of the harm."[151]

Drawing on English methods of choice of law for contracts, Morris advocated using the "proper law of torts." He asserted that "[i]f we adopt the proper law of the tort, we can at least choose the law which, on policy grounds, seems to have the most significant connection with the chain of acts and consequences in the particular situation before us. The task might not be easy, but at least we should be asking the right question."[152]

Influenced by the above writers, the New York Court of Appeals adopted the "center of gravity" approach in *Auten v. Auten*.[153] The critical issue in *Auten* was whether a wife had repudiated a separation agreement. The plaintiff wife and defendant husband had married in England and had two children. The husband deserted the wife, obtained a Mexican divorce, and, apparently, moved to New York. The wife traveled to New York to discuss their differences, and the parties entered into a separation agreement. Under the agreement, a trustee was to pay the wife £50 a month for the support of the wife and children, who would continue to live in England. The agreement stated that the parties were to live separately and provided that "neither should sue 'in any action relating to their separation' and that the wife should not 'cause any complaint to be lodged against . . . [the husband], in any jurisdiction, by reason of the said alleged divorce or marriage.'"[154]

The husband soon breached the agreement, leaving his family destitute. The wife brought an action against the husband in England for separation and asked for an order for the husband to pay alimony *pendente lite*. The wife allegedly filed this action to enable her to enforce the separation agreement, not with any thought of repudiating it. Apparently, the case never came to trial.

Several years later, the wife sued the husband in New York to recover $26,564 that the husband allegedly owed her under the separation agreement. The husband defended on the ground that the English action repudiated the separation agreement. The trial court granted summary judgment based on New York law, agreeing that the commencement of the English action had repudiated the separation agreement. An intermediate appellate court affirmed.

The New York Court of Appeals overturned the lower courts' decisions because English, not New York, law applied. In doing so, the court employed the "center of gravity" test.[155] "Under this theory, the courts, instead of regarding as conclusive the parties' intention or the place of making or performance, lay emphasis rather upon the law of the place 'which has the most significant contacts with the matter in dispute.'"[156] The court advocated this approach because "it gives to the place 'having the most interest in the problem' paramount control over the legal issues arising out of a particular factual context, thus allowing the forum to apply the policy of the jurisdiction 'most intimately concerned with the outcome of [the] particular litigation.'"[157] It also gives "effect to the probable intention of the parties and consideration to 'whether one rule or the other produces the best practical result.'"[158]

Using the center of gravity test, the court concluded that English law "must be applied to determine the impact and effect to be given the wife's institution of the separation suit."[159] The court thought that England had all the significant contacts with the case, whereas New York's only contacts with the dispute were that it was the place of the contract's making and the place where the trustee had his office. The court pointed out that the wife's sole purpose in making the trip to New York was to get her husband to support his family; she returned to England shortly after the agreement was signed. The separation agreement "fixed the marital responsibilities of an English husband and father and provided for the support and maintenance of the allegedly abandoned wife and children who were to remain in England."[160] The court concluded that "[t]here is no question that England has the greatest concern in prescribing and governing those obligations, and in securing to the wife and children essential support and maintenance."[161]

2. Currie's Governmental Interest Analysis Method

Although both academic commentators and judges suggested new approaches to choice of law, it was Professor Brainerd Currie who developed the first modern conflicts system.[162] Although only a few states have completely adopted his method,[163] Currie's governmental interest analysis dominated conflicts scholarship in the 1960s and 70s, and, although frequently attacked in recent years,[164] it remains a major conflicts theory today.[165] Even courts which do not profess to adopt Currie's methodology, nonetheless, often reflect his thinking in their written opinions.

Although Currie shared many of the criticisms the Realists had of vested rights, he was most troubled by the fact that the *First Restatement*'s rules could produce a result that did not advance the interest of any state.[166] For example, the last act might occur in a state with a tenuous, fortuitous connection to a case. Consequently, Currie defined the central problem of conflict of laws, "as that of determining the appropriate rule of decision when the interests of two or more states are in conflict—in other words, of determining which interest shall yield."[167]

One may summarize Currie's method as follows:

1. Even in cases involving multistate elements, a court should generally adopt forum law.
2. In cases where a party argues that another state's law should apply, the court should first examine the governmental policy behind forum law. Next, the court should determine whether the forum has a relation to the case that furnishes a legitimate basis for it to assert an interest in the application of its policy.
3. Next, the court should determine the policy behind the foreign law and whether the other state has an interest in applying its policy.
4. When the forum has no interest in applying its policy, but the other state does, the court should adopt the other state's law.
5. When the forum has an interest in employing its law, the court should adopt forum law, even though the other state has an interest in applying its law.[168]

As one can see from this summary, although Currie examined the policy behind the various states' laws, he advocated that a forum should generally apply its law. A forum should adopt foreign law only when it has no interest in employing its law. Currie declared that "the sensible and clearly constitutional thing for any court to do, confronted with a true conflict of interests, is to apply its own law. In this way it can be sure at least that it is consistently advancing the policy of its own state."[169]

Similarly, Currie expressly rejected the weighing of the states' interests in cases where each sovereign had an interest in having its own law applied.[170] He asserted that "[w]ho is to say which [state's interest] is the most important, or the most deserving, or the most enlightened? Not even the United States Supreme Court is in a position to do so."[171]

Currie's approach gave choice of law two key terms—"false conflicts" and "true conflicts." Under Currie's method, a false conflict (or false problem) exists when only one state has an interest in applying its law.[172] In such a case, a court should adopt the law of the state that has an interest in using its law. When two or more states have an interest in applying their laws, a true conflict exists, and, as mentioned above, forum law should apply.

Currie's analysis of *Milliken v. Pratt*[173] illustrates his method. In *Milliken*, Mrs. Pratt executed a guaranty of her husband's credit in favor of a Maine partnership. She executed the guaranty at her home in Massachusetts, and her husband mailed it to Maine. Mr. Pratt defaulted on his debts, and the partnership sued Mrs. Pratt on her guaranty in a Massachusetts court. Under a Maine statute, a married woman could be liable as a surety, but, under Massachusetts law, a married woman could not bind herself as a surety.

The Massachusetts Supreme Judicial Court reversed a trial court judgment for the defendant on the ground that Maine, rather than Massachusetts, law governed. The court analyzed Mrs. Pratt's guaranty as an offer for a unilateral contract that was accepted by goods being delivered to the buyer or to the buyer's carrier. Thus, because the goods were delivered in Maine, the wife's offer was accepted in Maine, and Maine law governed. Consequently, the Maine statute controlled, and the guaranty was valid.

Currie's method yields an opposite result.[174] Both Massachusetts and Maine had an interest in applying their laws. Massachusetts intended to protect married woman, who at that time, it believed, needed special protection. Maine, on the other hand, had an interest in freedom of contract and security of business transactions. Because the suit was filed in Massachusetts, the court should apply Massachusetts law, voiding the contract. Currie defended his notion by arguing, "[i]f one state's policy must yield, should not the court prefer the policy of its own state?"[175]

Governmental interest analysis is unilateralist because it does not require that the law of the most appropriate jurisdiction govern. The forum can adopt its law as long as it has an interest in doing so, even if another state has a greater interest in applying its law. As noted above, Currie believed that courts were not well suited to determine which of two (or more) interested states should prevail in cases of a true conflict, and thus he employed forum law as the deciding factor since at least the forum court is advancing its state's interest.[176]

Currie's approach is not only unilateralist, it is also consequentialist. As Professor Lea Brilmayer observed, his method focuses on "a decision's impact on the general social good, rather than the claims of the instant parties to fair treatment."[177] However, it is not a "universalistic consequentialist theory" in which a state adopts the "policy that it thinks is best for the world at large."[178] Rather, it is consequentialist "by its principle that if the values in the local statute would be furthered within the state by applying the law, then the state has a policy reason or 'interest' in having its law applied."[179]

Finally, although Currie advocated looking at both domiciliary and territorial factors, his analysis of cases focused on domiciliary connections. As Professor Brilmayer pointed out, "[u]nder Currie's scheme, a statute should in most cases be interpreted to apply to only those situations where a local person would benefit."[180] Similarly, Professor Friederich K. Juenger observed that Currie's system "merely substitutes a personal nexus for the First Restatement's territorial contacts."[181]

There have been several variations on Currie's classic formulation of governmental interest analysis. For example, at the end of his career, Currie himself suggested a modification to governmental interest analysis:

> In other cases analysis may at first indicate an apparent conflict of interests; . . . But no principle dictates that a state exploit every possible conflict . . . . On the contrary, to assert a conflict between the interests of the forum and the foreign state is a serious matter; the mere fact that a suggested broad conception of a local interest will create conflict with that of a foreign state is a sound reason why. The conception should be re-examined, with a more moderate and restrained interpretation both of the policy and of the circumstances in which it must be applied to effectuate the forum's legitimate purpose.[182]

Under this modification, a court will still adopt its law if it still has an interest in doing so after the more moderate and restrained interpretation of the reach of its own law even if another state's law has a greater claim to applicability.[183] Thus, Currie's modest adjustment to his conflicts methodology does not undermine the conclusion that his system of conflict resolution is unilateralist.

Professor William F. Baxter's comparative impairment approach is a multilateralist version of governmental interest analysis.[184] The first step in comparative impairment is the same as in Currie's method, namely, to determine whether an apparent conflict is, in reality, a false conflict. However, when a true conflict exists, instead of automatically choosing forum law, Professor Baxter determines which state's interest is more impaired—that is, he weighs the harm that is caused to a state's interest by adopting another state's law.[185] In other words, he looks for the law of the most appropriate jurisdiction in a consequentialist manner that focuses on state interests.

Bernhard v. Harrah's Club purported to employ both variations on Currie's method.[186] In *Bernhard*, a plaintiff was severely injured in a traffic accident by a drunken driver who had been served alcohol by a Nevada gambling casino. The casino, which advertised for patrons in California, continued to serve a California driver alcohol, despite the fact that she was visibly intoxicated. California law allowed civil suits against tavern owners, but Nevada law did not. However, Nevada law provided criminal penalties for selling or giving intoxicating liquor to any person who was drunk or who was known to be a habitual drunkard.

The California Supreme Court thought that California's interest would be severely impaired if its state policy was not adopted in this case: "It seems clear that California cannot reasonably effectuate its policy if it does not extend its regulation to include out-of-state tavern keepers such as defendants who regularly and purposely sell intoxicating beverages to California residents in places and under conditions in which it is reasonably certain these residents will return to California and act therein while still in an intoxicated state."[187]

The court felt that Nevada's interest, when comparatively assessed, was not as impaired. The court asserted that "[s]ince the act of selling alcoholic beverages to obviously intoxicated persons is already proscribed in Nevada, the application of California's rule of civil liability would not impose an entirely new duty requiring the ability to distinguish between California residents and other patrons."[188] The court added, "Nevada's interest in protecting its tavern keepers from civil liability of a boundless and unrestricted nature will not be significantly impaired when as in the instant case liability is imposed only on those tavern keepers who actively solicit California business."[189]

The court concluded, "[U]pon reexamining the policy underlying California's rule of decision and giving such policy a more restrained interpretation for the purpose of this case pursuant to the principles of law of choice of law discussed above, we conclude that California has an important and abiding interest in applying its rule of decision to the case at bench, that the policy of this state would be more significantly impaired if such rule were not applied and that the trial court erred in not applying California law."[190]

3. The Better Rule Approach

Several choice of law scholars have advocated a better rule approach to choice of law, some adopting it as the only criterion,[191] others as one of several factors.[192] Such an approach is neither unilateralist nor multilateralist, but rather it is a universalist, consequentialist theory that searches for the best rule for the world at large.

Professor Robert Leflar believed that judges used choice of law mechanisms, such as characterization and public policy, to hide the fact that they were seeking the just result.[193] Under his view, judges should not hide this preference, but rather should emphasize it.

Leflar's method comprises five choice of law influencing considerations:

(A) Predictability of results;

(B) Maintenance of interstate and international order;

(C) Simplification of the judicial task;

(D) Advancement of the forum's governmental interests;

(E) Application of the better rule of law.[194]

While Leflar emphasizes that courts should consider all five factors, his analyses and those of courts following his system rely on the better rule of law factor significantly more than the others.[195] Not surprisingly, although Leflar's approach theoretically is forum neutral, those states employing Leflar's system usually find their law to be the better rule.[196]

Minnesota adopted Leflar's method in *Milkovich v. Saari*.[197] The issue in this case was whether an Ontario guest statute barred a plaintiff's recovery for injuries received in an automobile accident that occurred in Minnesota, but in which all parties were Ontario residents. The lawsuit had originally been filed in Ontario, but the plaintiff dismissed and refiled in Minnesota, presumably because Ontario law would have precluded the action.

The court used Leflar's test to determine that Minnesota law governed. The court found that the "predictability of results" factor was unimportant because automobile accidents are not planned.[198] The court also quickly dismissed the "simplification of the judicial task" factor because the court could just as easily apply the Ontario guest statute as Minnesota's negligence rule.[199] The court then declared that "[i]nterstate and international relations are maintained without harm where, as here, the forum state has a substantial connection with the facts and issues involved."[200]

Concerning the forum's governmental interest, the court declared that "we are concerned that our courts not be called upon to determine issues under rules which, however accepted they may be in other states, are inconsistent with our own concept of fairness and equity."[201] Moreover, persons injured in an automobile accident in a state will probably require medical treatment in the state. The court added that "[i]n the instant case, plaintiff incurred medical bills in a Duluth hospital which have already been paid, but we are loath to place weight on the individual case for fear it might offer even minor incentives to 'hospital shop' or create litigation-directed pressures on the payment of debts to medical facilities."[202]

The court then averred that the Minnesota negligence rule was the better rule: "We can find little reason for the strict limitations of a host's liability to his guest beyond the fear of collusive suits and the vague disapproval of a guest 'biting the hand that feeds him.'"[203]

The dissent asserted that "the 'choice-influencing factor' in the majority opinion is simply that Minnesota law is 'better law' because, unlike Ontario law, this state has no guest statute."[204] The dissent further noted that "[w]e may assume that these Canadian citizens have concurred in the rule of law of their own government as just, so the law of this American forum is not for them the 'better' standard of justice."[205]

Professor Juenger also favors a substantive approach. He has declared that "[i]n its most radical form, the substantive law approach calls upon judges to play an active and open role in the creation of a 'true private international law.' In devising rules of decision to govern multistate disputes, they would act like international tribunals or central courts in federal or quasi-federal systems."[206]

Professor Patrick Borchers's analysis of *Pan American World Airways Inc. v. Boeing Co.*[207] illustrates Juenger's approach to choice of law. In this case, Pan Am, an airline centered in New York, sued Boeing, an aircraft manufacturer centered in Washington, for the negligent design of an aircraft. A Pan Am airplane had been destroyed in a crash while making an emergency landing at Boston when improperly stored hazardous chemicals caught fire, causing heavy smoke in the cockpit. Although Pan Am was negligent in loading the chemicals, it alleged that Boeing was also negligent because Boeing had not provided a device to evacuate the smoke.

The issue in the case was whether the New York rule—contributory negligence, which would bar Pan Am's claim—or the Washington rule—comparative negligence, which would allow the claim but reduce damages in proportion to Pan Am's negligence—governed the outcome. The New York federal district court, using New York's choice of law rule (that the law of the jurisdiction with the most interest in having its law applied should govern), adopted the New York rule—contributory negligence, and it dismissed the case.

Borchers, a follower of Juenger, criticized this result because it failed to examine substantive values, which he believes is necessary when interstate torts are involved.[208] In solving the choice of law question, Professor Borchers determines which rule "allocates the loss in the manner most consistent with modern standards, and which rule is aberrational."[209] In this case, Borchers would adopt comparative negligence because it is "[t]he most just and modern" based on the fact that "the substantive values that underlie loss-allocating rules are compensatory."[210]

4. The *Second Restatement*

Although the *Second Restatement* reflects the influence of several choice of law approaches, it is mainly multilateralist because its main test searches for the law of the state with the most significant relationship to the occurrence.[211] Section 6 sets out choice of law principles:

> (1) A court, subject to constitutional restrictions, will follow a statutory directive of its own state on choice of law.
>
> (2) When there is no such directive, the factors relevant to the choice of the applicable rule of law include
>
> (a) the needs of the interstate and international systems,
>
> (b) the relevant policies of the forum,
>
> (c) the relevant policies of other interested states and the relevant interests of those states in determination of the particular issue,
>
> (d) the protection of justified expectations,
>
> (e) the basic policies underlying the particular field of law,
>
> (f) certainty, predictability, and uniformity of results, and
>
> (g) ease in the determination and application of the law to be applied.

Professor Reese, reporter of the *Second Restatement*, has written that "the values stated in section 6 underlie the entire field of choice of law and that all of the black letter rules stem from these values."[212]

Section 145 presents the "most significant relationship test" for torts:

> (1) The rights and liabilities of the parties with respect to an issue in tort are determined by the local law of the state which, with respect to that issue, has the most significant relationship to the occurrence and the parties under the principles stated in § 6.
>
> (2) Contacts to be taken into account in applying the principles of § 6 to determine the law applicable to an issue include:
>
> (a) the place where the injury occurred,
>
> (b) the place where the conduct causing the injury occurred,
>
> (c) the domicile, residence, nationality, place of incorporation and place of business of the parties, and
>
> (d) the place where the relationship, if any, between the parties is centered.
>
> These contacts are to be evaluated according to their relative importance with respect to the particular issue.

The Second Restatement adopts similar tests for contracts,[213] property,[214] agency,[215] etc.

The Second Restatement also has specific rules for particular situations. For example, "[i]n an action for personal injury, the local law of the state where the injury occurred determines the rights and the liabilities of the parties unless, with respect to the particular issue, some other state has a more significant relationship under the principles stated in section 6 to the occurrence and the parties, in which event the local law of the other state will be applied."[216]

Schulze v. Illinois Highway Transp. Co. illustrates the *Second Restatement*'s most significant relationship test.[217] In *Schulze*, an Illinois 4-H club had chartered a bus from an Illinois corporation for a round trip to Dearborn, Michigan. The bus overturned while in Michigan, injuring several passengers. The Illinois plaintiffs sued in Illinois, alleging that the company "was negligent in failing to provide a bus that was in proper mechanical condition, failing properly to inspect the bus to determine its mechanical and roadway worthiness, failing to provide seatbelts, and employing an incompetent driver."[218]

The trial judge had determined that Illinois law should govern the case, but he certified this determination for immediate appeal to the Illinois Supreme Court. If Michigan law applied, the plaintiffs would not have to prove negligence, but they would be precluded from recovering some types of damages, and Michigan limited certain damages.[219]

In upholding the trial court's decision to adopt Illinois law, the court employed the *Second Restatement* sections set forth above.[220] The court examined four types of contacts under the most significant relationship test: (1) the place of the injury, (2) the place of the conduct causing the injury, (3) the parties' domiciles and places of business, and (4) the place where the parties entered into their relationship.[221] The court first looked at the quantity of the contacts: "[i]n this case contact 1 lies with Michigan, and contacts 3 and 4 lie with Illinois. As to contact 2, [the bus driver's] alleged negligent conduct occurred in Michigan, but [the bus company's] act or omission occurred in Illinois."[222]

The court, however, declared that counting contacts was not enough: "A court is also to consider the relative importance of the various contacts."[223] The court felt that the place of the injury "was a mere happenstance," so it carried little weight in the analysis.[224] The court also thought that the place of the negligence was secondary because negligence was not the issue. Because the right of recovery and the amount recoverable were the main issues, a key contact was the parties' domiciles, the jurisdictions "which personally will feel the social and economic impact of recovery or nonrecovery."[225] Also important was the place the parties' relationship was centered—"when, as here, . . . the injury was caused by an act done in the course of the relationship, then the place where the relationship is centered has an important contact with the parties and the occurrence."[226] Because the important contacts were with Illinois, the court held that Illinois law should govern the case.[227]

5. Hybrid Approaches

Some courts have adopted hybrid approaches to choice of law. For example, *Blakesley v. Wolford* combined elements of governmental interest analysis with the *Second Restatement*'s most significant relationship test.[228]

In *Blakesley*, a Pennsylvania woman had suffered nerve damage while having her wisdom teeth removed. Unable to find a Pennsylvania oral surgeon who could correct the problem, she consulted a Texas oral surgeon, who had a speaking engagement in Pennsylvania. The Texas oral surgeon told her about an operation in which he could repair the damaged nerve with another nerve and the prognosis for the procedure. She decided to go to Texas for the operation, after the oral surgeon told her that he would only perform the operation there. Before the operation, he again informed his patient about the procedure.

The operation failed to solve the problem, and it caused additional damage. One possible reason for the operation's failure was that the oral surgeon used a different nerve for the graft.

The patient filed suit in Pennsylvania, claiming lack of informed consent. The plaintiff argued that Pennsylvania law, which set an easier standard for proving lack of informed consent, should apply, while the defendant asserted that Texas law, which was intended to limit medical malpractice claims in order to lower health care costs and promote the availability of health care in Texas, should govern. The trial court adopted Pennsylvania law, and the jury returned an $800,000 verdict for the plaintiff.

The court stated that the Pennsylvania choice of law rule was

> [i]n determining which state has the greater interest in the application of

> its law, one method is to see what contacts each state has with the accident, the contacts being relevant only if they relate to the 'policies and interests underlying the particular issue before the court.' When doing this it must be remembered that a mere counting of contacts is not what is involved. The weight of a particular state's contacts must be measured on a qualitative rather than quantitative scale.[229]

The appellate court thought that a true conflict existed because Pennsylvania had an interest in fully compensating its citizens who were victims of physician malpractice, and Texas had an interest in limiting malpractice claims.[230] The court solved this true conflict by evaluating the states' contacts to the issue.

Both the appellate court and the district court examined three classes of contacts: (1) the parties' citizenships, (2) the place where the injury occurred, and (3) the place where the conduct causing the injury occurred.[231] Concerning the parties' citizenships, the court found that the contacts neutralized each other because of Pennsylvania's interest in protecting its citizens against medical malpractice and Texas's equally strong interest in holding down health care costs.

Concerning the place where the injury occurred, the court thought that the place was Texas, disagreeing with the lower court. The appellate court felt that the lower court had incorrectly focused on the place where the injury's effects were felt. The court declared that "[i]t is axiomatic that wherever the plaintiff lives, the effects of his or her personal injuries will be felt. However, looking to the place where the effects of an injury will be felt gives improper additional weight to the factor of the plaintiff's state of residence."[232]

The court found that the place where the conduct causing the injury occurred was also Texas.[233] The court concluded that, although the initial consultation happened in Pennsylvania, the final consent for the operation took place in Texas because the plaintiff had "testified that if she had been informed of all the risks entailed in using a different donor nerve at the Texas meeting, she would not have gone through with the operation."[234] The court also pointed out that "Blakesley's [the patient's] voluntary acceptance of Wolford's [the physician's] express condition that the operation take place in Texas, and her action in intentionally traveling to Texas for her operation, fully support a conclusion that Texas law should apply."[235] Under such conditions, "[i]nhabitants of a state should not be put in jeopardy of liability exceeding that created by their state's laws just because a visitor from a state offering higher protection decides to visit there."[236]

6. Modern Constitutional Constraints on Choice of Law

The current constitutional constraints on choice of law are minimal. State choice of law is constitutional as long as the state whose law is chosen has "a significant contact or significant aggregation of contacts, creating state interests, such that choice of law is neither arbitrary nor fundamentally unfair."[237] Thus, the modern constraints are unilateralist; a court can adopt a state's law, even if another state's law is more appropriate, as long as the above test is satisfied.

In *Allstate Ins. Co. v. Hague*, the case that established the minimal constraints, the plaintiff's husband had died in a motorcycle accident in Wisconsin.[238] The husband was a Wisconsin domiciliary at the time of his death, but he worked in Minnesota. The other parties involved in the accident had no insurance, but the decedent had insured three automobiles with Allstate that included uninsured motorist coverage with a $15,000 limit per automobile.

After the accident, the widow moved to Minnesota, where she remarried, and Minnesota appointed her personal representative of her husband's estate. As personal representative, she filed an action in Minnesota "seeking a declaration under Minnesota law that the $15,000 uninsured motorist coverage on each of her husband's three automobiles could be 'stacked' to provide a total coverage of $45,000."[239] The defendant alleged that Wisconsin law prohibited stacking and that Wisconsin law governed because (1) the insurer had delivered the policy in Wisconsin, (2) the accident had occurred there, and (3) all relevant persons were Wisconsin residents at the time of the accident.[240]

Although the Minnesota trial court agreed that Wisconsin law prevented stacking, it entered summary judgment for the plaintiff because Minnesota choice of law rules required the adoption of Minnesota law on the ground that the antistacking rule was "inimical to the public policy of Minnesota."[241] The Minnesota Supreme Court affirmed, using Leflar's approach to choice of law, particularly the fifth factor—application of the better rule.[242]

The sole issue in *Allstate* was whether Minnesota's choice of its law was constitutional.[243] The Court declared that it had long accepted that more than one state's law might be applicable to a controversy.[244] In addition, the Court had traditionally examined the contacts of the state whose law was being applied with the parties and occurrence or transaction under both the due process and full faith and credit clauses.[245] The Court noted that it had struck down the use of a state's law when such contacts were lacking.[246] The Court then cited cases (*Alaska Packers, Cardillo,* and *Clay*) where the Court had upheld choice of law decisions when there were significant contacts with the state whose law governed.[247]

The Court found "three contacts with the parties and the occurrence giving rise to the litigation": (1) the decedent worked in Minnesota and he commuted to work from Wisconsin to Minnesota, (2) Allstate did business in Minnesota, and (3) the widow moved to Minnesota before the litigation.[248] Concerning the first contact, the Court stated that "[e]mployment status is not a sufficiently less important status than residence."[249] Concerning the second contact, the Court pointed out that "[b]y virtue of its presence, Allstate can hardly claim unfamiliarity with the laws of the host jurisdiction and surprise that the state courts might apply forum law to litigation in which the company is involved."[250] Finally, concerning the third contact, the Court noted, "Respondent's residence and subsequent appointment in Minnesota as personal representative of her husband's estate constitute a Minnesota contact which gives Minnesota an interest in respondent's recovery, an interest which the court below identified as full compensation for 'resident accident victims' to keep them 'off welfare rolls' and able 'to meet financial obligations.'"[251]

While the *Allstate* standard would allow most state choice of law decisions, a state's choice of law can violate this standard in extreme cases. For example, *Phillips Petroleum Co. v. Shutts* used the *Allstate* standard to invalidate a state court's choice of law in a class action.[252] In *Shutts*, a petroleum company had leased land in eleven states, and it had paid royalties on natural gas taken from the land.[253] The company requested several price increases from the Federal Power Commission on the natural gas it sold. Under the Commission's regulations, the company could collect the tentative higher prices while awaiting final approval. If the Commission rejected the higher prices, the company would have to make refunds to the buyers.

The petroleum company, however, did not pass on the additional royalties from the tentative higher prices to the landowners. Rather, it gave the landowners the increase only if they posted a bond or indemnity for the increase, plus interest, should the rate be disapproved. A few owners agreed to the indemnity, but most did not receive a royalty on the unapproved portion of the increase. Although the Commission approved all increases the company requested, the company did not pay the landowners interest on the withheld royalties when it distributed the withheld funds.

Three landowners filed a class action in Kansas state court, and the court certified the class.[254] The trial court held the company liable for interest on the suspended royalties, and the company appealed.[255] On appeal to the Kansas Supreme Court, the company maintained that the trial court had erred in applying Kansas law to all claims, including those where the land lay outside of Kansas. The Kansas Supreme Court affirmed, stating that "generally the law of the forum controlled all claims unless compelling reasons existed to apply a different law."[256]

The Supreme Court held that the Kansas courts' application of Kansas law to all claims was unconstitutional.[257] The Court first determined whether Kansas law conflicted with the other states' laws, finding that apparently there were conflicts.[258]

The Court then applied the *Allstate* standard "that for a State's substantive law to be selected in a constitutionally permissible manner, that State must have a significant contact or significant aggregation of contacts, creating state interests, such that choice of law is neither arbitrary nor fundamentally unfair."[259] The Court examined the contacts in the Kansas Supreme Court opinion to see if they satisfied the standard, and it rejected all these contacts as constitutionally insignificant.[260] First, the Court disagreed with the contention that there was a common fund in Kansas.[261] Second, the Court held that the plaintiffs' desire to have Kansas law employed, indicated by their failure to opt out, was irrelevant: "In most cases, the plaintiff shows his obvious wish for forum law by filing there."[262]

The Court also rejected the argument that Kansas could apply its law to all claims because there was a nationwide class action.[263] The Court asserted that the existence of jurisdiction and the presence of the due process procedural guarantees of notice and adequate representation were not enough to satisfy due process. Moreover, the fact that it might be difficult to comply with constitutional limitations because of the large number of transactions involved cannot change those limitations.

Finally, application of Kansas law to non-Kansas leases did not conform to the parties' expectations; the parties had no understanding that Kansas law might govern when the leases were executed.[264] Consequently, "Kansas 'may not abrogate the rights of parties beyond its borders having no relation to anything done or to be done within them.' "[265]

D. RECENT CHOICE OF LAW SCHOLARSHIP

In recent years, several scholars have harshly criticized Professor Currie's method.[266] For example, some commentators have questioned whether governmental interests really exist or are useful in making choice of law decisions.[267] Other scholars have also criticized governmental interest analysis because it is not forum neutral, which allows a case's outcome to hinge on where the suit was filed.[268]

In the place of Currie's policy based method, several of these scholars have proposed systems that choose law based on rights. This section will examine three such approaches.

1. Lea Brilmayer's Negative Rights Approach

Professor Lea Brilmayer advocates an approach based on negative rights against the government.[269] Her proposal is not a comprehensive method for choosing law; rather, it is an approach to determining what law a court *can* choose, much like constitutional limitations on choice of law. Accordingly, Brilmayer's proposal may allow the law of several jurisdictions to be applied to a situation—it is unilateralist. Professor Brilmayer asserts that "[a] negative rights-based argument might rule out the application of state A law without dictating a choice between B and C's."[270]

Brilmayer rejects choice of law systems predicated on furthering social policy because "one cannot simply take for granted the fairness of using a multistate litigant as a means to that end."[271] Instead, Brilmayer focuses on the individual, and she adopts a deontological approach that sets out "[a] political rights model of choice of law [that] requires a state to justify its exercise of coercive authority over an individual aggrieved by the application of the state's law."[272] In other words, "a state must be able to justify the burdens that it imposes, as well as explain the benefits it seeks to achieve, when it applies its law."[273]

Under Brilmayer's approach, a court must "identify the circumstances under which the state has, or lacks, an adequate justification for coercion."[274] First, the court must determine the connection between the state and the party burdened by the application of that state's law. An adequate connection between the state and the burdened party might comprise: (1) the party's status as a local domiciliary, (2) the party's consent to the application of the state's law, or (3) the party's voluntary affiliation with the state by engaging in local conduct or activities with foreseeable legal consequences in the state.[275] Second, the court must examine the connection between the state and the party who is to be benefitted by the choice of law. Brilmayer asks, "[i]s there the sort of connection that would allow application of local law if the tables were turned and he or she thus stood to lose?"[276] Ideally, a court will adopt the law of a state with connections to both parties.

2. Perry Dane's Vestedness Approach

Like Brilmayer's approach, Professor Perry Dane's approach to choice of law is not a full-fledged system, but a constraint on choice of law.[277] In his article, Dane attacks choice of law systems based on *lex fori*—that favor forum law. Instead, Dane advocates a multilateralist approach, which he calls "vestedness," that requires that "the court of any forum should, in selecting the criteria governing the substantive elements in an adjudication, apply choice of law criteria that could be expected to generate the same set of substantive criteria if they were applied by any other forum in an actual adjudication."[278]

Dane notes that vestedness does not guarantee identical results.[279] First, it does not require that all jurisdictions adopt the same choice of law rule. Rather, it mandates that the conflicts rule a jurisdiction employs produce the same substantive criteria if used by a different forum.[280] Second, vestedness might not produce the same substantive result even if jurisdictions use the same choice of law rule. Nonsubstantive elements may generate different outcomes. Moreover, two judges in different forums might view an identical controversy differently, which, of course, is also true of two judges sitting in the same jurisdiction.

3. Larry Kramer's Interpretive Method

Larry Kramer advocates an interpretive method of choice of law that retains Currie's basic insight concerning the applicability of standard methods of statutory interpretation to conflicts.[281] Professor Larry Kramer observes that choice of law problems are not limited to multistate situations but may occur in domestic lawsuits. He suggests that one can apply techniques for solving domestic choice of law problems to multistate situations.

Kramer proposes a two-step method of choice of law: (1) one must ascertain whether there is a conflict of laws and (2) if there is a conflict, one must employ a "second-order rule of interpretation to choose between these laws."[282] Obviously, a court does not have to choose between laws unless two laws can govern a case. Kramer calls establishing whether more than one law might be applicable "determining a law's prima facie applicability."[283]

Kramer adopts a positivistic approach in ascertaining a law's prima facie applicability. He examines whether a law creates a right that might apply to the case. In other words, has the legislature, expressly or implicitly, intended that the law govern the situation? Such analysis "has two components: (1) ascertaining the purpose that led to the adoption of a law in wholly domestic cases, and (2) presuming that the law applies only when that purpose is advanced in that state."[284]

The above analysis may generate three results: (1) no law creates a right, (2) one law creates a right, or (3) both laws create a right. In many situations, this analysis will end the inquiry because the case falls within the first two categories; if there is no right or only one law furnishes a right, there is no choice of law problem. If two laws provide a right, then a court must go to the next step—resolving true conflicts.

Kramer resolves true conflicts by using second-order principles—canons of construction that eclectically draw on other conflicts methods.[285] These canons include: (1) "if there is a conflict between two states' laws, and a failure to apply one of the laws would render it practically ineffective, that law should be applied;"[286] (2) "in a conflict between a substantive policy and a procedural policy, the law reflecting the substantive policy should prevail unless the forum's procedural interest is so strong that the forum should dismiss on grounds of *forum non conviens*;" (3) "in contract cases, true conflicts should be resolved by applying the law chosen by the parties, or, if no express choice is made, by applying whichever law validates the contract;" (4) "where one of two conflicting laws is obsolete . . . the other law should be applied;" and (5) "where two laws conflict, but the parties actually and reasonably relied on one of them, that law should be applied."

E. CHOICE OF LAW AT THE END OF THE CENTURY

Choice of law in the twentieth century has moved from a fairly uniform, multilateralist choice of law method dominant at the beginning of the century to several systems coexisting awkwardly at the end. According to one scholar, in 1997 in torts, eleven states used the traditional method (a variation on Beale), three states a significant contacts approach,[287] twenty states the *Second Restatement* approach, three states interest analysis, three states a *lex fori* approach (always adopt forum law as long as doing so is constitutional),[288] five a better law approach, and six a combined modern method.[289] Similarly, in contracts, ten states employed the traditional method, five states a significant contacts approach, twenty-five the *Second Restatement*, two a better law approach, and ten a combined modern approach.[290]

This inconsistency in state choice of law methods cannot continue. As later chapters show in detail, the disarray that is now the dominant feature of conflicts law can be significantly reduced by returning to multilateralism in both choice of law methodology and constitutional constraints on state choice of law.

NOTES

1. JOSEPH BEALE, A TREATISE ON THE CONFLICT OF LAWS (1935) [hereinafter BEALE, TREATISE]; RESTATEMENT OF THE LAW OF CONFLICT OF LAWS (1934) [hereinafter FIRST RESTATEMENT] (Beale was the principle draftsman of the FIRST RESTATEMENT); Joseph Beale, *What Law Governs the Validity of a Contract*, 23 HARV. L. REV. 1 (1909); JOSEPH H. BEALE, JR., A SELECTION OF CASES ON THE CONFLICT OF LAWS (1900, 1902). Other important choice of law studies in the period include HERBERT F. GOODRICH, HANDBOOK ON THE CONFLICT OF LAWS (1927) and RALEIGH C. MINOR, CONFLICT OF LAWS (1901).

2. JOSEPH STORY, COMMENTARIES ON THE CONFLICT OF LAWS § 18, at 19 (1st ed. 1834).

3. *Id.* § 20, at 21.

4. According to Morton Horwitz, Duncan Kennedy coined the term. *See* MORTON J. HORWITZ, THE TRANSFORMATION OF AMERICAN LAW, 1870–1960: THE CRISIS OF LEGAL ORTHODOXY 273 n.1 (1992); *see also* Duncan Kennedy, *Towards an Historical Understanding of Legal Consciousness: The Case of Classical Legal Thought in America, 1850–1940*, 3 RES. LAW & SOC. 3 (1980).

5. HORWITZ, *supra* note 4, at 10; G. EDWARD WHITE, TORT LAW IN AMERICA: AN INTELLECTUAL HISTORY 6 (1985) [hereinafter WHITE, TORT LAW].

6. Thomas C. Grey, *Langdell's Orthodoxy*, 45 U. PITT. L. REV. 1, 5 (1983).

7. GRANT GILMORE, THE AGES OF AMERICAN LAW 62 (1977); HORWITZ, *supra* note 4, at 16–17; WHITE, TORT LAW, *supra* note 5, at 6; *see generally* Grey, *supra* note 6. For a defense of the period's legal thought that tries to view it in its original context, *see* Marcia Speziale, *Langdell's Concept of Law as Science: The Beginning of Anti-Formalism in American Legal Thought*, 5 VT. L. REV 1 (1980).

8. G. Edward White, *From Sociological Jurisprudence to Realism: Jurisprudence and Social Change in Early Twentieth-Century America*, in PATTERNS of AMERICAN LEGAL THOUGHT 99, 101–102 (1978) [hereinafter, White, *Sociological Jurisprudence*].

9. HORWITZ, *supra* note 4, at 17–19.

10. WHITE, TORT LAW, *supra* note 5, at 33.

11. HORWITZ, *supra* note 4, at 17–18.

12. Grey, *supra* note 6, at 11.

13. HORWITZ, *supra* note 4, at 35.

14. *Id.*

15. Grey, *supra* note 6, at 5.

16. Elizabeth Mensch, *The History of Mainstream Legal Thought*, *in* THE POLITICS OF LAW 16, 24–25 (David Kairys ed., 1982) (emphasis in original).

17. 95 U.S. 714 (1878).

18. *Id.* at 722.

19. *Id.* at 727.

20. *Id.*

21. *Id.* at 734.

22. 1 BEALE, TREATISE §§ 4.12, 5.2, *supra* note 1, at 46, 52.

23. FIRST RESTATEMENT § 377, *supra* note 1.

24. *Id.* §§ 332, 377.

25. 2 BEALE, TREATISE § 384.1, *supra* note 1, at 1298, 3 BEALE, TREATISE APPENDIX § 73, at 1967–69. "A right having been created by the appropriate law, the recognition of its existence should follow everywhere. Thus an act valid where done cannot be called into question anywhere." *Id.* at 1969. Beale derived his notion of vested rights from the English theorist A. V. Dicey. *See* A. V. DICEY, A DIGEST OF THE LAW OF ENGLAND WITH REFERENCE TO THE CONFLICT OF LAWS 22 (1896); *see also Joseph H. Beale, Dicey's "Conflict of Laws,"* 10 HARV. L. REV. 168 (1896).

26. Slater v. Mexican Nat'l R.R. Co., 194 U.S. 120, 126 (1904).

27. Smith v. Firemens Ins. Co. of Newark, 590 A.2d 24, 27 (Pa. Super. 1991).

28. STORY §§ 23, 29, 32-38, *supra* note 2, at 24–25, 30, 33–37.

29. *E.g*, Levy v. Daniels U-Drive Auto Renting Co., 143 A. 163, 164–65 (Conn. 1928). I discuss this case in Chapter 5.

30. FIRST RESTATEMENT, § 612, *supra* note 1.

31. 2 BEALE, TREATISE §377.2, *supra* note 1, at 1287.

32. *Id.* at 1288.

33. *Id.* § 378.1 at 1288–89.

34. Characterization and the public policy exception might change this in a small number of cases.

35. *Id.* § 4.12, at 46.

36. The fact that Beale's method might result in the adoption of a law with a tenuous connection to a controversy does not affect his system's multilateralist character. Although one might criticize the effectiveness of Beale's last act criterion, he was still trying to find the most appropriate legal system.

37. In addition to the cases discussed in this section, see *Home Ins. Co. v. Dick*, 281 U.S. 397 (1930); *Mutual Life Ins. Co. v. Liebing*, 259 U.S. 209 (1922); *Western Union Tel. Co. v. Brown*, 234 U.S. 542 (1914).

38. 246 U.S. 357 (1918).

39. *Id.* at 372.

40. *Id.* at 365–66.

41. *Id.* at 366–67.

42. *Id.* at 373.

43. *Id.* at 369, 371.

44. *Id.* at 373–77.

45. *Id.* at 377.

46. Hartford Accident & Indem. Co. v. Delta & Pine Land Co., 292 U.S. 143, 149 (1934).

47. 286 U.S. 145 (1932).

48. *Id.* at 151.

49. *Id.* at 153.

50. *Id.* at 158.

51. *Id.* at 159.

52. 2 BEALE, TREATISE § 398.2, *supra* note 1, at 1318.

53. HORWITZ, *supra* note 4, at 6.

54. *Id.* at 198–206. This attack began in the first decade of the Twentieth Century. *See, e.g.*, Roscoe Pound, *Mechanical Jurisprudence*, 8 COLUM. L. REV. 605 (1908).

55. Lochner v. New York, 198 U.S. 45, 76 (1905) (J. Holmes dissenting).

56. HORWITZ, *supra* note 4, at 202, 208–10; White, *Sociological Jurisprudence*, *supra* note 8, at 122, 124–25; *see also*, Roscoe Pound, *The Theory of Judicial Decisions*, 36 HARV. L. REV. 641, 645–6, 954–55 (1923).

57. Felix Cohen, *Transcendental Nonsense and the Functional Approach*, 35 COLUM. L. REV. 809, 824 (1935).

58. HORWITZ, *supra* note 4, at 199.

59. Standard Oil v. United States, 221 U.S. 1 (1911).

60. United States v. Carroll Towing Co., 159 F.2d 169, 173 (2d Cir. 1947).

61. Walter W. Cook, *Scientific Method of the Law*, 13 A.B.A. J. 303, 307 (1927).

62. *Id.* at 308.

63. *Id.* Felix Cohen, a leading realist scholar, declared that "I think that creative legal thought will more and more look behind the traditionally accepted principles of 'justice' and 'reason' to appraise in ethical terms the social values at stake in any choice between two precedents." *Cohen, supra* note 57, at 833.

64. *E.g.*, David F. Cavers, *A Critique of the Choice-of-Law Problem*, 47 HARV. L. REV. 173, 173–76 (1933) [hereinafter Cavers, *Critique*]; Hessel E. Yntema, *The Hornbook Method and the Conflict of Laws*, 37 YALE L.J. 468 (1928); Walter W. Cook, *The Logical and Legal Bases of the Conflict of Laws*, 33 YALE L.J. 457, 458–60 (1924) [hereinafter Cook, *Conflict*]; Ernest G. Lorenzen, *Territoriality, Public Policy and the Conflict of Laws*, 33 YALE L.J. 736, 743–46 (1924).

65. Cook, *Conflict, supra* note 64, at 460, 475–76, *passim.*

66. *Id.* at 460.

67. Yntema, *supra* note 64, at 481.

68. *E.g.*, Lorenzen, *supra* note 64, at 743, 745, 748–50.

69. *Id.* at 748; Cavers, *supra* note 64, at 178–79; 187–89; *passim.*

70. Lorenzen, *supra* note 64, at 745.

71. Cook, *Conflict, supra* note 64, *passim*; Cavers, *supra* note 64, at 208.

72. LEA BRILMAYER, CONFLICT OF LAWS 25–27 (1995) [hereinafter BRILMAYER, CONFLICT].

73. Cook, *Conflict, supra* note 64, at 475–76; *see also* Cavers, *supra* note 64, at 175–76.

74. Erie R.R. Co. v. Thompkins, 304 U.S. 64, 79 (1938).

75. Lorenzen, *supra* note 64, at 746–47.

76. *Id.* at 747.

77. Cook, *Conflict, supra* note 64, at 469 (emphasis in original). Cook partially derived his local law theory from Judge Hand's opinion in *Guinness v. Miller*, 291 F. 769 (S.D.N.Y. 1923).

78. Cook, *Conflict, supra* note 64, at 475.

79. DAVID CAVERS, THE CHOICE-OF-LAW PROCESS 9 (1965) [hereinafter CAVERS, PROCESS]; *see also* Cavers, *Critique, supra* note 64, at 194.

80. CAVERS, PROCESS, *supra* note 79, at 9.

81. 294 U.S. 532 (1935).

82. 306 U.S. 493 (1938).

83. *Alaska Packers*, 294 U.S. at 542.

84. *Id.* at 537.

85. *Id.* at 538.

86. *Id.*

87. *Id.*, *citing*, Quang Ham Wah Co. v. Industrial Accident Comm'n, 192 P. 1021 (Cal. 1920).

88. *Alaska Packers*, 294 U.S. at 538.

89. *Id.* at 533–37.

90. *Id.* at 535.

91. *Id.* at 536 (emphasis added).

92. *Id.* at 537.

93. *Id.*

94. *Id.* at 539–43.

95. *Id.* at 540–41.

96. *Id.*

97. *Id.*

98. *Id.* at 542.

99. *Id.*

100. *Id.* at 543.

101. *Id.* at 544–550.

102. *Id.* at 545.

103. *Id.* at 547.

104. *Id.*

105. *Id.* at 548.

106. *Id.* at 547–48.

107. 306 U.S. at 493.

108. *Id.* at 500 ("[T]he constitutionality [under the due process clause] of the provisions of the California statute awarding compensation for injuries to an employee occurring within its borders, and for injuries as well occurring elsewhere, when the contract of employment was entered into within the state, is not open to question.").

109. *Id.* at 503.

110. *Id.*

111. *Id.* at 504.

112. *Alaska Packers*, 294 U.S. at 548.

113. 348 U.S. 66 (1954); *see also* Cardillo v. Liberty Mut. Ins. Co., 330 U.S. 469, 476 (1947).

114. *Watson*, 348 U.S. at 69.

115. *Id.* at 72.

116. Carroll v. Lanza, 349 U.S. 408 (1955); *see also* Nevada v. Hall, 440 U.S. 410, 421–24 (1979).

117. *Carroll*, 449 U.S. at 420.

118. *See* BRAINERD CURRIE, SELECTED ESSAYS ON THE CONFLICT OF LAWS (1963).

119. *See* Symeon C. Symeonides, *Choice of Law in American Courts in 1997*, 46 AM. J. COMP. L. 233, 266 (1997). Professor Brilmayer has observed that "[w]hile a surprisingly large number of states still adhere to the First Restatement of Conflicts, they do so less because of its status as an immutable truth than the simple facts that change is costly and that the alternatives don't seem perfect either." BRILMAYER, CONFLICT, *supra* note 72, at 4–5.

120. Paul A. Freund, *Chief Justice Stone and the Conflict of Laws*, 59 HARV. L. REV. 1210, 1223–25 (1946).

121. *Id.* at 1225.

122. *Id.* at 1223–24.

123. CURRIE, *supra* note 118, at 107, 163, 180, 189, 726.

124. Freund, *supra* nore 120, at 1223–24.

125. *Id.* at 1224.

126. *Id.*

127. Moffatt Hancock, *Choice-of-Law Policies in Multiple Contact Cases*, 5 U. TORONTO L.J. 133, 140–46 (1943).

128. *Id.* at 141.

129. *Id.* at 141–42.

130. *Id.* at 143.

131. *See* Emery v. Emery, 289 P.2d 218 (Cal. 1955); Grant v. McAuliffe, 264 P.2d 944 (Cal. 1953). I discuss both of these cases in detail in Chapter 5.

132. 129 P.2d 691 (Cal. 1942).

133. *Id.* at 693.

134. *Id.* at 697.

135. *Id.*

136. *Id.*

137. Antecedents of the *Second Restatement* go back at least as far as Savigy's "seat of the relationship" test. FRIEDRICH CARL VON SAVIGNY, PRIVATE INTERNATIONAL LAW 27, 94–95 (1869); *see also* JOHN WESTLAKE, A TREATISE ON PRIVATE INTERNATIONAL LAW 288 (1922) ("[T]he law by which to determine the intrinsic validity and effect of a contract will be selected in England on substantial considerations, the preference given to the country with which the transaction has the most real connection, and not the place of the contract as such."). For a discussion of Savigny's importance for modern choice of law in contracts cases, see Mathias Reiman, Savigny's Triumph? Choice of Law in Contracts Cases at the Close of the Twentieth Century, 39 VA. J. INT. L. 571 (1999). Professor Reiman has

declared that "[t]oday, both the American and the European approaches to contracts conflicts [in the absence of a contractual choice of law clause] employ essentially the same technique: they combine the broad principle of the 'most significant relationship' or 'closest connection' with specific rules. These rules are phrased as presumptions and subject to escape clauses." *Id.* at 587. "On the European side, the Rome Convention is drafted in terms of the closest connection." *Id.* at 581.

138. ELLIOT E. CHEATHAM ET. AL., CASES AND MATERIALS ON CONFLICT OF LAWS 411 (1941).

139. *Id.*

140. Elliot E. Cheatham and Willis L. M. Reese, *Choice of the Applicable Law*, 52 COLUM. L. REV. 959 (1952).

141. These factors resemble the choice of law factors in § 6 of the *Second Restatement*, which are discussed below.

142. *Id.* at 972.

143. *Id.* at 973.

144. *Id.* at 975.

145. *Id.*

146. FOWLER VINCENT HARPER AND CHARLES W. TAINTOR II, CASES AND OTHER MATERIALS ON JUDICIAL TECHNIQUE IN CONFLICT OF LAWS 173–75 (1937); *see also* Fowler V. Harper, *Policy Bases of the Conflict of Laws: Reflections on Reading Professor Lorenzen's Essays*, 56 YALE L.J. 1155, 1161–67 (1947).

147. HARPER AND TAINTOR, *supra* note 146, at 173.

148. J. H. C. Morris, *The Proper Law of a Tort*, 64 HARV. L. REV. 881 (1951).

149. *Id.* at 893.

150. *Id.* at 885–86.

151. *Id.* at 886.

152. *Id.* at 888.

153. 124 N.E.2d 99 (N.Y. 1954). Chapter 5 criticizes the court's reasoning. A few earlier cases also took a similar approach to contracts, *e.g.*, *Jansson v. Swedish American Line*, 185 F.2d 212, 218–19 (1st Cir. 1950); *Rubin v. Irving Trust Co.*, 113 N.E.2d 424, 431 (N.Y. 1953); *W. H. Barber Co. v. Hughes*, 63 N.E.2d 417, 423 (Ind. 1945), but I am discussing *Auten* in detail because scholars and courts have frequently analyzed this case.

154. *Id.* at 100.

155. O. von Gierke apparently coined the term. *See* 1 O. VON GIERKE, DEUTSCHES PRIVATRECHT 217 (1895).

156. *Auten*, 124 N.E.2d at 102.

157. *Id.*

158. *Id.*

159. *Id.*

160. *Id.* at 103.

161. *Id.*

162. Currie fully acknowledged his predecessors. CURRIE, *supra* note 118, at 87, 612–15.

163. *See* Symeonides, *supra* note 119, at 266.

164. *See* the section "Recent Choice of Law Scholarship" below.

165. Governmental interest analysis's vitality is reflected in the extensive symposium recently devoted to it at Mercer Law School. *See Choice of Law: How It Ought to Be*, 48 MERCER L. REV. 623, 623–916 (1997).

166. CURRIE, *supra* note 118, at 180. As Professor Roosevelt has noted, "interest analysis makes a very important advance by conceiving of multistate cases as clashes between sovereigns, each attempting to impose its own regulatory scheme in furtherance of its own policies." Kermit Roosevelt III, *The Myth of Choice of Law: Rethinking Conflicts*, 97 MICH. L. REV. 2448, 2463 (1999).

167. Currie, *supra* note 118, at 178.

168. *Id.* at 183–84.

169. *Id.* at 119.

170. *Id.* at 181–83, 601–2.

171. *Id.* at 117.

172. *E.g.*, *id.* at 107, 163, 180, 189, 726. While I am critical of much of Professor Currie's method, a modified version of "false conflict" is central to my approach.

173. 125 Mass. 374 (1878).

174. CURRIE, *supra* note 118, at 77–127.

175. *Id.* at 90.

176. *Id.* at 117, 119, 181–83, 601–02.

177. BRILMAYER, CONFLICT, *supra* note 72, at 228.

178. *Id.* at 299.

179. *Id.*

180. *Id.* at 85; *see also* FRIEDERICH K. JUENGER, CHOICE OF LAW AND MULTISTATE JUSTICE 100 (1993).

181. JUENGER, *supra* note 180, at 135.

182. Brainerd Currie, *The Disinterested Third State*, 28 LAW AND CONT. PROBLEMS 754, 757 (1963) [hereinafter, Currie, *The Disinterested Third State*]; *see also* Bernkrant v. Fowler, 360 P.2d 906 (Cal. 1961).

183. CURRIE, *The Disinterested Third State, supra* note 182, at 758.

184. William F. Baxter, *Choice of Law and the Federal System*, 16 STAN. L. REV. 1 (1963).

185. *Id.* at 9–22.

186. 546 P.2d 719 (Cal. 1976).

187. *Id.* at 725.

188. *Id.*

189. *Id.*

190. *Id.* at 725–26.

191. *E.g.*, JUENGER, *supra* note 180; Patrick J. Borchers, *The Origins of Diversity Jurisdiction, the Rise of Legal Positivism, and a Brave New World for Erie and Klaxon*, 72 TEX. L. REV. 79 (1993).

192. *See* ROBERT A. LEFLAR, AMERICAN CONFLICTS LAW 180–81 (3d. ed. 1977). One can see the continuing strength of the better rule approach in a recent symposium on whether there should be a new *Restatement of Conflicts* in which several scholars advocated the use of a better rule approach or a better rule criterion. Friedrich K. Juenger, *A Third Conflicts Restatement*, 75 IND. L.J. 403 (2000); Louise Weinberg, *A Structural Revision of the Conflicts Restatement*, 75 IND. L.J. 473 (2000); Bruce Posnak, *The Restatement (Second): Some Not So Fine Tuning for a Restatement (Third): A Very Well-Curried Leflar over Reese with Korn on the Side (Or Is It Cob)*, 75 IND. L.J. 561 (2000); William A. Reppy, Jr., *Codifying Interest Analysis in the Torts Chapter of a New Conflicts Restatement*, 75 IND. L.J. 591 (2000); Joseph William Singer, *Pay No Attention to the Man Behind the Curtain: The Place of Better Law in a Third Restatement of Conflicts*, 75 IND. L.J. 659 (2000).

193. *Id.* at 180–81.

194. *Id.* at 195.

195. *E.g.*, Clark v. Clark, 222 A.2d 205 (N.H. 1966); Heath v. Zellmer, 151 N.W.2d 664 (Wis. 1967); Brown v. Church of the Holy Name of Jesus, 252 A.2d 176 (R.I. 1969).

196. William A. Reppy, Jr., *Eclecticism in Choice of Law: Hybrid Method or Mishmash?* 34 MERCER L. REV. 645, 691 n.216 (1983); BRILMAYER, CONFLICT, *supra* note 72, at 71.

197. 203 N.W.2d 408 (Minn. 1973).

198. *Id.* at 414, 417.

199. *Id.* at 416–17.

200. *Id.* at 417.

201. *Id.*

202. *Id.*

203. *Id.*

204. *Id.*

205. *Id.* at 417–18.

206. JUENGER, *supra* note 180, at 194–95. Juenger would allow "alternate reference rules" to "facilitate the transition from the classical method to a value-oriented approach." *Id.* at 195–96.

207. 500 F.Supp. 656 (S.D.N.Y. 1980).

208. Borchers, *supra* note 191, at 128.

209. *Id.*

210. *Id.* at 129.

211. The *Second Restatement* originally "was to contain rules, not policies, in its black letter formulations . . ." Herma Hill Kay, *Theory into Practice: Choice of Law in the Courts*, 34 MERCER L. REV. 521, 553 (1983). However, while it was being drafted, the *Second Restatement* received considerable criticism, particularly concerning its failure to consider Currie's scholarship. *Id.* at 553–55. "The Restatement Second was thus promulgated with two vastly different conceptions about how a choice of law problem should be addressed." *Id.* at 555. Chapter 4 examines the dual origins of the *Second Restatement.*

212. Willis L. M. Reese, *The Second Restatement of Conflicts Revisited*, 34 MERCER L. REV. 501, 516 (1983).

213. RESTATEMENT (SECOND) OF CONFLICT OF LAWS § 188 (1971).

214. *Id.* at § 222.

215. *Id.* at § 291.

216. *Id.* at § 146.

217. 423 N.E.2d 278 (Ill. 1981).

218. *Id.* at 279.

219. *Id.*

220. *Id.* at 279–81.

221. *Id.* at 280.

222. *Id.*

223. *Id.*

224. *Id.*

225. *Id.*

226. *Id.*

227. *Id.* at 281.

228. 789 F.2d 236 (3d. Cir. 1986).

229. *Id.* at 239.

230. *Id.* at 240.

231. *Id.* at 241.

232. *Id.*

233. *Id.* at 242–43.
234. *Id.* at 243.
235. *Id.* at 242.
236. *Id.* at 243, *quoting*, *Cipolla v. Shaposka*, 267 A.2d 854, 856–57 (Pa. 1970).
237. Allstate Ins. Co. v. Hague, 449 U.S. 302, 313 (1981).
238. *Id.* at 305.
239. *Id.*
240. *Id.* at 306.
241. *Id.*
242. *Id.* at 306–07. Chapter 3 discusses the Minnesota Supreme Court's opinion.
243. *Id.* at 307.
244. *Id.*
245. *Id.* at 308, *citing*, Clay v. Sun Ins. Office Ltd., 377 U.S. 179, 183 (1964).
246. *Allstate*, 449 U.S. at 309, *citing*, John Hancock Mut. Life Ins. Co. v. Yates, 299 U.S. 178 (1936) and Home Ins. Co. v. Dick, 281 U.S. 397 (1930).
247. *Allstate*, 449 U.S. at 311–313.
248. *Id.* at 313–20.
249. *Id.* at 317.
250. *Id.* at 317–18.
251. *Id.* at 319.
252. 472 U.S. 797 (1985).
253. *Id.* at 799–800.
254. *Id.* at 800.
255. *Id.* at 802.
256. *Id.* at 808.
257. *Id.* at 814–23.
258. *Id.* at 816–18.
259. *Id.* at 819.
260. *Id.* at 819–23.
261. *Id.* at 819–20.
262. *Id.* at 820.
263. *Id.* at 820–23.
264. *Id.* at 822.
265. *Id.* On remand, the Kansas Supreme Court determined that the other interested states would calculate interest in roughly the same manner as Kansas did. *Shutts v. Phillips Petroleum Co.*, 732 P.2d 1286 (Kan. 1987).
266. *E.g.*, BRILMAYER, CONFLICT, *supra* note 72, 76–119; Lea Brilmayer, *Interest Analysis and the Myth of Legislative Intent*, 78 MICH. L. REV. 392 (1980); Lea Brilmayer, *Methods and Objectives in the Conflict of Laws: A Challenge*, 35 MERCER L. REV. 555 (1984); Harold L. Korn, *The Choice of Law Revolution: A Critique*, 83 COLUM. L. REV. 772 (1983); JUENGER, *supra* note 180, at 131–39; *see also* the articles cited below in this section. I present my critique of governmental interest analysis in Chapter 2 and discuss its constitutionality in Chapter 3.
267. JUENGER, *supra* note 180, at 131–39; Harold G. Maier, *Finding the Trees in Spite of the Metaphorist: The Problem of State Interests in Choice of Law*, 56 ALB. L. REV. 753, 759 (1993).
268. *E.g.*, BRILMAYER, CONFLICT, *supra* note 72, at 77; JUENGER, *supra* note 180, at 139; Perry Dane, *Vested Rights, 'Vestedness,' and Choice of Law*, 96 YALE L.J. 1191, 1205–6 (1987); Luther L. McDougal III, *Comprehensive Interest Analysis Versus Reformulated Governmental Interest Analysis: An Appraisal in the Context of Choice-of-*

Law Problems Concerning Contributory and Comparative Negligence, 26 UCLA L. REV. 439, 449–51 (1979); *see also*, John Hart Ely, *Choice of Law and the State's Interest in Protecting Its Own*, 23 WM & MARY L. REV. 173 (1981).

269. BRILMAYER, CONFLICT, *supra* note 72, at 219–63.

270. *Id.* at 223.

271. *Id.* at 235–36.

272. *Id.* at 240.

273. *Id.* at 262.

274. *Id.* at 240.

275. *Id.* at 241–53, 262.

276. *Id.* at 262; *see also id.* at 253–59.

277. Dane, *supra* note 268, at 1209.

278. *Id.* at 1205.

279. *Id.* at 1207–1209.

280. This is what makes his method multilateralist.

281. Larry Kramer, *Rethinking Choice of Law*, 90 COLUM. L. REV. 277 (1990).

282. *Id.* at 291.

283. *Id.*

284. *Id.* at 299.

285. *Id.* at 323–38. Kramer's canons resemble David Caver's "principles of preference." *See* CAVERS, PROCESS, *supra* note 79.

286. This canon resembles Professor Baxter's comparative impairment approach discussed above.

287. This is another name for the center of gravity approach that the New York court used in *Auten*.

288. *See* Foster v. Leggett, 484 S.W.2d 827, 829 (Ky. 1972).

289. *See* Symeonides, *supra* note 119, at 266.

290. *Id.* at 266.

Chapter 2

A Normative View of Choice of Law

All choice of law approaches contain underlying normative assumptions. Professor Brilmayer has asserted that "[t]he fundamental and unavoidable problem in choice of law is one of perspective. What normative perspective should a court adopt in making the choice between the law of one state and the law of another? This is a question of the proper normative grounding, of what is the appropriate foundation for choice of law?"[1]

This chapter presents this author's normative view of choice of law, then discusses the major modern conflicts methods in relation to this normative view.

A. CHOICE OF LAW CRITERIA

Choice of law should try to satisfy the following criteria:

1. Choice of law should be grounded in positive law,
2. Choice of law should be substantively neutral,
3. Choice of law should be forum neutral,
4. Choice of law should be predictable,
5. Choice of law should be fair to the individual litigants, and
6. Choice of law should reflect the relevant states' interests.

These criteria balance a respect for state sovereignty with the need to protect individual rights.[2]

1. Choice of Law Should Be Grounded in Positive Law

Legal thinkers in the late nineteenth and early twentieth centuries conceived of law as *a priori*—law existed before government, and the judge's role was to "find" this preexisting law.[3] A few early-twentieth-century legal scholars and judges rejected this natural law view, arguing instead that the only law that existed was positive law—law created by the state. Justice Holmes stated that "the life of the law has not been logic: it has been experience,"[4] and he fought against "the brooding omnipresence in the sky [natural law]."[5] Similarly, Justice Brandeis rejected the notion that there was federal common law because there was no pre-existing law that a judge could use as a basis for federal common law.[6]

Professor Wesley Hohfeld asserted that all law was positive law, and he revolutionized legal thinking by categorizing property into four pairs of correlative relations—right/duty, privilege/no right, power/liability, and immunity/disability, which he considered to be the lowest common denominators in the law.[7] Legal scholars have used these correlative relations in numerous contexts, and they are useful in thinking about choice of law.[8]

Although a few legal thinkers still view law as being based on natural law,[9] most modern scholars adopt a positive law approach—law must be enacted by a legislature, made by a judge, or promulgated by an administrative agency under proper authority. Moreover, requiring a positive law source for all law respects state sovereignty. Accordingly, choice of law must be grounded in positive law—a choice of law analysis must begin by looking at the legal relations created by the relevant states.

To be grounded in positive law, a choice of law method must select a law that the lawmaker (the legislature, the judge, or the agency) meant to encompass the situation that is being litigated. It is not enough that a law exists if it does not apply to the facts.[10] This requirement corresponds with the need to respect state sovereignty; choice of law hinders state sovereignty when it selects a law that the lawmaker did not intend to a apply to a dispute instead of a law that a different lawmaker did intend to apply. It is also unfair to an individual to have a state's law govern an issue when the lawmaker did not mean for it to apply to that issue. As the second part of this chapter shows, certain choice of law systems sometimes ignore this requirement and select a law that the lawmaker did not intend to govern a particular case.

Although determining a law's scope can often be difficult, some methods, particularly Professor Kramer's interpretative approach, do a fairly good job of establishing a law's scope.[11] Chapter 5 discusses the problem of establishing a law's scope in greater detail.

In *Allstate v. Hague*,[12] a Minnesota trial court had applied a Minnesota law that allowed stacking of uninsured motorist coverage in automobile insurance policies to a controversy that the Minnesota legislature probably did not intend it to apply to, thus, showing no respect for the sovereignty of Wisconsin, the state whose law should have governed. In *Hague*, the Supreme Court upheld this adoption of Minnesota's law in a case where the plaintiff's husband had been killed in a traffic accident. The decedent had been domiciled in Wisconsin at the time of his death, the insurance policy had been written there, and the accident had occurred there. On the other hand, the decedent had worked in Minnesota, Minnesota allowed Allstate to sell insurance there, and the plaintiff moved to Minnesota after her husband's death. Minnesota's law allowed stacking of insurance policies, whereas Wisconsin's did not.

A court could properly apply Wisconsin law to this case. The Wisconsin antistacking rule obviously encompasses an insurance policy written in Wisconsin for a Wisconsin domiciliary.

On the other hand, Minnesota probably did not intend its stacking rule to govern an insurance contract written in Wisconsin insuring a Wisconsin domiciliary and his property. A state generally regulates insurance policies written in that state or that cover its citizens or property with a situs in the state. A state usually does not regulate foreign insurance policies that insure noncitizens and foreign property.[13]

Similarly, the contacts with Minnesota do not support the conclusion that Minnesota intended its stacking rule to apply to this case. First, states do no normally regulate automobile insurance policies just because a person works in that state. Second, the fact that Minnesota licensed Allstate to sell insurance there is irrelevant. Licensing an insurance company to do business in a state does not mean that that state can regulate insurance sold in other states. Finally, the fact that the plaintiff moved to Minnesota after her husband's death is also irrelevant. The pertinent law is the law that governed at the time of the accident; the law of an after-acquired domicile cannot create a right for a preexisting tort.

Minnesota should not have been able to apply its law to the case even if the accident had occurred in Minnesota. The issue is what law governs the relationship between a nationwide insurance company and a Wisconsin citizen on a Wisconsin automobile insurance policy concerning the insured's coverage. The location of an accident covered by that policy is irrelevant to this issue.[14]

2. Choice of Law Should Be Substantively Neutral

A judge should not choose law based on how the judge feels a case should come out.[15] Choice of law is a method for ascertaining what law applies; it should not be a mechanism for substantive justice. When it is used for substantive justice, it interferes with state sovereignty and individual rights.

Substantive justice should be accomplished at the substantive level by the proper lawmaker, not at the choice of law level by a judge who just happened to draw a case. If a rule is substantively unjust, the sovereign that created the rule should change it; a judge should not have the unfettered discretion to use choice of law to undermine the authority of the sovereign that enacted the rule. The states have varying views on what the law should be, and courts in a federal union should be tolerant of another state's policy choices,[16] especially when that other state is more closely connected to the controversy than the forum. For example, one state may want unlimited medical malpractice damages to give injured patients full recovery, while another state may want to cap malpractice damages because damage ceilings may encourage larger numbers of medical providers to locate in that state, improving health care for all. Moreover, states have different needs and respond to different economic conditions; one should not expect that New York law and Alabama law will always be the same.

How do judges decide which substantive rule is the fairest one?[17] As Professor P. John Kozyris has asked, "[d]oes it really make sense to mix substantive justice with conflicts justice? Under what authority, from what source and in what practical way may a judge decide that one of two potentially applicable systems of justice is more just?"[18] The only possible method a judge can use to make such a decision is the judge's innate sense of justice—that is, natural law.[19] Should we allow a judge to reject the postivistic nature of American law in favor of natural law in conflicts when it has been overwhelmingly rejected in all other areas of law?

Contemporary products liability law illustrates the difficulty judges face in choosing the better substantive rule. Beginning in the 1960s, courts and legislatures developed rules to protect consumers from defective products.[20] However, in recent years, some jurisdictions have decided that such rules go too far and that damages should be limited to protect a manufacturer's solvency.[21]

Accordingly, how is a judge to decide which of these products liability rules is the better rule? There is no objective way to determine which of the above rules is the better one. As Professor Laycock has observed, "[t]here is no higher authority, no lawgiver in the sky, empowered to decide which state's laws is better."[22] Similarly, Professor Joseph William Singer has rejected any notion of "basic policies underlying the particular field of law" or "policies all states share."[23] He has declared that "the reason we have a conflicts case is because the laws of the two states conflict. They do not have a shared policy, and it is misleading to pretend that they do . . . . There is simply no basic policy of tort or contract law—these areas involve accommodations between conflicting interests in freedom and security."[24]

Consequently, a judge can follow her own sense of justice and decide for the plaintiff or manufacturer depending on which rule she feels is better. However, such an *ad hoc* judgment substitutes the judge's values for the values of the states that passed the laws, a solution that interferes with state sovereignty. In addition, since judges will have differing views as to which rule is just, there will be inconsistency among the courts, leading to an unworkable solution.

Equally important, where do judges get the power to apply their sense of justice to choice of law? When a case is governed by legislation, a judge cannot make law; he must follow the dictates of the appropriate legislature. Does the fact that a case involves two or more sovereigns and hence a choice of law change this rule? Likewise, how can a judge from one state overrule judge made law from another state? As Professor Silberman has asked, "can the state of Minnesota bind the nation?"[25]

A substantive approach to choice of law is also unfair to the individual litigants—it does not respect individual autonomy.[26] An individual should be judged by the rule of the most appropriate jurisdiction, not the rule that a single judge thinks is the most just for the world at large. Fairness to an individual does not only involve having the (supposedly) fairest substantive rule govern his or her activities; fairness also means having consistent, predictable rules applied to an individual's conduct.[27]

3. Choice of Law Should Be Forum Neutral

Choice of law should be forum neutral; a case's outcome should not depend on the forum in which it was filed.[28] Lack of forum neutrality in choice of law impedes both individual liberty and state sovereignty.

A forum should not be able to further its policies at the expense of justice to individual litigants in a private lawsuit. In particular, a jurisdiction should not be able to further its interests in a way that is unfair to nonresidents. A state cannot justify a consequentialist, utilitarian approach to choice of law when the person being burdened is not a citizen of that state. Consequently, when a state imposes its law on a nonresident, that state should have a very substantial connection to the case.

Lack of forum neutrality promotes forum shopping—a plaintiff will search for favorable law even if that law is from a state with a tenuous connection to a case. Although some conflicts scholars favor *lex fori* because they want law to be pro-plaintiff,[29] choice of law should favor neither plaintiffs nor defendants; it should choose the law of the most appropriate jurisdiction (the one with the closest connection to the controversy), regardless of which party that law favors. If a jurisdiction wants to be pro-plaintiff, it should do so at the substantive level. Why should a plaintiff have an increased right of recovery solely because multistate elements are involved? Moreover, sometimes more than one litigant might be able to file suit; winning the race to the court house should not determine a case's outcome.

Lack of forum neutrality also infringes on state sovereignty. When a state adopts its law because it is forum law, it is showing no respect for the sovereignty of other states that might be more closely connected to the dispute. Such a lack of respect for other states' sovereignty violates the structure of our federal union in which states must respect other states' sovereignty and enforce their laws when appropriate.

Choice of forum determined the outcome in *Allstate*. If the case had been filed in Wisconsin, a Wisconsin court would have applied its antistacking rule to an insurance policy that was executed in Wisconsin by a Wisconsin domiciliary. By imposing its own rule, Minnesota ignored the need for forum neutrality (and interfered with state sovereignty and individual autonomy) simply because it felt its prostacking rule was the fairer rule. Would Minnesota have thought that it was fair if the opposite situation had occurred—If Allstate had filed a declaratory judgement action in Wisconsin to establish that a Minnesota citizen could not stack under her

Minnesota insurance policy?

Rosenthal v. Warren[30] vividly illustrates the unfairness in "conflicts localism"—"cases favoring local substantive law when the forum state's relation to the controversy is clearly less than the place providing conflicting law."[31] In *Rosenthal*, a wrongful death case, the plaintiff's husband, a New York domiciliary, had gone to a Massachusetts hospital for an operation. The husband died while under the doctor's care, and the plaintiff sued the doctor and hospital for malpractice. The question was whether Massachusetts law that limited wrongful death damages or New York law that permitted unlimited recovery applied. All connections to the case, except for the husband's and wife's domiciles, were with Massachusetts. Most important, as the dissent pointed out, "the decedent made a deliberate choice to undergo the operation in Massachusetts at the defendant hospital."[32] Nevertheless, the New York (federal) court applied New York law, allowing unlimited recovery.[33] However, a forum-neutral court would have adopted Massachusetts law because Massachusetts clearly had the closest connection to the controversy.[34]

Not adopting Massachusetts law was unfair to the defendants. The defendants would have expected that an operation performed in a Massachusetts hospital by Massachusetts doctors on a patient who voluntarily came to Massachusetts for the operation would be governed by Massachusetts law, whereas a New York citizen would not have expected that he could carry New York law wherever he went. Similarly, Massachusetts's sovereignty was impeded because it clearly had the closest connection to the case.

4. Choice of Law Should Be Predictable

A major goal of any legal system should be predictability. Individuals need to know how the law governs their behavior so that they can conform their behavior to the law. Similarly, businesses need to be able to predict what the law will be so that they can conduct their affairs with certainty. Consequently, any choice of law system should be as predictable as possible.

The criteria discussed above affect predictability. For example, when choice of law is not content neutral, it is difficult to predict what rule will control a situation. *Allstate* illustrates the point. Because the court in that case used a better rule approach, insurers suffer the uncertainty of not knowing whether they can rely on the law of the state where an insurance policy was executed or whether they might be subject to the law of *any* state in which the plaintiff can obtain *in personam* jurisdiction that has a different rule. Similarly, a manufacturer will not be able to predict which state's products liability damages rule will govern the sale of its products. Although many choice of law scholars have little sympathy for insurance companies and product manufacturers, these businesses should be allowed to predict their possible liability in order to adjust prices and determine the amount of insurance they should buy. In addition, not all litigants who are hurt by unpredictable choices of law are big companies; individuals also need to predict how they should conduct their lives.

Lack of forum neutrality also destroys the law's predictability. If a forum can apply its law to a situation regardless of the fact that another state's law might be more appropriate, forum selection is outcome determinative. In such a situation, it is difficult for individuals and businesses to conduct their affairs with certainty, for they cannot predict where a particular plaintiff might bring suit.

As pointed out above, in both *Allstate* and *Rosenthal*, choice of forum determined the outcome. If those cases had been filed in Wisconsin and Massachusetts, respectively, their outcomes would have been exactly the opposite. Such a situation is unacceptable, especially in the United States where individuals are often subject to suit in several jurisdictions.

5. Choice of Law Should Be Fair to the Litgants

The primary goal of choice of law should be fairness to the litigants.[35] Although a lawsuit may affect society in general, and courts cannot ignore the impact its decision will have on future cases, a lawsuit's main purpose is individual justice. Yet, many choice of law systems ignore fairness to the litigants, instead taking a parochial approach that favors forum law or uses some other consequentialist criteria.

Conflicts justice differs from substantive justice. Conflicts justice is achieved by adopting the law of the most appropriate jurisdiction, not necessarily by applying the rule that may be the best one substantively. A court should respect the parties' reasonable expectations and avoid unfair surprise, even if some scholars may criticize the approach because it sometimes fails to adopt the better substantive rule. As Justice Antonin Scalia has pointed out, sometimes the "perfect" answer is not the most important value in litigation.[36] Or, as Ronald Dworkin has written, "Hercules [the ideal judge] is prevented from achieving integrity viewed from the standpoint of justice alone—coherence in the substantive principle of justice that flows throughout his account of what the law now is—because he has been seeking a wider integrity that gives effect to principles of fairness and procedural due process as well."[37]

Moreover, it is a fundamental principle of fairness that a person not be subjected to inconsistent or ambiguous laws. Justice Scalia made the point nicely when he declared, "Rudimentary justice requires that those subject to the law must have the means of knowing what it prescribes."[38] Similarly, Lon Fuller has written that "[c]ertainly there can be no rational ground for asserting that a man can have a moral obligation to obey a legal rule that does not exist, or is kept secret from him, or that came into existence only after he had acted, or was unintelligible, or was contradicted by another rule of the same system, or commanded the impossible, or changed every minute."[39] Professor Fuller continued, "Government says to the citizen, in effect, 'These are the rules we expect you to follow. If you follow them, you have our assurance that they are the rules that will be applied to your conduct.'"[40]

Professor Laycock has transferred these jurisprudential principles to choice of law: "People cannot obey the law unless they know it; they cannot know the law unless they know which law to learn. If I am to know the law that governs an act or transaction, I must be able to identify, before the act, the one state empowered to govern."[41]

The factors discussed above—lack of content neutrality, forum-favoring choice of law, and lack of predictability—create inconsistent laws and otherwise affect fairness to the litigants. A choice of law system that is not substantively neutral is not fair to the litigants because a rule might control a case that would not be applied absent a multistate setting. Similarly, a system that is not forum neutral is unfair because the place of the filing of the suit can affect a case's outcome. Justice is not served on any level by allowing forum selection to be outcome determinative, especially considering that this creates inconsistent laws. Finally, a system that is not predictable is not fair because individuals will be subject to inconsistent laws, and they will not be able to conform their behavior and affairs to the law.

6. Choice of Law Should Reflect the Relevant States' Interests

If a legal system is based on positive law, then choice of law should reflect the interests of the states that created those laws. Courts should not choose law in a vacuum. Rather, choice of law should reflect the policies and interests a state had when it passed the law.

Allowing communities to have differing values is one reason to have subdivisions of a national state. Professor Seth F. Kreimer has written that "[o]ne of the virtues of a territorial federalism is precisely that it allows conflicting communities of commitment to coexist within a single national polity, while allowing individuals to move fluidly among them. On issues of fundamental life choices, America has often been a house divided, with the individualized citizens entitled to decide the rooms in which they wish to live."[42]

Some choice of law systems, such as governmental interest analysis, use state interests as the major factor when choosing law. However, these approaches stress state interests by allowing a state to select forum law whenever a forum has an interest in doing so, thus ignoring the interests of other states that are more closely connected to the controversy. Not only should a choice of law system reflect state interests, that system should also select the law of the state that has the *most* interest in having its law applied—the state that has the closest connection to the controversy.[43]

My view on how state interests should be respected reflects Professors Kramer's and Brilmayer's writings on the importance of interstate cooperation and maximizing state policy objectives through choice of law.[44] Professor Kramer, for example, discusses the role of reciprocity in choice of law.[45] Kramer compares conflicts to the classic prisoner's dilemma in game theory.[46] Both states would be better off if they cooperated in the choice of law. By cooperating, a state's law governs when it is especially important to that state's interest, but the state would step aside when it is more important to the other state that its laws apply. That way both states' policies would be furthered in the long run. Obviously, a state would be better off if the other state cooperated, but it did not. In other words, there is an incentive to cheat. However, this incentive to cheat is lessened by the fact that the game is reiterated. If State A cheats on the first play, State B will feel free to cheat on the second play. Professor Kramer does not believe that cooperation will always result, but that both parties will be better off if they do so.

A system that chooses law based on which state has the closest connection to a controversy furthers interstate cooperation and maximizes state policy objectives. A state's law will govern when it has the most interest in having its law applied—when that state has the closest connection to a case, but it will yield to another state's law when the other state has the greater interest in having its law control—when that state has the closest connection to the dispute.

B. A NORMATIVE VIEW OF MODERN CHOICE OF LAW SYSTEMS

This section tests modern choice of law systems against the normative criteria set forth above. The methods it examines include (1) Beale's vested rights method, (2) Currie's governmental interest analysis, (3) the better rule approach, and (4) the *Second Restatement*'s most significant relationship test.

1. Beale's Vested Rights Method

Despite the fact that it is multilateralist, Beale's method fails all the normative criteria set forth above. First, vested rights is grounded in positive law in one sense; it adopts the law of the state where the last act occurred. However, because of the rigid last act rule, in a few cases, it employs the law of a state that did not intend its law to govern those circumstances.

For example, assume that a Mississippi husband and wife are involved in an automobile accident in Alabama, caused by the husband's negligence. Alabama does not allow a spouse to recover from the other spouse if the spouse is merely negligent, but Mississippi does.[47] Under the last act rule, the wife could not recover because the Alabama immunity governs. However, it is doubtful Alabama intended its spousal immunity rule to apply to spouses domiciled in other states.

Vested rights is substantively neutral in its main choice of law rules; as the Realist critics pointed out,[48] it does not consider a rule's content when choosing law. However, escape devices, such as characterization and refusing to adopt foreign law based on the forum's public policy, limit vested rights' substantive neutrality. For instance, a judge can characterize a rule she dislikes as procedural, rather than substantive, allowing her to apply forum law, or she can characterize an issue as being governed by contract law, rather than tort law, permitting a different rule to govern.

For example, a traffic accident occurs in Washington, where there is a one-year statute of limitations for wrongful death actions. Thirteen months after the accident, the plaintiff files suit in Montana, which has a two-year torts statute of limitations. Under Beale's approach, Washington law governs substantive issues because it is the place of the injury. Washington law creates a right to recover for the injury, but the action is barred if a statute of limitations is substantive. A Montana judge who believes that the plaintiff should be compensated can overcome the bar of the Washington statute of limitations by characterizing the limitations issue as procedural, allowing her to adopt the longer Montana statute.

Similarly, characterization of the category of a substantive right (*i.e.*, tort or contract) can be outcome determinative. For example, P rents a car in Arizona, and he is injured in a traffic accident in New Mexico due to the car's improper preparation. The rental contract contains a limitation of damages clause that precludes recovery for pain and suffering. Arizona enforces such clauses; New Mexico does not. If the court characterizes the action as contract, the limitation of damages clause will limit the damages that P can recover because the law of the place of the contract governs in contract actions. However, if the court characterizes the action as tort, it can apply New Mexico law to invalidate the limitations clause and give P pain and suffering damages because the law of the place of the injury controls for torts.

Although vested rights is forum neutral in its main rules, the escape devices can destroy this forum neutrality. The main problem is the public policy exception—a state can refuse to enforce a rule of another state if that rule violates the forum's public policy. For example, the defendant incurs a debt at a Nevada gambling casino, which is in a state where gambling is legal. The defendant moves to Utah, where gambling is illegal. Because the gambling debt was incurred where the debt was legal, a vested right to collect the debt in favor of the casino should generally be honored in any state. However, under the public policy exception, Utah can refuse to recognize the debt. Thus, there is no forum neutrality; if the case is brought in Nevada, a court will enforce the debt; however, if the case is filed in Utah, a court will not enforce it.

Although vested rights should be highly predictable in theory, the escape devices, including characterization and the public policy exception, limit its predictability. If a judge can recharacterize an issue or refuse to enforce a vested right on public policy grounds, law loses its predictability.

Beale's method is sometimes unfair to the individual litigants. Although Beale's method is concerned with rights, his notion of rights is very different from that of contemporary conflicts scholars. Beale is enforcing rights created by positive law; he is not otherwise concerned with fairness to the litigants. On the other hand, when contemporary scholars, such as Professors Dane and Brilmayer, talk about rights, they are usually referring to constraints on the application of a state's law—constraints that involve fairness to the litigants.[49]

Vested rights is unfair to the litigants when the last act occurs in a state with only a tenuous connection to the controversy. Consider, for example, a case involving a waiver of liability clause. D is a railroad incorporated and operating mainly in Missouri, with one train a week taking passengers to Kansas City, Kansas. P, a Missouri resident, buys a ticket on D's train to travel from St. Louis, Missouri to Kansas City, Kansas. Assume D's ticket contains a waiver of liability clause in favor of the railroad. Missouri refuses to enforce such clauses, but Kansas does enforce them. D's mechanic negligently repairs the train's brakes in St. Louis. Other of D's employees fail to properly inspect the train's brakes in Kansas City,

Missouri. The brakes fail while the train is in Missouri, causing it to go out of control. Shortly after the train has passed into Kansas, it jumps the tracks, and P is injured.

Because P is injured in Kansas, under vested rights, the law of the place of the injury controls, and P will not be able to recover for his injuries. Is this fair? P and D are both Missouri residents, the negligence occurred there, and most of the train trip was in Missouri.

Finally, the main rules of vested rights do not consider state interests at all; they are intended to enforce the litigants' preexisting rights. The sole exception is the public policy exception, which, as has been noted, considers only the forum's interest.

In sum, Beale's multilateralist vested rights method violates the six normative criteria to some degree. This, however, does not mean that all multilateralist approaches will violate the criteria. As Professor Brilmayer has pointed out, "[w]e should not reject a rights-based approach to choice of law without first trying to discover what the best possible rights-based theory might have to offer."[50]

2. Currie's Governmental Interest Analysis and Variations

Professor Currie's governmental interest analysis also fails all the normative criteria to some extent. Because he considers whether a state has an interest in having its law applied, Currie's system generally adopts law that the lawmaker intended to apply to the facts. However, Professor Brilmayer has argued that interest analysis lacks a positive law source in the defining of interests. She has written that interest analysts "need no positive law source for their pronouncements—they rely on pure rationality and can disregard legislative preferences that contradict their objective conclusions."[51] In other words, the interests that Currie's method uses are often hypothetical interests—a plaintiff *may* become a public charge, a hospital *might* not be paid, a plaintiff's spouse and children *may* become destitute.[52]

Governmental interest analysis is not substantively neutral. Rather, as noted in the previous chapter, it is consequentialist and instrumentalist—judges under Currie's system use choice of law as an instrument of social change. As Professor Brilmayer has observed, judges evaluate alternative rules of law "according to the desirability of their consequences."[53]

One can make numerous criticisms of the consequentialist element of governmental interest analysis.[54] However, the most fundamental one is Kantian: governmental interest analysis "is indifferent to what the parties deserve"—"the individual is treated only as a means to an end."[55] In criminal law, a court would not punish an innocent person just because the deterrence value of such punishment would benefit society as a whole. Why should courts be allowed to do something similar in choice of law when they enforce state interests at the expense of individual autonomy?

Similarly, governmental interest analysis is not forum neutral. In fact, a unilateralist method, like governmental interest analysis, cannot be forum neutral.

This lack of forum neutrality leads to forum shopping, which is unfair to the litigants, hinders state sovereignty, and destroys predictability.

For example, in *Milliken v. Pratt*,[56] a Massachusetts wife had guaranteed her husband's contract with a Maine partnership. Under Massachusetts law a married woman could not be a surety on a contract, whereas under Maine law she could. As mentioned in the previous chapter, Currie would have applied Massachusetts law because that state was the forum and it had an interest in protecting its married women. However, if the lawsuit had been filed in Maine, Currie would have selected Maine law because Maine was the forum and it had an interest in freedom of contract. In other words, *Milliken*'s outcome under governmental interest analysis hinges *solely* on the forum in which the action was filed.[57]

As I observed in Chapter 1, one reason Currie proposed the rule that courts should adopt forum law when true conflicts exist was because he thought that, when a judge weighed interests, he was legislating.[58] Currie declared that "[b]ut the assessment of the respective values of the competing legitimate interests of two sovereign states, in order to determine which is to prevail, is a political function of a very high order. This is a function that should not be committed to courts in a democracy."[59] Similarly, he asserted that "[t]he only virtue of the method proposed here is that at least it makes the choice of interests on a rational and objective basis: the forum consistently applies its own law in the case of conflict, and thus at least advances its domestic policy. This is not an ideal; it is simply the best that is available."[60]

Although there are problems in weighing interests, I think that there are ways to resolve true conflicts other than by weighing. The problem with Beale's method was that he mechanically chose law based on a single factor in a controversy. A multilateralist system does not have to be mechanical, as the *Second Restatement* demonstrates.

Lack of substantive and forum neutrality makes governmental interest analysis unpredictable.[61] Consequently, it is impossible for individuals and businesses to conduct their lives and affairs with any certainty because a case's outcome often depends on where a case is filed. In addition, this lack of predictability can hinder settlement and lead to protracted litigation, including costly appeals.[62]

Governmental interest analysis ignores fairness to the litigants in favor of furthering state interests—it does not examine whether choice of law is fair to individuals at all. Why should state interests be emphasized at the expense of fairness to individuals in private litigation? The outcome of private litigation is crucial to the individuals before the court, but the outcome of one case has little effect on state policies. A conflicts method that disregards fairness to the litigants is as unsatisfactory as a system that uses mechanical rules to choose law.

In addition, as noted above, the state interests are often hypothetical. Should a court sacrifice individual interests in favor of hypothetical state interests? Isn't this a new type of formalism?[63] Another formal assumption of interest analysis is that in every lawsuit involving a true conflict, the "competing" states have a deep and potentially controlling interest in the adjustment of rights between private litigants.

Some critics of interest analysis have argued that Currie's system defines state interests too narrowly emphasizing interests that protect domiciliaries, which is unfair to individual litigants who are nondomiciliaries.[64] For instance, Professor Singer has asserted that states have a "legitimate moral policy of protecting outsiders within its borders."[65] Similarly, Professor Brilmayer has suggested that "friendly relations with outsiders can make excellent business sense."[66]

Most important, as noted above, even though Currie's method uses state interests as the main factor in choosing law, his approach often ignores the state with the greatest interest in having its law applied because the forum can adopt its law whenever it has an interest in doing so, however slight. If governmental interest analysis were applied to *Allstate*, Minnesota could employ its law because it has an interest in adopting its law—Allstate did business in Minnesota and the decedent worked in Minnesota. However, these interests, even if valid, pale in comparison to Wisconsin's interest in regulating insurance contracts made in that state with its domiciliaries. Considering the above, is governmental interest analysis the best way to protect state interests? It appears to protect the forum's interests even when another state has a greater interest, as long as those interests are defended by Currie and his adherents.

Professor Baxter's comparative impairment approach eliminates some, but not all, of the problems in classic governmental interest analysis. Because he weighs interests rather than automatically adopting forum law with true conflicts, his system seems to eliminate forum bias. However, the difficulty that Currie saw in weighing discussed above can allow a court to weigh interests, but still unfairly favor forum interests. For example, which interest is more important: a state's interest in protecting it citizens who are spendthrifts or a state's interest in freedom of contract? The next chapter presents an example that shows how comparative impairment can be used to choose a state's law when another state has a much closer connection to the case.

Most important, comparative impairment is unfair to individuals because, like classic governmental interest analysis, it ignores their interests completely. Determining which state's interest is more impaired does not protect the litigant's interest in a fair outcome in individual cases. Rather, it furthers state interests at the expense of individual ones.

3. The Better Rule Approach

The better rule approach also does not meet the normative criteria set forth above.[67] First, it is not grounded in positive law. Rather, it emphasizes "justice" at the expense of positive law. Judges who base their choice of law decision primarily on which of the competing jurisdictions has the preferable rule often select a law which was not intended to apply to an interstate conflict. For example, in their zeal for the better rule, the judges of the Minnesota Supreme court inappropriately applied forum law to the defendant in *Hague v. Allstate Ins. Co.*[68]

Obviously, the better rule approach is not substantively neutral. The central tenet of this approach is to choose the rule that is the most just. As to the legitimacy of this inquiry, Professor Larry Kramer makes a telling point: "Because states are co-equal sovereigns, true conflicts present a dispute between competing but equally legitimate versions of what is just in a particular case."[69]

Although, theoretically, a better rule approach is forum neutral, in practice, it generally is not. As noted previously, most courts think their rule is the better one. This preference, of course, is not surprising. If the rule were inferior, the appropriate governmental organ of the state would change it. Note, also, that Leflar's better rule system does not purport to be forum neutral: one of the factors relevant to choosing the appropriate law is that of advancing the forum's interest.[70]

Another deficit of the better rule approach is that outcomes are unpredictable. The outcome of choice of law under this approach often depends on where the plaintiff files his case. Further, at the trial level, the choice of the "better rule" hinges on a single judge's view of the relative merits of the competing laws. Consider, for example, the following hypothetical: The defendant, a railroad company, operates solely in Texas. Texas has a rule that passengers on railways can contractually waive their right to recover from railroad companies for negligence. D's ticket has such a waiver that is valid under Texas law. P, an Oklahoma resident, is injured through D's negligence while a passenger on D's railroad. Oklahoma allows recovery for damages when its residents are injured by another's negligence, regardless of where the accident occurs. In addition, Oklahoma would not enforce the waiver of liability clause.

Under a better rule approach, the Texas court might decide that the Oklahoma rule is the better rule and apply it because the Texas rule is antiquated and Texas law generally favors compensating negligence victims. Similarly, the plaintiff might file the case in Oklahoma, which would probably consider its rule the better one. Thus, the railroad cannot plan its affairs with certainty, even though it only does business in Texas. Although many scholars believe that compensation of torts victims is one of the law's major goals, the law should achieve this goal by changing the substantive law, not by manipulating choice of law. If the Texas legislature believes that waiver of liability clauses should not be enforced, it can pass such a law.

In one sense, a better rule approach is fair to the litigants because it (supposedly) adopts the rule which is the most just. However, as noted above, choice of law should not be concerned with substantive justice; substantive justice should be considered when the legislature passes a law, a court makes a law, or an administrative agency promulgates a rule. Fair in the choice of law context means that a court should employ the law of the jurisdiction with the closest connection to the controversy, which will usually meet the parties' expectations concerning choice of law.

Finally, a better rule approach ignores states' interests. A court will adopt the better rule regardless of whether another state has a stronger interest in having its rule apply. While individual interests are more important than state interests in choice of law, courts should not disregard state interests.[71] A state's law should govern when it has the closest connection to the controversy because this allows the values of the most interested state to prevail.

4. The Most Significant Relationship Test

The *Second Restatement*'s most significant relationship test (standing alone) generally meets my normative criteria.[72] Although not specifically stating that choice of law should be grounded in positive law, it will usually choose a law that the lawmaker intended to apply to a situation because the state with the most significant relationship to a controversy generally provides a legal relation that governs the case. Similarly, the most significant relationship test is usually substantively and forum neutral because it does not look at the laws' content or use forum-favoring choice of law criteria, although section 6 considerations might affect this under certain circumstances.

The most significant relationship test is more predictable than governmental interest analysis or the better rule approach because it is substantively and forum neutral. Any predictability problems in this test will occur because judges may apply its criteria differently.

The most significant relationship test is usually fair to the individual litigants because it adopts the law of a jurisdiction that is closely connected to the controversy. Moreover, a court using this test is supposed to consider the parties' justified expectations under section 6.

Finally, by choosing the law of the state with the most significant relationship to a case, a court is considering state interests because a the law of a state with a close connection to the controversy should govern. Moreover, section 6 requires a court to consider the relevant policies of the forum and other interested states.

NOTES

1. LEA BRILMAYER, CONFLICT OF LAWS 1 (1995).
2. The introduction discussed these background considerations in depth.
3. G. EDWARD WHITE, THE AMERICAN JUDICIAL TRADITION 107, 148–49 (1988).
4. OLIVER W. HOLMES, THE COMMON LAW 1 (1881).
5. Southern Pac. Co. v. Jensen, 244 U.S. 205, 222 (1917) (Holmes, J., dissenting).
6. Erie R.R. Co. v. Tompkins, 304 U.S. 64, 78–79 (1938).
7. Wesley Newcomb Hohfeld, *Some Fundamental Legal Conceptions as Applied in Judicial Reasoning*, 23 YALE L.J. 16 (1913) ("[I]f X has a right against Y that he shall stay off the former's land, the correlative (and equivalent) is that Y is under a duty to stay off the place." *Id.* at 32.); Wesley Newcomb Hohfeld, *Fundamental Legal Conceptions as Applied in Judicial Reasoning*, 26 YALE L.J. 710 (1917).
8. *See* Chapter 5.
9. *E.g.*, JOHN FINNIS, NATURAL LAW AND NATURAL RIGHTS (1980).
10. As Larry Kramer has pointed out, "alleging or even proving that the defendant did something does not entitle the plaintiff to anything." Larry Kramer, *Rethinking Choice of Law*, 90 COLUM. L. REV. 277, 282 (1990).
11. See the discussion of these methods in Chapter 1.
12. Allstate Ins. Co. v. Hague, 449 U.S. 302, 308 (1981). Chapter 1 discussed this case in depth.
13. Chapter 3 argues that to allow a state to do so is unconstitutional.

14. Of course, the choice of law might have been different if the issue had concerned recovery by a person who was not a party to the insurance contract.

15. Other writers who advocate multilateralism also believe that choice of law should be substantively neutral. *See, e.g.,* Dirk H. Bliesener, *Fairness and Choice of Law: A Critique of the Political Rights-Based Approach to Conflict of Laws*, 42 AM. J. COMP. L. 687, 707–9 (1994).

16. For a similar view, see Joseph William Singer, *Real Conflicts*, 69 B.U. L. REV. 1, 53 (1989) [hereinafter Singer, *Real Conflicts*].

17. Professor Juenger writes that "[t]he large majority of cases reveals a simple clash between two rules of decision, one of which is clearly superior to the other." FRIEDRICH K. JUENGER, CHOICE OF LAW AND MULTISTATE JUSTICE 206 (1992). As is obvious from the accompanying text, I strongly disagree with this statement because there is no basis for determining which rule is superior.

18. P. Jon Kozyris, *Reflections on Allstate–The Lessening of Due Process on Choice of Law*, 14 U.C. DAVIS L. REV. 889, 906 (1981); *see also* Harold P. Southerland, *Sovereignty, Value Judgments, and Choice of Law*, 38 BRANDEIS L.J. 451, 485 (2000).

19. As Professor Laycock has pointed out, choice of law systems that use substantive justice as the main criteria invoke "a general common law not derived from any sovereign." Douglas Laycock, *Equal Citizens of Equal and Territorial States: The Constitutional Foundations of Choice of Law*, 92 COLUM. L. REV. 249, 312 (1992).

20. *E.g.,* Greenman v. Yuba Power Products, 377 P.2d 897 (Cal. 1962); Henningsen v. Bloomfield Motors, Inc., 161 A.2d 69 (N.J. 1960); Larsen v. General Motors Corp., 391 F.2d 495 (8th Cir. 1968).

21. *E.g.,* IND. CODE § 31-51-3-4 (1995) (limiting punitive damages); KAN. STAT. ANN. § 60-19a01 (1988) (limiting pain and suffering damages); KAN. STAT. ANN. § 60-19a02 (1988) (limiting noneconomic damages).

22. Laycock, *supra* note 19, at 312.

23. Singer, *Real Conflicts, supra* note 16, at 45–47.

24. *Id.* at 46. This observation, however, has led Professor Singer to conclude that generally a "case should be resolved by applying what the forum understands as the better law." *Id.* at 128.

25. Linda Silberman, *Can the State of Minnesota Bind the Nation?: Federal Choice of Law Constraints after Allstate Insurance Co. v. Hague*, 10 HOFSTRA L. REV. 103 (1981).

26. The introduction discussed individual autonomy.

27. I will develop these ideas in greater depth below.

28. As Gene Shreve has noted, "[m]ultilateralism strives for uniform results in choice of law." Gene R. Shreve, *Choice of Law and the Forgiving Constitution*, 71 IND. L.J. 271, 282 (1996).

29. Joseph William Singer, *A Pragmatic Guide to Conflicts*, 70 B.U. L. REV. 731, 738 (1990) [hereinafter Singer, *A Pragmatic Guide*]; Michael E. Solimine, *An Economic and Empirical Analysis of Choice of Law*, 24 GA. L. REV. 49, 56, 81–89 (1989). For example, Robert Sedler has written, "When two states are involved with an interstate case, so that both states can constitutionally exercise jurisdiction and can constitutionally apply their own law, the plaintiff should be able to make a choice of forum and obtain the benefit of the law of the state with the plaintiff-favoring rule." Robert A. Sedler, *A Real World Perspective on Choice of Law*, 48 MERCER L. REV. 781, 818 (1997). However, Professor Gottesman has observed, "It is simply not fair that one party gets to choose, after the fact, what legal regime will govern the parties' dispute." Michael H. Gottesman, *Adrift on the Sea of Indeterminancy*, 75 IND. L.J. 527, 529 (2000).

30. 475 F.2d 438 (2d Cir. 1973).

31. Shreve, *supra* note 28, at 271.

32. *Rosenthal*, 475 F.2d at 447 (Justice Lumbard, dissenting).

33. Several scholars have strongly criticized this decision. *E.g.*, Harold L. Korn, *The Choice-of-Law Revolution: A Critique*, 83 COLUM. L. REV. 772, 903–42 (1983); Frederic L. Kirgis, Jr., *The Role of Due Process and Full Faith and Credit in Choice of Law*, 61 CORNELL L. REV. 185, 225–27 (1976); Willis L. M. Reese, *Legislative Jurisdiction*, 78 COLUM. L. REV. 1587, 1605–6 (1978).

34. I will return to this case in Chapter 3 in connection with constitutional constraints on choice of law.

35. Other choice of law scholars who stress fairness to the litigants include BRILMAYER, *supra* note 1, at 219–63; Perry Dane, *Vested Rights, "Vestedness" and Choice of Law*, 96 YALE L.J. 1197 (1987); Terry Kogan, *Toward a Jurisprudence of Choice of Law, the Priority of Fairness over Comity*, 62 N.Y.U. L. REV. 651 (1987).

36. *See* Antonin Scalia, *The Rule of Law as a Law of Rules*, 56 U. CHI. L. REV. 1175, 1178 (1989).

37. RONALD DWORKIN, LAW'S EMPIRE 404 (1986).

38. Scalia, *supra* note 36, at 1179. As Justice Scalia has noted, "[it] is said that one of emperor Nero's nasty practices was to post his edicts high on the columns so that they would be hard to read and easier to transgress." *Id.*

39. LON L. FULLER, THE MORALITY OF LAW 39 (1964).

40. *Id.* at 39–40.

41. Laycock, *supra* note 19, at 319; *see also* Gottesman, *supra* note 29, at 528–29.

42. Seth F. Kreimer, *Territoriality and Moral Dissensus: Thoughts on Abortion, Slavery, Gay Marriage and Family Values*, 16 QUINNIPIAC L. REV. 161, 163 (1996); *see also* Linda J. Silberman, *Can the Island of Hawaii Bind the World? A Comment on Same-Sex Marriage and Federalism Values*, 16 QUINNIPIAC L. REV. 191, 204 (1996) ("Hawaii has no legitimate basis for imposing its social choice on other communities which have adopted quite different norms on a matter which has generated so much controversy [same-sex marriage].").

43. Chapter 5 presents such a method.

44. Kramer, *supra* note 10, at 339–44; BRILMAYER, *supra* note 1, at 169–218.

45. Kramer, *supra* note 10, at 339–44.

46. *Id.* at 341 n.224.

47. Unless citing a specific case or statute, the examples in this book are hypotheticals and do not necessarily reflect actual state law.

48. *See* Chapter 1.

49. Dane, *supra* note 35; BRILMAYER, *supra* note 1, at 219–263.

50. BRILMAYER, *supra* note 1, at 223; *see also* Kermit Roosevelt III, *The Myth of Choice of Law: Rethinking Conflicts*, 97 MICH. L. REV. 2448, 2471 (1999); John Bernard Corr, *Interest Analysis and Choice of Law: The Dubious Dominance of Domicile*, 1983 UTAH L. REV. 651, 673–76 (1983).

51. BRILMAYER, *supra* note 1, at 112. Professor Brilmayer has added: "Legislatures are the source of substantive policies; the interest analysts are the source of choice of law decisions." *Id. See also* Lea Brilmayer, *The Role of Substantive and Choice of Law Policies in the Formation and Application of Choice of Law Rules*, 252 RECUIL DES COURS D'ACADEMIE DE DROIT INTERNATIONAL 107–8 (1989).

52. BRILMAYER, *supra* note 1, at 229–30.

53. *Id.* at 225.

54. *Id.* at 224–32.

55. *Id.* at 232.

56. 125 Mass. 374 (1878).

57. Professor Shreve has pointed out that uniformity is not central to unilaterists, including Currie. Rather, these scholars believe that unilaterist approaches, such as interest analysis, can produce a better result. Shreve, *supra* note 28, at 284–85.

58. BRAINERD CURRIE, SELECTED ESSAYS ON THE CONFLICT OF LAWS 181–83 (1963).

59. *Id.* at 182.

60. *Id.* at 169.

61. Professor Gottesman has noted that modern "conflicts scholarship is unique in its utter disregard for the values of determinancy." Gottesman, *supra* note 29, at 529.

62. *Id.*

63. Professor Singer has noted that conflicts scholars who reject territorial approaches "have engaged in formalism by identifying these policies [compensating plaintiffs, deterring wrongful conduct, and promoting reliance on agreements] as 'shared' or 'basic' or 'emerging' or 'prevalent' or 'better,' without confronting the conflicting values and policy arguments that are faced by those who debate the substantive content of law." Singer, *Real Conflicts, supra* note 16, at 75.

64. *E.g.*, Brilmayer, *supra* note 1, at 85–91; Singer, *Real Conflicts, supra* note 16, at 35–45.

65. Singer, *Real Conflicts, supra* note 16, at 39.

66. BRILMAYER, *supra* note 1, at 89.

67. For further criticism of the better rule approach, see Gary J. Simson, *Resisting the Allure of Better Rule of Law*, 52 ARK. L. REV. 141, 146–56 (1999).

68. 289 N.W.2d 43 (Minn. 1978), *aff'd*, 449 U.S. 302 (1981).

69. Kramer, *supra* note 10, at 280. Many better rule advocates fail to see that there can be more than one legitimate approach to many legal questions. For example, Professor Juenger has recently asserted concerning "tort law reform," "nowdays in many instances inferior domestic law [law that limits recovery of damages], which is the product of astute lobbying rather than judicious reevaluation of existing rules, conflicts with superior foreign law [pro-plaintiff rules]." Friederich K. Juenger, *A Third Conflicts Restatement?* 75 IND. L.J. 403, 413 (2000).

70. ROBERT A. LEFLAR, AMERICAN CONFLICTS LAW 195 (3d. ed. 1977).

71. When done in the right way, protecting state interests can be compatible with protecting individual interests.

72. Other SECOND RESTATEMENT criteria can affect whether the most significant relationship test meets the normative criteria. See my discussion of the problems with the SECOND RESTATEMENT as a whole in Chapter 4.

Chapter 3

Constitutional Constraints on Choice of Law

Because of the numerous positive and normative approaches to conflicts mentioned in Chapters 1 and 2, a major problem in American choice of law is the lack of constraints on the choice of law methods that courts can use. This lack of constraints has helped create the "dismal swamp" in modern American conflicts.

On the international level, there are no legal constraints that limit a nation's choice of law rules absent a voluntary agreement with other nations. Choice of law rules are internal; one sovereign cannot thrust its choice of law rules on another sovereign. Thus, in the international setting, a country with jurisdiction over the defendant is free to apply its own law.

When there are no external constraints on choice of law, one might expect a nation to adopt a unilateralist approach and apply its law in most instances. Why should a sovereign yield to another sovereign's law in its own courts? In fact, a *lex fori* approach might be mandatory in those countries that employ a separation of powers political structure unless there are other limitations. As Professor David Currie has noted, "[a]s a matter of separation of powers, you can't refuse to do what your legislature tells you to do just because there's another state that also has a law that it would like to apply."[1]

American states, however, are different from sovereign nations. Although states have some characteristics of sovereignty, they are part of a federal union and subject to the United States Constitution.[2] Consequently, constraints on choice of law emanate from the Constitution. The main clauses that might provide such constraints when two or more states are concerned are the due process clause of the Fourteenth Amendment, which limits a state's power over the individual and protects individual liberty, and the full faith and credit clause, which draws the structural lines that regulate the relations of the states and preserves state sovereignty.[3]

Current constitutional constraints on choice of law, however, are minimal. The prevailing standard from *Allstate* says that a "[s]tate must have a significant contact or significant aggregation of contacts, creating state interests, such that choice of law is neither arbitrary nor fundamentally unfair."[4] Under this minimalist constraint, a court can adopt a state's law (often its law) even if another state's law has a significantly closer connection to the dispute.

Although most choice of law scholars advocate retaining the present minimalist constitutional constraints on choice of law,[5] a few scholars have called for greater limitations.[6] For example, Professor Douglas Laycock has declared, "The choice of law revolution has proceeded in disregard of the Constitution," and he has argued, following Justice Robert H. Jackson, that "choice of law within the United States is inherently constitutional law."[7]

Stricter constitutional constraints are needed to overcome the great confusion in American choice of law and to protect individual liberty and state sovereignty. Accordingly, there should be a new constitutional standard for choice of law derived from the due process and full faith and credit clauses: Choice of a state's law is unconstitutional when another state has a significantly closer connection to the controversy. Furthermore, certain choice of law criteria—choosing forum law because it is forum law and selecting the better rule—should be unconstitutional even when the above standard is satisfied because these criteria interfere with individual liberty under the due process clause and state sovereignty under the full faith and credit clause.

Chapter 1 examined the current constitutional constraints on choice of law and how they evolved from a multilateralist basis to a unilateralist one. The first part of this chapter evaluates the modern constitutional constraints and concludes that they are inadequate. The second part presents my approach to constitutional constraints on choice of law. The third part applies the new standard to existing choice of law methods, finding that several methods should be unconstitutional. Finally, the fourth part examines choice of law in close cases and concludes that even in close cases certain choice of law criteria are unconstitutional.

A. EVALUATION OF MODERN CONSTITUTIONAL CONSTRAINTS ON CHOICE OF LAW

The current constitutional constraints on choice of law misinterpret the effect of the due process and full faith and credit clauses on choice of law.[8]

1. General Criticisms

First, applying the same analysis to the due process and full faith and credit clauses ignores the fundamental differences between these clauses. As Justice Stevens observed in his concurrence in *Allstate*,[9] the due process clause concerns fairness to the defendant, while the full faith and credit clause involves the relations of sovereigns (the states) in our federal system. Although it is conceivable that the constraints on choice of law might be similar under both clauses, the analysis to determine those constraints must be different.[10]

Second, the Court should not give greater scrutiny to personal jurisdiction than choice of law. As Professor Louise Weinberg has pointed out, the "Court employs restrictive scrutiny in personal jurisdiction cases, but minimal scrutiny in conflicts cases."[11] Why should courts give greater scrutiny to the place of the trial than the governing law—the governing law directly affects the trial's outcome, while absent an effect of forum on choice of law, personal jurisdiction mainly involves convenience.[12] As Professor Linda Silberman has declared, "[t]o believe that a defendant's contacts with the forum state should be stronger under the due process clause for jurisdictional purposes than for choice of law is to believe that an accused is more concerned about where he will be hanged than whether [he will be]."[13] Moreover, as Professor Terry S. Kogan has noted, "[i]f courts usually apply their own law, they will tend to overlook whether it is fair for a plaintiff to invoke that law once the question of adjudicative [personal] jurisdiction has been decided."[14]

Finally, the *Allstate* standard seems to be combining the language of The *Second Restatement*'s "most significant relationship test" ("a significant contact or a significant aggregation of contacts")[15] with governmental interest analysis ("creating state interests"),[16] two choice of law approaches that seem incompatible.[17]

2. Criticisms of the Court's Current Due Process Analysis

The Court's due process analysis for choice of law ignores general principles of due process and allows states to treat an individual unfairly. First, the Court's due process analysis of choice of law differs substantially from its due process analysis in all other areas. Second, *Allstate* stresses state interests over individual liberty interests, countervening the purpose of the due process clause—the protection of individual liberty. Third, the current standard is unfair to the individual because it permits a state's law to govern when another state has a significantly closer connection to the matter. Fourth, *Allstate* is unfair to the individual because it authorizes inconsistent laws, with choice of forum often determining choice of law, and it fails to give the individual notice of the applicable law. Finally, the present standard allows an individual to be subjected to parochial laws without political redress.

a. The current standard ignores due process analysis in other areas. First, the Court employs a different due process analysis in *Allstate* than it uses in all other areas.[18] In fact, neither *Allstate* nor *Shutts* cites a due process case outside of choice of law or personal jurisdiction. Below I propose an alternate due process analysis that considers normal due process concepts.

b. There is no justification for Allstate's emphasis on state interests at the expense of the individual's interest. Second, related to the Court's failure to employ the proper due process analysis, *Allstate* inappropriately emphasizes state sovereignty interests at the expense of fairness to the individual.[19] The problem with this emphasis on state interests is that due process has nothing to do with the relations of the states (horizontal federalism); rather, it concerns the relationship of a state to the individual—the due process clause is one of the Constitution's countermajoritarian clauses.[20]

The due process clause states that "nor shall any State deprive any person of life, liberty, or property, without due process of law. . . ."[21] Obviously, there is no explicit reference to horizontal federalism in this clause. Similarly, normal due process analysis does not consider federalism or sovereignty conflicts. As Professor Martin Redish observed in 1981 while discussing the misplaced federalism emphasis in the due process analysis of personal jurisdiction, "[i]n virtually every other context, due process—in both its substantive and procedural manifestations—has been construed as a protection of private parties from some form of injustice."[22] In 1982, the Court backed off the federalism emphasis in the due process analysis of jurisdiction, declaring that "[t]he restriction on state sovereignty power described in *World-Wide Volkswagen Corp.*, however, must be seen as ultimately a function of the individual liberty interest preserved by the Due Process Clause."[23] Finally, with the existence of the full faith and credit clause to protect state sovereignty in choice of law, it is hard to understand why the Court has incorporated horizontal federalism into due process.

A state's emphasis on its interests in choice of law at the individual's expense disregards the jurisprudential basis of the due process clause.[24] For a state to favor its interests requires a utilitarian approach to choice of law: that something is fair when it does the greatest good for the greatest number.[25] Under a Kantian approach—an individual is not a means to an end, even if the end promotes the general welfare[26]—a state should not favor its interests over the individual's in choice of law.

Substantive due process is usually based on individual rights, not utilitarianism. As James Hilliard has written, "[s]ubstantive due process reflects the American political reality that at the very basis of conduct or action are rights inherent to all individuals."[27]

When a state favors its interests over the individual's interest in choice of law, it is using the individual as a means to an end. There is little justification for this emphasis. As the previous chapter mentioned, most lawsuits are private disputes, and the outcome of private disputes will have little tangible impact on state interests. As Professor Kogan has observed, "abstract conflicts between states that result from competing state regulatory policies are not as important as the effects of those conflicts on individual citizens."[28]

c. The current standard is unfair to the individual because it allows a state's law to govern an individual's conduct when another state has a significantly closer connection to the dispute. If one ignores the misplaced federalism emphasis in *Allstate* discussed above, requiring a state to have significant contacts to a case before that state's law can govern *might* satisfy due process because it might be fair to the parties. Professor Brilmayer has noted that "[b]y defining the reach of state authority, the due process clause does more than protect the rights of other states, it also prescribes the rights and obligations of individuals."[29]

The third question, then, is whether the current standard, which allows a state to apply its law to a matter even though another state has a significantly closer connection, is fair to the individual. I think it is not. This negative conclusion flows from my conviction that there are two inquires in the due process analysis of choice of law: (1) whether a state can legitimately apply its law to an occurrence or transaction and (2) whether a court can adopt a state's law when another state's law might also legitimately govern under the first inquiry. The *Allstate* standard does well enough with the first inquiry, but it completely fails to consider the second.

The first inquiry is whether a state can constitutionally apply its law to a controversy. Significant contacts between the state and the parties, transaction, or occurrence that relate to the law should satisfy this requirement. Although I would not use, as *Allstate* does, the language of "state interests," the *Allstate* standard fulfills the first requirement.

Allstate, however, sets no limit when two states' laws could legitimately govern under the first inquiry—that is, cases involving true conflicts.[30] There are many cases where a court could apply a state's law absent a true conflict, but where the court cannot fairly adopt that law because the controversy is significantly more closely connected to another jurisdiction under the second inquiry. This signal limitation concerns whether a state has the power to apply its law to a controversy, not as an interference with another state's sovereignty, but as an infringement on individual liberty. In other words, a litigant should have a due process right not to have a state's law applied when another jurisdiction has a *significantly* closer connection to the matter, even if there is a political basis (significant contacts) for adopting the first state's law.

Conceptually, the difference between my view of the effect of the due process clause on choice of law and the current standard is a multilateralist notion of constitutional constraints on choice of law versus a unilateralist one. Under a unilateralist approach, a court need only determine whether a state's law can be constitutionally adopted; the court does not have to consider whether another state's law has a stronger claim for application. However, under a multilateralist approach, determining whether the use of a state's law is constitutionally legitimate is not enough; a court must also decide whether adoption of that state's law is proper when another state's law might also govern.

As Chapter 1 demonstrated, the virtual constitutionalization of vested rights in *Dodge*, *Hartford*, and similar cases was a multilateralist approach to constitutional constraints on choice of law. Those cases required that a court use highly mechanical, territorial criteria to connect the controversy to the most appropriate jurisdiction. Justice Stone began the transition from this multilateralist constitutional approach to choice of law to a unilateralist one in *Alaska Packers* when he adopted a due process standard that ascertained whether a state had a legitimate interest in applying its law, thus sometimes allowing more than one state's law to govern. The current standard is unilateralist because it only considers the first inquiry—whether a state can constitutionally apply its law to a controversy; it does not examine whether another state's law might be more fitting. Finally, my proposal below is multilateralist in that it requires a court to try to find the most appropriate legal system.[31]

d. The current standard is unfair to the individual because it subjects the individual to inconsistent laws and fails to give the individual notice of the applicable law. Fourth, as mentioned in the previous chapter in connection with the normative criteria, it is a fundamental principle of fairness that a person not be subjected to inconsistent or ambiguous laws and that a person have notice of the applicable law. The current constitutional constraints allow the existence of inconsistent laws because they often permit a court to choose from the laws of several jurisdictions, even one that is only tenuously connected to a case. For example, *Allstate*'s outcome was dictated solely by choice of forum, not any material factor in the case. Thus, Allstate had no notice of the governing law, and it was impossible for it to determine which law it had to comply with—Minnesota's or Wisconsin's, an unfair result.

e. The current standard permits an individual to be subjected to unfair choice of law without political redress. Finally, an individual often lacks political protection from unfair choice of law. When a state applies its law to a nonresident, despite the fact that the case has a significantly closer connection to another state, the nonresident lacks political redress, such as the right to vote in the jurisdiction applying its parochial law. As Professor James R. Pielemeier has noted, "[l]egitimate state power in the United States is premised on political accountability, and assertion of power entailing no opportunity for redress by those potentially most directly affected should thus be viewed as constitutionally suspect."[32] Similarly, Professor Brilmayer has written concerning consequentialist approaches like Currie's, "[t]he claims of one of the parties are being sacrificed to further the general good of a community of which he or she may not even be a part."[33] Thus, the due process clause should protect an individual when he or she lacks a political remedy.

3. Criticisms of the Court's Full Faith and Credit Analysis

Allstate adopted a unilateralist reading of the full faith and credit clause,[34] rendering it meaningless and ignoring the horizontal structural lines set forth in the Constitution.[35] A state can employ its law as long as it has political contacts with the matter; a state does not have to give *any* credit to another state's law. As Justice Stone pointed out the opposite interpretation is equally ludicrous: "Whenever the conflict arises, the statute of each state must be enforced in the courts of the other, but cannot be in its own."[36] Obviously, neither extreme is appropriate.

The current standard permits "interested" parties—the states—to choose law without any restrictions on furthering their parochial interests. This is like allowing the home team to umpire a baseball game or letting one of the litigants be the judge in a lawsuit. As one court has asserted, "to vest the power of determining the extraterritorial effect of a State's own laws and judgments in the State itself risks the very kind of parochial entrenchment on the interests of other States that it was the purpose of the Full Faith and Credit Clause and other provisions of Art. IV of the Constitution to prevent."[37] Similarly, Justice Richard Neely has demonstrated the danger of allowing interested parties to choose the applicable law: "I'm not the only appellate judge in America who wants to sleep at night. As long as I am allowed to redistribute wealth from out-of-state companies to insured in-state plaintiffs, I will continue to do so. Not only is my sleep enhanced when I give someone else's money away, but so is my job security, because the in-state plaintiffs, their families, and their friends will reelect me."[38]

Moreover, parochial choice of law interferes with democracy and pluralism. As Professor Pielemeier has observed, "[w]hen the law applied is different from that of the community where a substantial portion of the litigation-creating occurrence took place, that community's consensus on the appropriate legal consequences is frustrated."[39]

Why has the Court given such a limited reading to constraints on choice of law under the full faith and credit clause? As Judge Wilkinson of the Fourth Circuit Court of Appeals has declared (in another context), courts should "refrain from being textually selective" in constitutional interpretation.[40] He added, "How one clause can be robust and the other anemic is a mystery when both clauses, after all, are part of our Constitution."[41] Placing greater structural limitations on the states is particularly important in light of the new judicial activism, which gives states greater authority than they enjoyed during most of the last half of the twentieth century.[42]

Notably, Article 4, section 1, does not distinguish among "public Acts, Records, and judicial Proceedings," and for a time the Court gave statutes and case law the same full faith and credit as judgments.[43] Although there are differences between acts and judgments, there is no reason to require stringent full credit to judgments and almost none to statutes and case law.

Allstate's minimalist reading of the full faith and credit clause for choice of law is related to the rejection of Beale's vested rights.[44] As stated above, previous constitutional analysis of choice of law virtually constitutionalized vested rights. The Court was correct to reject Beale's method and jurisprudence, but it should not have rendered the full faith and credit clause meaningless when applied to statutes and case law, as it seems to be under *Allstate*.

On the other hand, a proper multilateralist approach would give both the forum and foreign state's law full faith and credit and respect the horizontal structural lines set forth in the Constitution: a state gives full faith and credit to the laws of another state without yielding its power to apply its laws when it adopts the law of the most appropriate jurisdiction.

B. CONSTITUTIONAL LIMITATIONS ON CHOICE OF LAW

1. Due Process Limitations on Choice of Law

The due process analysis of choice of law should reflect due process analysis in other areas. Although distinctions between choice of law and other areas require some differences,[45] a due process standard for choice of law should not ignore normal due process principles.

a. Due process analysis in general. There are two main types of due process under the Fourteenth Amendment: (1) procedural due process and (2) substantive due process. Procedural due process requires "a fair decision-making process before the government takes some action directly impairing a person's life, liberty or property."[46] Under procedural due process, "[i]t is only necessary that a fair decision making process be used; the ultimate rule to be enforced need not be a fair or just one."[47] On the other hand, substantive due process is "the judicial determination of the compatibility of the substance of a law or a governmental action with the Constitution."[48] In other words, "[t]he Court is concerned with the constitutionality of the underlying rule rather than with the fairness of the process by which the government applies the rule to the individual."[49] Substantive due process "places absolute limits on the State's ability to act against an individual, not withstanding the procedural protections in place."[50]

Determining the constitutionality of state choice of law falls under substantive due process because the Court is testing the compatibility of choice of law rules with the Constitution. Moreover, a law's scope (the situations to which it applies) is substantive because a law's scope is an integral part of the law.[51]

The Fourteenth Amendment due process clause limits the power of state governments.[52] Professor Hilliard has written that "the doctrine of substantive due process inhibits the legislature [and state courts] in exercising its law-making power which tends to affect an individual's liberty."[53] "The concept of due process evolved in order to protect individuals from the arbitrary and capricious acts of legislative will."[54] "In the context of due process, arbitrary action means willful and unreasonable action: action that depends on the governmental will alone rather than reason or judgment."[55] "Since arbitrary action is equivalent to unreasonableness, substantive due process is a test of reasonableness."[56]

The degree of scrutiny a court gives a law under substantive due process usually depends on whether the law involves economic and social welfare or fundamental rights. A court will generally find that an economic or social welfare law satisfies due process as long as the law "bears a reasonable relation to the state's legitimate purpose" in creating that law.[57]

The modern approach is found in *Williamson v. Lee Optical*, where the Court declared, "The day is gone when this Court uses the Due Process Clause of the Fourteenth Amendment to strike down state laws, regulatory of business and industrial conditions, because they may be unwise, improvident, or out of harmony with a particular school of thought."[58] The Court added that "[f]or protection against abuses by legislature, the people must resort to the polls, not to the courts."[59]

Similarly, in *Ferguson v. Skrupa*, the Court wrote,

> Under the system of government created by our Constitution, it is up to legislatures, not courts, to decide on the wisdom and utility of legislation. There was a time when the Due Process Clause was used by this Court to strike down laws which were thought unreasonable, that is, unwise or incompatible with some economic or social philosophy. In this manner the Due Process Clause was used, for example, to nullify laws prescribing maximum hours for work in bakeries, outlawing "yellow dog" contracts, setting minimum wages for women, and fixing

the weight of loaves of bread.[60]

The Court cited Justice Holmes who had declared, "The criterion of constitutionality is not whether we believe the law to be for the public good."[61]

One can see the application of these principles in *Exxon Corp. v. Governor of Maryland.*[62] In this case, Maryland passed a statute prohibiting petroleum producers and refiners from operating retail service stations within Maryland and requiring producers to extend temporary price restrictions to all stations they supply (rather than just company-owned stations). Several petroleum companies challenged the statute on due process grounds.

The Court rejected the petroleum companies substantive due process challenge. The Court declared that "[t]he evidence presented by the refiners may cast some doubt on the wisdom of the statute, but it is, by now, absolutely clear that the Due Process Clause does not empower the judiciary to sit as a superlegislature to weigh the wisdom of legislation."[63] The Court refused to consider the economic wisdom of the statute (the companies had vigorously argued that the statute was irrational and counterproductive) and concluded that the statute bore a reasonable relation to the purpose for which it had been enacted.

On the other hand, a state may regulate fundamental rights only for a compelling state interest, and such regulations must be narrowly drawn to express only the compelling state interest.[64] The Court has found only a few fundamental interests within the due process (and equal protection) clause. These include (1) the freedom of association;[65] (2) the right to vote and participate in the electoral process;[66] (3) the right of interstate travel;[67] (4) a right to fairness in the civil process;[68] (5) a right of fairness in procedures involving claims against the government concerning deprivations of life, liberty, or property;[69] and (6) the right of privacy.[70]

Although the Supreme Court has generally limited strict scrutiny to fundamental rights, it has recently applied a seemingly heightened substantive due process analysis to state punitive damages awards. As the introduction noted, in *BMW of America v. Gore,*[71] the Court invalidated excessive punitive damages on substantive due process grounds because Alabama did not have a legitimate interest in assessing such an award.[72]

Gore involved BMW's nondisclosure of the fact that it had repainted the plaintiff's car before delivery.[73] BMW had a nationwide policy of not disclosing predelivery damage when that damage did not exceed 3 percent of the car's suggested retail price. At trial, BMW argued that Gore's car was as good as if it had a factory finish.

The jury returned a verdict of $4,000 compensatory damages and $4 million punitive damages. On a posttrial motion to set aside the punitive damages, BMW argued its nondisclosure policy was consistent with the law of approximately twenty-five states. It asserted that, since its conduct was not illegal in those states, its actions in those jurisdictions could not be the basis of punitive damages. The trial judge denied BMW's motion. The Alabama Supreme Court rejected BMW's claim that the award was unconstitutional, but it reduced the damages to $2 million because the jury had improperly computed them.

In holding the award violated the due process clause, Justice Stevens pointed out that "[p]unitive damages may properly be imposed to further a State's legitimate interests in punishing unlawful conduct and deterring its repetition."[74] A state has flexibility in calculating punitive damages as long as they are necessary to vindicate a state's legitimate interests of punishment and deterrence.[75] "Only when an award can fairly be categorized as 'grossly excessive' in relation to those interests does it enter the zone of arbitrariness that violates the Due Process Clause of the Fourteenth Amendment."[76] A state cannot impose its policy on its neighbors.[77] Not only is a state limited by the federal power over interstate commerce, it "is also constrained by the need to respect the interests of other States."[78] Accordingly, "it follows from these principles of state sovereignty and comity that a State may not impose economic sanctions on violations of its laws with the intent of changing the tortfessors' lawful conduct in other States."[79] Equally important, "[e]lementary notions of fairness enshrined in our constitutional jurisprudence dictate that a person receive fair notice not only of the conduct that will subject him to punishment, but also the severity of the penalty that a State may impose."[80]

Based on these principles, Justice Stevens struck down the punitive damages award. He held that (1) BMW's conduct did "not establish the high degree of culpability that warranted a substantial punitive damages award," (2) the ratio of compensatory to punitive damages was suspicious, and (3) the award exceeded criminal and civil penalties for similar conduct.[81]

b. Due process analysis of choice of law. As stated earlier in this chapter, applying the above principles to choice of law requires a two-step analysis. First, one must determine whether a state can constitutionally apply its law to a dispute, ignoring, in this step, the possibility that another state's law might also apply. Second, one must establish whether choice of a state's law satisfies due process when another state's law might also apply under step one.

A court should analyze a state's decision concerning the scope of its laws (when the scope does not conflict with another sovereign's laws) under rational basis analysis. A court should not interfere with a state's determination as to its law's scope as long as there is a reasonable relation between the law's reach and its legitimate purpose. Otherwise, the court would be sitting as a superlegislature weighing the wisdom of the law's scope. As noted earlier, the Supreme Court's due process analysis in *Allstate* is satisfactory for this step.

The rational basis test (and *Allstate*), however, is not appropriate when there is a true conflict of laws. When a court is determining whether a state can apply its law to a case when there is a true conflict, the court is not evaluating whether the first state's law can extend that far; rather, it is deciding whether the state can adopt its law instead of the law of another state. Although courts should not interfere with a state's value judgments when that state is the only one that has sovereignty over the matter (as long as those judgments are otherwise constitutional), heightened scrutiny is required when two jurisdictions are trying to assert their sovereignty over an individual when a true conflict exists. Due process should protect an individual from competing states. Thus, a reasonable relation between a law's scope and its purpose is not enough for true conflicts.[82]

Cases in which the Court has struck down state regulations that substantially interfere with interstate commerce are analogous to where one state's law substantially conflicts with another state's law. The Court will allow a state regulation that has some effect on interstate commerce as long as "it does not materially restrict the free flow of commerce."[83] However, the Court will invalidate a state law that substantially interferes with interstate commerce.[84]

In *Southern Pacific*, the Court struck down an Arizona statute that regulated the length of trains because it violated the commerce clause, even though the Arizona Supreme Court had found that the statute bore a reasonable relation to its purpose.[85] Justice Black's dissent attacked the majority on the ground that it was acting as a "superlegislature."[86] He declared that

> I am therefore compelled to reach the conclusion that today's decision is the result of the belief of a majority of this Court that both the legislature of Arizona and the Congress made wrong policy decisions in permitting a law to stand which limits the length of railroad trains. I should at least give the Arizona statute the benefit of the same rule which this Court said should be applied in connection with state legislation under attack for violating the Fourteenth Amendment, that is, that legislative bodies have "a wide range of legislative discretion, . . . and their conclusions respecting the wisdom of their legislative acts are not reviewable by the courts."[87]

The majority, however, was not acting as a superlegislature in *Southern Pacific*. It was not interfering with a decision that was solely within Arizona's sovereignty. By severely restricting the length of interstate trains passing through its jurisdiction, Arizona was imposing its judgment on states and individuals outside its sovereignty. It was this imposition that the Court struck down. Arizona cannot decide how far its sovereignty constitutionally extends; only the Supreme Court can establish these structural lines. The same analysis should apply to the structural lines that regulate choice of law.

Although having a particular state's law govern a controversy is probably not a "fundamental right," *Gore* provides some guidance as to the degree of scrutiny that a court should use when evaluating choice of law under due process. *Gore* demonstrates that there are some situations where a state's law can violate due process even when a fundamental right is not implicated.[88] A state's unreasonable choice of law is similar to a state's assessment of excessive punitive damages. As was true of excessive punitive damages, when a state adopts its law when another state has a significantly closer connection to the controversy, it has imposed its law on its neighbors; other states' interests are not respected, and, more important for due process, neither are the interests of the citizens of those states. Moreover, the unreasonable choice of law often makes conduct that is lawful in the state that has the closest connection to the matter unlawful solely because the forum state extended its reach beyond appropriate limitations. Such choice of law is unfair to the individual who is burdened by having the law of a state with a tenuous connection to a case decide the controversy. Accordingly, the due process clause should protect individuals from overreaching by a state—a person has a right not to have a state's law applied to a case when another jurisdiction has a significantly closer connection, even if the first state could apply its law absent a conflict. Such a limitation would also comport with *Gore*'s requirement that an individual have notice of the conduct that will subject him or her to punishment, as well as fair notice of the extent of that punishment.

The constraint proposed here would not interfere with state sovereignty. When a court rules that a state cannot apply its law because another state has a significantly closer connection to a controversy, it is not intruding upon that state's sovereignty; rather, it is saying that the state lacks sufficient connections to exercise sovereignty over the matter. This is very different from substituting the court's judgment as to the economic or social wisdom of a law for the state's judgement, the major impetus behind the rational basis test. Indeed, what often happens under the current constitutional approach to choice of law is that a state simply chooses to substitute its judgment for that of a sister state.

2. Full Faith and Credit Limitations on Choice of Law

The full faith and credit clause places constraints on choice of law that are similar to those imposed by the due process clause. However, as noted above, the source of these constraints is different. Due process is based on individual liberty, while full faith and credit is predicated on respect for state sovereignty and the structural lines of horizontal federalism.[89]

The full faith and credit clause states: "Full Faith and Credit shall be given in each State to the public Acts, Records, and Judicial Proceedings of every other State. And Congress may by general Laws prescribe the Manner in which such Acts, Records and Proceedings shall be proved, and the Effect thereof."[90]

The first question under the full faith and credit clause is its scope. It is generally accepted that the full faith and credit clause applies to all sources of state law—statutes, case law, and judgments.[91]

The more difficult question is the effect of the full faith and credit clause on choice of law. An examination of the relation of the states in our federal system provides the starting point for this question. States are quasi-sovereigns: They have their independent spheres of sovereignty in many areas, but they are subject to the United States Constitution and the supremacy clause, which declares that the federal government is supreme in areas in which it is competent to act.[92] Within this framework, the states are independent sovereigns as to each other.[93] "[T]he States stand on an equal level or plane under our constitutional system . . .,"[94] and they "are equal to each other in power, dignity, and authority, each component to exert that residuum of sovereignty not delegated to the United States by the Constitution itself."[95] Moreover, "[o]ur federal system depends on one jurisdiction's respect for the sovereignty of another."[96]

Absent a treaty, independent sovereigns do not have to enforce foreign law. When they do enforce foreign law, it is based on comity—"the principle that courts of one state or jurisdiction will give effect to laws and judicial decisions of another state out of deference and mutual respect, rather than out of duty."[97] However, the full faith and credit clause "substituted a command for the earlier principles of comity" for American states, and it requires them to give full faith and credit to the statutes and case law of sister states.[98] As the Supreme Court recently stated, the clause's purpose "was to alter the status of the several states as independent foreign sovereignties, each free to ignore obligations created under the laws or by the judicial proceedings of the others, and to make them integral parts of a single nation throughout which a remedy upon a just obligation might be demanded as of right, irrespective of the state of its origin."[99]

A middle ground approach to full faith and credit can respect the sovereignty of independent states, but still give meaning to the clause. As Professor Douglas Laycock has pointed out, the key word in the clause is "full":

> A state does not owe some credit, partial credit, or credit where it would be wholly unreasonable to deny credit, which seems to be the Supreme Court's current interpretation. Rather, each state owes *full* faith and credit to the law of sister states. *Full* faith and credit is what a state affords its own law . . . . Thus, the Clause is most plausibly read as requiring each state to give the law of every other state the same faith and credit as its own law—to treat the law of sister states as equal in authority to its own.[100]

How does a court "treat the law of each state as equal in authority to its own?" The most practical solution is to determine which state has the closest connection to the controversy and adopt the law of the state with the closest connection. Consequently, choice of a state's law should violate the full faith and credit clause whenever another state has a significantly closer connection to the matter—that is, whenever a state has imposed its policy on its neighbors[101] and, in doing so, has failed to respect the superior interests of other states. Thus, a state shows appropriate respect for another state's sovereignty by yielding its interest when that other state has a significantly closer connection to the dispute, and it can assert its interest when it has a significantly closer connection. As Justice Jackson observed, "[a]nything taken away from a state by way of freedom to deny faith and credit to law of others is thereby added to the state by way of a right to exact faith and credit for its own."[102]

3. Application of Due Process and Full Faith and Credit Constraints to Create a Constitutional Standard for Choice of Law

Although the bases for judging the constitutionality of choice of law under the due process and full faith and credit clauses are different, the standard derived from these clauses is the same—choice of law should be unconstitutional if a court adopts a state's law when another state has a significantly closer connection to the controversy. The basis of the constraint under the due process clause is individual liberty, whereas under the full faith and credit clause it is state sovereignty.

This standard requires a multilateralist approach to the determination of the constitutionality of choice of law. Thus, a court must examine the applicability of *all* laws that might govern a matter; it cannot stop when it thinks that forum law might be applicable, as it can under *Allstate*. It also requires a court to adopt an objective, deontological view of choice of law. A court cannot favor forum law because it is forum law. Similarly, a court cannot employ a rule that the court thinks is the better law, when the state whose law is not "better" has a significantly closer connection to the dispute.

The above standard still allows for differences of opinion concerning which state's law should be employed. Different methods of determining which state has the closest connection, different interpretations of the facts, and differing views on the importance of connections will occur. This is why the standard includes "significantly." Reasonable differences of opinion should not attain constitutional status.

Some critics might label my approach to constitutional constraints on choice of law as conservative. In comparison, governmental interest analysis furthers state policies, and the better rule approach searches for the rule that is the most just. Moreover, as Chapter 2 noted, many modern choice of law systems, including governmental interest analysis and the better rule approach, are often pro-plaintiff.

My standard, however, is neither conservative nor liberal. It allows the substantive values of the state with the closest connection to the controversy to prevail regardless of forum. Thus, if a state chooses to prevent stacking in order to safeguard insurance companies' solvency, another state with a tenuous connection to the controversy cannot interfere with that decision. Similarly, if a state wants to protect plaintiffs through unlimited damages or easier standards of proof, another state cannot refuse to apply those laws when the first state has a significantly closer connection to the matter. In other words, the standard preserves a state's judgments no matter how controversial or unpopular.

4. The Effect of Other Constitutional Clauses on Choice of Law

Some scholars have suggested that the Constitution's antidiscrimination clauses—Article IV's privileges and immunities clause, the Fourteenth Amendment's equal protection clause, and the commerce clause—might constrain state choice of law.[103] In short, these clauses might limit a state's ability to favor its residents over nonresidents through its choice of law rules.

Douglas Laycock, for example, has written a convincing article that argues that the antidiscrimination clauses (along with other constraints such as the full faith and credit clause and the principle of territorial states) substantially limit choice of law.[104] From the antidiscrimination clauses, Professor Laycock derives "the principle of equal citizens: States must treat the citizens of sister states equally with their own."[105] He asserts that choice of law rules that prefer local litigants violate this principle.[106] For example, he concludes that interest analysis is unconstitutional because it prefers insiders and disregards outsiders' interests.[107] He declares that "[i]nterest analysis is discriminatory because it effectively creates three sets of rules. There is the local rule, the other state's rule, and the local rule for outsiders, which is the least advantageous of the three."[108]

Although Professor Laycock's article is persuasive, a combination of the due process and full faith and credit clauses places strict limits on choice of law and makes use of other clauses unnecessary. My proposed standard that a state's choice of law is unconstitutional if another state has a significantly closer connection to the controversy should eliminate discriminatory choice of law rules. As Professor Laycock has noted, "It is . . . possible to get anomalous results with territorial rules, but it is not possible to get systematically self-interested results."[109]

C. APPLICATION OF THE PROPOSED CONSTITUTIONAL STANDARD TO EXISTING CHOICE OF LAW METHODS

My proposed standard for choice of law is substantially stricter than the *Allstate* standard, and it limits the possible choice of law methods a court can use. For example, when two states' laws might govern, the forum cannot automatically choose its law; the other state's law might have a significantly closer connection to the controversy and thus would have priority. Similarly, courts cannot always adopt the "better rule" because the state with the other rule might be significantly more closely connected to the case.

1. Governmental Interest Analysis

a. Professor Currie's original method. Currie's governmental interest analysis would not survive the above standard because it adopts forum law when there is a true conflict—when the laws of two or more states might govern a controversy.[110] The first step in Currie's analysis—determine which states have interests in applying their laws—complies with the constitutional standard set forth above. In this step, he is trying to determine which states' laws might govern, and his system is effective for determining whether there is a reasonable relation between a law's scope and its legitimate purpose.

The problem with Currie's method lies in its second step—adopting forum law in all cases where there is a true conflict. Such a rigid approach disregards the fact that another jurisdiction might have a significantly closer connection to the controversy. Consequently, Currie's forum-centered approach infringes upon individual liberty under the due process clause. As stated above, an individual has a due process right not to have a state's law govern his or her conduct when another state has a significantly closer connection to the controversy. In addition, there is nothing in the Constitution to support stressing state interests over individual interests.[111] Similarly, governmental interest analysis infringes on state sovereignty because it allows a forum to adopt its law when another state is more closely connected to the case, permitting it to further its interests at the expense of the interests of the more interested state.

Rosenthal v. Warren illustrates the constitutional problems with interest analysis.[112] In *Rosenthal*, a New York citizen sued a Massachusetts hospital and doctor in federal court in New York to recover for the wrongful death of her husband. The husband had gone to Boston for an operation, and he had died there eight days later. The issue was whether New York's unlimited wrongful death damages or Massachusetts's $50,000 limit on wrongful death damages governed.

The court unhesitatingly adopted New York law based on New York's governmental interest analysis choice of law rules, declaring that "[t]his review of [New York] case law leaves us with the overwhelming conclusion that . . . the strong New York public policy against damage limitations has triumphed over the contrary policies of sister states in every case where a New York domiciliary has brought suit."[113] The court quickly dismissed the defendants' interests: "Even if expectations, real or constructive, could be hypothesized, they would be legally irrelevant. Despite the argument that looking to the expectations of the parties to solve choice of law problems promotes 'an unconscious acceptance of legality and [the] legal order,' . . . this contractual type of approach to multistate tort problems has been 'summarily rejected' by the New York Court of Appeals."[114]

The court also disregarded Massachusetts's interest, calling Massachusetts's law "the vestigial remains of a mistaken view that there was no common law action for wrongful death."[115] The court continued, "In any event, it is our considered view that the New York Court of Appeals would view the Massachusetts limitation, in the words of Judge Hatch, as 'so absurd and unjust' that the New York policy of fully compensating the harm for wrongful death would outweigh any interest Massachusetts has in keeping down in this limited type of situation the size of the verdict (and in some cases insurance premiums)."[116]

The majority also rejected the dissent's argument that adopting New York law would violate the full faith and credit clause: "The fact that Massachusetts was the situs of the tort and the residence of the defendant would not be sufficient to require as a matter of full faith and credit that the limits in the Massachusetts law control, in light of the very strong New York policy against wrongful death limitations in connection with its citizens and next of kin and in light of the interstate aspects of the transaction."[117]

The application of New York law in *Rosenthal* was unconstitutional because the dispute had a significantly closer connection to Massachusetts.[118] The malpractice took place in Massachusetts, and the defendants were Massachusetts domiciliaries. Significantly, there was no evidence that they had solicited patients outside Massachusetts.[119] Moreover, the malpractice insurance premium was apparently calculated with the Massachusetts damages limitation in mind.[120] In addition, although the decedent and his widow were New York domiciliaries, the decedent voluntarily came to Massachusetts for the operation. As the dissent pointed out, "I cannot see how the alleged malpractice and subsequent death of plaintiff's decedent can be classified as anything other than a local incident."[121]

The adoption of New York law interfered with the defendants' liberty interests because law with a tenuous connection to the case governed their conduct. Similarly, the court completely ignored the parties' expectations. As noted in the previous chapter, a doctor and a hospital operating in Massachusetts could reasonably expect that their conduct would be governed by Massachusetts law, but a New York resident who voluntarily travels to Massachusetts should not expect that New York law should apply. Notably, under *Rosenthal*'s reasoning, the patients' domiciles might govern in *all* cases, regardless of where the patients are from, giving the defendants no notice of what law applies, thus violating *Gore*[122] and making it impossible for health care providers to plan their conduct with certainty.

Adopting New York law also impeded Massachusetts's sovereignty because Massachusetts had a significantly closer connection to the case. The court ignored Massachusetts's interest because New York had a strong policy of giving its residents full compensation. However, one state's policy should not be allowed to trump another state's policy when the second state has a significantly closer connection to the controversy. This is the type of situation the full faith and credit clause was designed to deal with: where one state extends its policy so far as to interfere unreasonably with another state's sovereignty.[123] Such interference might be legitimate with independent sovereigns, but not with quasi-sovereign states subject to the provisions of the Constitution, especially the full faith and credit clause. As Professor Peter Hay has observed, "federalism is designed to preserve, protect, and nurture pluralism. Any notion of intersystem cooperation, however, also must include restraint, lest pluralism should equal the sum of parochial self-interests and the objective of the union be lost."[124]

b. A more moderate and restrained interpretation of state interests. Although Currie's "more moderate and restrained interpretation of state interests"[125] might prevent some of the more extreme constitutional problems in his original system, it does not solve all of them. If a true conflict remains even after the more moderate and restrained interpretation, the forum can—and should under Currie's view—still adopt its law despite the fact that another state has a significantly closer connection to the matter.

A recent forum on governmental interest analysis that discussed *Rosenthal* illustrates the problem.[126] In analyzing *Rosenthal* based on a more moderate and restrained interpretation of state interests, Professor John Rees still found a true conflict.[127] In analyzing New York's interest, he declared, "The policy of our state in not limiting damages is to provide full compensation to the family of the victim of wrongful death, at least where the victim and his family are domiciliaries of this state. Since the victim and his family are citizens of this state, we have an interest in the application of our law in this case."[128] He concluded, "According to Currie, if upon reconsideration the court finds that a conflict between the legitimate interests of the two states is unavoidable, it should apply the law of the forum. Thus, our rule of unlimited damages applies in this case."[129]

c. Professor Baxter's comparative impairment approach. Another variation on governmental interest analysis is Professor Baxter's comparative impairment approach.[130] Choice of law in *Rosenthal* under comparative impairment would probably be the same as under traditional interest analysis. As stated above, *Rosenthal* strongly downplayed Massachusetts's interest as compared with New York's,[131] despite the fact that Massachusetts had the stronger connection to the dispute. Professor David Currie has recently stated that he doubted that the case's outcome would be different under Professor Baxter's approach.[132] Perhaps the outcome would vary if another court were applying Baxter's approach, but the court that decided *Rosenthal* would probably adhere to the decision.

A proper application of comparative impairment would satisfy the full faith and credit clause in many cases. Determining how much the failure to apply a state's law will affect that state's interest shows respect for that state's sovereignty. However, the above analysis of *Rosenthal* demonstrates that comparative impairment is no guarantee that a state's sovereignty would not be infringed by a sister state.

The major problem with comparative impairment is that it fails to consider the individual's interest under the due process clause. Although application of a state's law might not significantly impinge on another state's interest, the application of that law might still treat unfairly the individual subjected to its coercive force. Assuming we accept *Rosenthal*'s dubious conclusion that Massachusetts's interest was not significantly impaired, it still seems unfair to the defendants that the law of the state with such a tenuous connection to the dispute was permitted to govern their conduct.

2. The Better Rule Approach

Application of the better rule approach would be unconstitutional under my standard. The Minnesota Supreme Court's decision in *Allstate* illustrates the constitutional problems with this approach.[133] As mentioned in Chapter 1, Minnesota's contacts with the case were tenuous: (1) the decedent worked in Minnesota, (2) the decedent's widow moved to Minnesota after her husband's death, and (3) the defendant did unrelated business in Minnesota. Notably, none of these contacts is directly related to the accident. On the other hand, Wisconsin's contacts with the case were substantial and related to the cause of action: (1) the decedent was a Wisconsin domiciliary, (2) the decedent bought the policy in Wisconsin, and 3) the accident occurred in Wisconsin.

Despite the overwhelming connections to Wisconsin, the Minnesota court upheld the application of Minnesota law, mainly based on the fact that its prostacking rule was the better rule.[134] Concerning the better rule, the court declared,

> Minnesota follows a majority of jurisdictions in allowing stacking . . . . Although majority status is not by itself sufficient to make a rule "better," the decisions on stacking are fairly recent and well considered in light of current use of automobiles . . . . We believe that it is preferable to compensate victims of accidents to the full extent of their injuries . . . . The Minnesota rule is better because it requires the cost of accidents with uninsured motorists to be spread more broadly through insurance premiums than does the Wisconsin rule.[135]

Minnesota's adoption of the better rule violated the Constitution because Wisconsin had a significantly closer connection to the dispute. Wisconsin's connections were the fundamental ones: the decedent was domiciled there, he bought the insurance there, and the accident occurred there. On the other hand,

Minnesota's connections were very tenuous. First, Minnesota did not have an "interest" in protecting nonresidents who were injured in other states, even if they worked in Minnesota. Second, Minnesota did not have an interest in regulating the behavior of foreign corporations in other states, even if they did unrelated business in Minnesota. Finally, the fact that the widow moved to Minnesota after the accident was irrelevant because such later occurrences cannot affect preexisting legal relations.

Thus, this case resembles *Gore*. In *Gore*, Alabama unconstitutionally tried to regulate conduct in other states through its excessive award of punitive damages. In *Allstate*, Minnesota unconstitutionally tried to regulate conduct in another state by extending its law too far.

Minnesota's decision violated the due process clause because it did not respect Allstate's interest. Because Allstate wrote the policy in Wisconsin for a Wisconsin resident and the accident occurred in Wisconsin, Allstate had the reasonable expectation that Wisconsin law would govern stacking. Moreover, Allstate had a state's law applied to it that had a questionable connection to the controversy. That Mrs. Hague might have been more sympathetic than Allstate should not have affected the analysis.[136] If a law is wrong, the law should be changed; a court should not manipulate choice of law on a case by case basis to fit its sense of justice.

Minnesota also hindered Wisconsin's sovereignty. Wisconsin had the sovereignty to regulate its domiciliaries and companies doing business in Wisconsin, accidents that occurred in Wisconsin that involved mainly local interests, and insurance policies written in Wisconsin concerning accidents that took place there. For Minnesota to apply its policy despite Wisconsin's strong connection to the case was a blatant usurpation of Wisconsin's sovereignty and a violation of the horizontal structural lines in the full faith and credit clause. The fact that a jurisdiction has a strong policy does not mean that jurisdiction can force its policy on the world.[137]

Emphasizing individual liberty and state sovereignty in the constitutional analysis of choice of law demonstrates in general the problems with the better rule approach. As mentioned previously, individual justice requires predictability in legal rules so that an individual can conform his or her conduct to those rules. That choice of law might depend on a single, idiosyncratic judge's notion of the better rule violates this principle.[138] As stated earlier, a person has the right not to have the law of a jurisdiction with a tenuous connection to a controversy govern that individual's conduct. Fairness in choice of law should mean that the choice involves the law of the most appropriate political entity, not the fairest rule from a natural law standpoint. As noted earlier, substantive fairness should be established at the substantive level, not the choice of law level.

The better rule approach allows one sovereign to substitute its values for those of a competing sovereign. Application of the rule violates the full faith and credit clause in those instances where a state with significantly fewer connections to a case than a sister state nonetheless applies the "better" rule. In many instances, there are reasonable grounds supporting both sovereigns' rules; making value judgments is a part of sovereignty. Professor Kogan has observed that "[g]ranting each state independent police power promotes experimentation with different policies, enabling the fifty states to 'serve as laboratories for the development of new social, economic, and political ideas.'"[139] In other cases, even if one sovereign's rule is clearly not the better one, that fact alone does not give another sovereign (in our interstate system) the power to ignore the first sovereign's judgment. Part of sovereignty is the power to be wrong (within constitutional limits, of course), without interference from a sovereign that thinks it knows better. As Professor David Currie has noted, the full faith and credit clause's purpose "is to make it easier for a state to regulate its own affairs, not to enable it to fiddle with the affairs of others."[140] Or, as Professor Laycock has observed, "[i]f each state is equal in authority to the other forty-nine, then no state is required to conform its law to that of the others, or to follow the trend that other states find more in keeping with the times."[141]

3. Beale's Approach

Although a unilateralist approach that is generally applied cannot be constitutional under my standard because it fails to analyze all laws that might govern a controversy,[142] not all multilateralist systems satisfy the standard. Beale's vested rights approach occasionally violates the proposed standard because it sometimes chooses law based on tenuous connections. As mentioned above, under Beale's system, the law of the place of the last act—the injury—governs in tort cases. In a few instances, the place of the injury might have a fortuitous connection to the dispute.

Reconsider, for example, the waiver of liability case discussed in Chapter 2. P, a Missouri resident, bought a ticket on D's train to travel from St. Louis, Missouri to Kansas City, Kansas. The ticket included a waiver of liability clause, which absolved the railroad of liability for its negligence. Kansas enforces such clauses, but Missouri does not. D's mechanic negligently repaired the train's brakes in St. Louis, and other employees failed to properly inspect the train's brakes in Kansas City, Missouri. The brakes failed while the train was in Missouri. Shortly after the train passed into Kansas, it jumped the tracks, and P was injured. D was incorporated and doing business mainly in Missouri, with one train a week traveling from St. Louis to Kansas City, Kansas.

Under Beale's method, the law of the place of injury controls, and P will not be able to recover because the waiver is valid under Kansas law. Such a decision violates my proposed constitutional standard because the matter has a significantly closer connection to Missouri; everything but the injury occurred there. Thus, choice of Kansas law infringes upon the plaintiff's liberty interest and Missouri's sovereignty.

4. The *Second Restatement*'s "Most Significant Relationship" Test

The *Second Restatement*'s "most significant relationship" test (by itself) is constitutional under my standard.[143] First, the most significant relationship test evaluates all relevant laws—so it is multilateralist. Second, it chooses the law of the state with the most significant relationship to the dispute, which should fulfill the requirement that a court should not select a state's law if another state has a significantly closer connection to the case. Third, section 145 (2) sets out criteria that are relevant to making a sound determination of the state with the most significant relationship. Finally, nothing under the general principles of section 6 requires a court to be forum favoring or adopt law solely because it is the better law.

Schulze v. Illinois Highway Transp. Co., which was also discussed in Chapter 1, demonstrates that the *Second Restatement*'s most significant relationship test satisfies the proposed constitutional standard.[144] In this case, members of an Illinois club, which had chartered a bus from an Illinois corporation for a round trip to Michigan, were injured when the bus overturned in Michigan. The Illinois plaintiffs sued in Illinois, and the trial court decided that Illinois law should apply to the issues of damages and damages limitations.

The Illinois Supreme Court affirmed the trial court's decision to adopt Illinois law, using the *Second Restatement*'s most significant relationship test.[145] The court analyzed four types of contacts: (1) the place of the injury, (2) the place of the conduct causing the injury, (3) the parties' domiciles and places of business, and (4) the place where the parties entered into their relationship.[146] The court first examined the quantity of the contacts, finding that the place of the injury was Michigan, that the place of the conduct causing the injury was both Illinois and Michigan, and that the parties' domiciles and places of business, as well as the place where the parties entered into their relationship, was Illinois.[147]

As mentioned in Chapter 1, the court also examined the "quality" of the contacts.[148] The court thought that the place of the injury was insignificant because it was fortuitous.[149] It also believed that the place of the negligence was unimportant because negligence was not the issue. On the other hand, since the type of damages recoverable and the amount recoverable were the important issues, the parties' domicile—Illinois—was important because that was where the social and economic impact of recovery or nonrecovery would be felt.[150] The place the parties' relationship was centered—also Illinois—was also significant because the injuries occurred in connection with that relationship.[151] The court concluded that Illinois law should govern the case because the significant contacts were with Illinois.[152]

The above approach satisfies my proposed constitutional standard. As the court's analysis shows, the issues had a significantly closer connection to Illinois because the most important connections were with Illinois: (1) the parties were domiciled there and (2) their relationship was centered there. Since Illinois had a significantly closer connection to the dispute than Michigan, choice of its law complies with both the due process and full faith and credit clauses.

D. CHOICE OF LAW IN CLOSE CASES

1. Cases Where the Adoption of Two or More States' Laws Might be Constitutional

My proposed constitutional standard significantly limits choice of law methods. However, it does not require that there be one right answer in close cases; the standard only gives the outer limits for permissible choice of law. There will be some cases in which the court could choose more than one state's law without violating the Constitution because neither state has a *significantly* closer connection to the dispute. In other words, the connections between the states are almost even, and choice of law will depend on the judge's reasoned judgment of what connections are most important for that case.

Cases involving a tavern owner's liability for an automobile accident in another state are typical of close cases.[153] For example, P, an Indiana resident, is injured in Indiana by a drunken driver. P wants to sue the Kentucky tavern owner who served the driver the alcohol. Indiana allows recovery from a tavern owner by persons injured by drivers who were served excessive amounts of alcohol by the tavern owner; Kentucky does not impose liability on the owner.

In this case, the connections are virtually equal. The tavern owner is a Kentucky domiciliary, and he served the drinks in Kentucky. The Kentucky law is intended to protect tavern owners from liability for drunk driving accidents, presumably because Kentucky believes that it is difficult to tell when someone is too drunk to drive. On the other hand, the injured party is an Indiana resident, and the accident occurred there. The Indiana law is intended to protect motorists who drive on its roads; Indiana believes that holding tavern owners liable will reduce drunken driving accidents. Courts that have faced this issue have come out on both sides.[154]

I would pick Indiana law because the location of the accident seems more significant than the place where the liquor was served. In addition, the plaintiff had no connection to Kentucky and would not expect Kentucky law to apply, whereas a Kentucky tavern owner should be aware that a person to whom he served alcohol might drive to Indiana. However, there are sufficient connections with Kentucky that an opposite decision would not be unconstitutional under the proposed standard.

2. Unconstitutional Choice of Law Criteria in Close Cases

Although the Constitution does not require a single right answer in close cases, courts should not use certain criteria to choose law in close cases. The criteria that should be unconstitutional, even as tie breakers, are adopting forum law solely because it is forum law and employing the better rule.[155]

Adopting forum law solely because it is forum law intrudes on individual liberty under the due process clause even in close cases. As noted earlier, a state's interest in what law should apply should never be superior to the individual's interest in the governing law in a private dispute.[156] Lawsuits are between people, not state policies. Courts should judge people based on the legal norms they are expected to follow, not what law would further the forum's policy.

Similarly, this criterion violates the full faith and credit clause because the forum does not give full credit to the foreign law when the deciding criterion for adopting forum law is that it is forum law. As Douglas Laycock noted, "[i]f an employer hired black applicants only when they were clearly superior to the white applicants, and hired whites whenever the comparison between the applicants was fairly debatable, we would easily concluded that the employer discriminated."[157]

Using the better rule criterion as a tie breaker also violates individual liberty and state sovereignty. It is not fair to a person who has complied with the rule that should govern to be told that his conduct is unlawful because another court thinks another rule is the better substantive rule. As the previous chapter noted, fairness means more than substantive fairness. A litigant has a right to have appropriate criteria applied to the decision-making process, even if the case is close enough that a good faith application of these criteria would produce reasonable disagreement.

Likewise, to refuse to follow a state's rule because another court thinks it is not the better rule is an egregious usurpation of that state's sovereignty and a violation of the allocation of authority among the states created by the full faith and credit clause. If a state has the power to make a value judgment under the due process rational basis test without a court being able to interfere with that judgement (as discussed above), why should a court be able to interfere with that judgment under the guise of better rule choice of law? As Professor Kogan has written, "any approach to choice of law that directs a court to apply the 'better law' violates the constitutionally mandated neutrality towards sister states' visions of the Good."[158]

E. CONCLUSION

The above has criticized the current minimalist constraints on choice of law and advocated a stricter standard: A court cannot choose a state's law if another state has a significantly closer connection to the dispute. The above has also argued that certain choice of law criteria—choosing forum law because it is forum law and selecting the better rule—should always be unconstitutional because they interfere with individual liberty under the due process clause and state sovereignty under the full faith and credit clause.

Use of the above constraints would preclude several existing choice of law systems, including any that are forum favoring or based on the better rule. Thus, under this standard, Currie's governmental interest analysis and Leflar's and Juenger's better rule method would be unconstitutional. In addition, Beale's approach would be unconstitutional because it sometimes chooses the law of a state with a tenuous connection to the controversy.

My proposal for a new constitutional standard for choice of law constitutes a radical reorientation in American conflicts law. However, such a reorientation is necessary to clean up the dismal swamp of American choice of law.[159]

NOTES

1. David Currie et al., *Choice-of-Law Symposium Transcript*, 48 MERCER L. REV. 639, 682 (1997) [hereinafter Currie, *Symposium*].

2. I discuss state sovereignty in greater depth below.

3. Other clauses that might constrain state choice of law include Article IV's privileges and immunities clause, the Fourteenth Amendment's equal protection clause, and the commerce clause. I will discuss these clauses below.

4. Allstate Ins. Co. v. Hague, 449 U.S. 302, 313 (1981).

5. *E.g.*, LEA BRILMAYER, CONFLICT OF LAWS 129-68 (1995); Earl M. Maltz, *Visions of Fairness—The Relationship between Jurisdiction and Choice of Law*, 30 ARIZ. L. REV. 751 (1988); Louise Weinberg, *Choice of Law and Minimal Scrutiny*, 49 U. CHI. L. REV. 440 (1982); Ralph U. Whitten, *The Constitutional Limitations on State Choice of Law: Due Process*, 9 HASTINGS CONST. L.Q 851 (1982) (arguing that the *Allstate* standard is *too* restrictive); Ralph U. Whitten, *The Constitutional Limitations on State Choice of Law: Full Faith and Credit*, 12 MEM. ST. U.L. REV. 1 (1981); Robert A. Sedler, *Constitutional Limitations on Choice of Law: The Perspective of Constitutional Generalism*, 10 HOFSTRA L. REV. 54 (1981); Robert A. Leflar, *Constitutional Limits on Free Choice of Law*, 28 LAW & CONTEMP. PROBS. 706 (1963).

6. Kermit Roosevelt III, *The Myth of Choice of Law: Rethinking Conflicts*, 97 MICH. L. REV. 2448 (1999) ("Interstate conflicts are a chief concern of the Constitution, and the Constitution will allow us to deal with them." *Id.* at 2453.); Douglas Laycock, *Equal Citizens of Equal and Territorial States: The Constitutional Foundations of Choice of Law*, 92 COLUM. L. REV. 249 (1992); Terry S. Kogan, *Toward a Jurisprudence of Choice of Law: The Priority of Fairness over Comity*, 62 N.Y.U. L. REV. 651 (1987); *see also* Gene R. Shreve, *Choice of Law and the Forgiving Constitution*, 71 IND. L.J. 271 (1996); Peter Hay, *Full Faith and Credit and Federalism in Choice of Law*, 34 MERCER L. REV. 709 (1983); James R. Pielemeier, *Why We Should Worry about Full Faith and Credit to Laws*, 60 S. CAL. L. REV. 1299 (1987).

7. Laycock, *supra* note 6, at 336, 250, *citing*, Robert H. Jackson, *Full Faith and Credit—The Lawyer's Clause of the Constitution*, 45 COLUM. L. REV. 1, 2, 6–7 (1945).

8. Several scholars have criticized *Allstate* based on the application of the standard to the facts, although these writers generally agree with the standard. *E.g.*, Linda Silberman, *Can the State of Minnesota Bind the Nation?: Federal Choice-of-Law Constraints After Allstate Insurance Co. v. Hague*, 10 HOFSTRA L. REV. 103, 104–05 (1981); Willis L. M. Reese, *The Hague Case: An Opportunity Lost*, 10 HOFSTRA L. REV. 195, 200 (1981); Arthur T. von Mehren & Donald T. Trautman, *Constitutional Control of Choice of Law: Some Reflections on* Hague, 10 HOFSTRA L. REV. 35, 43–44 (1981). Authors who have made more fundamental criticisms of current constitutional constraints on choice of law are listed *supra* note 6.

9. *Allstate*, 449 U.S. at 320 ("The first inquiry [full faith and credit] implicates the federal interest in ensuring that Minnesota respect the sovereignty of the State of Wisconsin; the second [due process] implicates the litigants' interest in fair adjudication of their rights." *Id.*); *see also* Hay, *supra* note 6, at 712–13.

10. *Allstate* fails to give a cogent reason for using the same analysis for both clauses. *Allstate*, 449 U.S. at 308.

11. Weinberg, *supra* note 5, at 454 (Weinberg advocates minimal scrutiny for both).

12. *See* Bruce Posnak, *The Court Doesn't Know Its Asahi from Its Wortman, A Critical View of the Constitutional Constraints of Jurisdiction on Choice of Law*, 41 SYRACUSE L. REV. 875, 876–79 (1989); Martin Redish, *Due Process, Federalism and Personal*

Jurisdiction: A Theoretical Evaluation, 75 NW. U.L. REV. 1112, 1133–34 (1981) [hereinafter, Redish, *Due Process*].

13. Linda Silberman, *Shaffer v. Heitner: The End of an Era*, 53 N.Y.U. L. REV. 33, 88 (1978).

14. Kogan, *supra* note 6, at 677.

15. RESTATEMENT (SECOND) OF CONFLICT OF LAWS § 145 (1971).

16. *See generally*, BRAINERD CURRIE, SELECTED ESSAYS ON THE CONFLICT OF LAWS (1963).

17. See the discussion of these approaches in Chapter 1.

18. I will discuss the Court's usual approach to due process below.

19. *Allstate*, 449 U.S. at 313–320. Terry Kogan has also attacked the modern emphasis on state interests: "Responsibility lies squarely with modern common law conflicts theory and its concept of 'state interest.' In their zeal to rid conflicts law of the nineteenth-century metaphysic of vested rights, the realist-influenced scholars replaced one metaphysic with another—state interest. A state in a federal union may well have an interest in regulatory policies being furthered. However, modern commentators have so elevated that interest that constitutional protections afforded to individuals have been completely ignored." Kogan, *supra* note 6, at 680–81.

20. *See* Martin H. Redish, *Procedural Due Process and Aggregation Devices in Mass Tort Litigation*, 63 DEF. COUNS. J. 18, 25 (1996) ("It is easy to lose sight of enduring values when immediate needs become pressing. But it is precisely for this reason that the framers of the U.S. Constitution choose to codify those values in the form of countermajoritianism."). Based on the neofederalist view that sovereignty under the Constitution lies in the people rather than the state, and that, under this view, a fundamental feature of the Constitution is that it protects individual rights from state infringement, Professor Kogan argues that "[i]n the context of legislative jurisdiction, the Constitution should be viewed as primarily concerned with protecting individuals, not states, from overreaching by other states." Kogan, *supra* note 6, at 699 n.230, *citing*, Akil Reed Amar, *Of Sovereignty and Federalism*, 96 YALE L.J. 1425, 1426 n.9 (1987).

21. U.S. Constitution, amend. XIV, § 1.

22. Redish, *Due Process, supra* note 12, at 1113; I discuss the proper due process analysis below.

23. Insurance Corp. of Ireland, Ltd. v. Compagnie des Bauxites de Guinee, 456 U.S. 699, 702–03 n.10 (1982).

24. I made a similar argument based on normative grounds in the previous chapter. Also see the discussion of Kantianism in the introduction.

25. *See* JEFFRIE G. MURPHY & JULES L. COLEMAN, PHILOSOPHY OF LAW: AN INTRODUCTION TO JURISPRUDENCE 70–75 (1990). The introduction discussed utilitarianism and Kantianism.

26. *Id.* at 71, 75–82.

27. James W. Hilliard, *To Accomplish Fairness and Justice: Substantive Due Process*, 30 J. MARSHALL L. REV. 95, 112 (1996).

28. Kogan, *supra* note 6, at 694.

29. BRILMAYER, *supra* note 5, at 135.

30. *Allstate*, 449 U.S. at 308.

31. *See* the section "Constitutional Limitations on Choice of Law" below.

32. Pielemeier, *supra* note 6, at 1333.

33. BRILMAYER, *supra* note 5, at 235.

34. *See* Chapter 1.

35. See the discussion in the introduction of the new judicial activism in which judges are structural referees.

36. Alaska Packers Ass'n v. Industrial Accident Comm'n, 294 U.S. 532, 547 (1935).

37. Thomas v. Washington Gas Light Co., 448 U.S. 261, 272 (1980); *see also* William F. Baxter, *Choice of Law and the Federal System*, 16 STAN. L. REV 1, 23 (1963).

38. RICHARD NEELY, THE PRODUCT LIABILITY MESS: HOW BUSINESS CAN BE RESCUED FROM THE POLITICS OF STATE COURTS 4 (1988) (arguing for tort reform).

39. Pielemeier, *supra* note 6, at 1336; *see also* Roosevelt, *supra* note 6, at 2505 ("But to tell a state that its interests are inferior is a serious infringement on its power to determine the relative importance of particular policies. Surely it is for each state to decide which interests are more important to it.").

40. Brzonkala v. Virginia Polytechnic Institute, 169 F.3d 820, 894 (4th Cir. 1999) (Wilkinson, J., concurring).

41. *Id.* at 895.

42. This seems to be what the Court was doing in *Saenz v. Roe*, 119 S.Ct. 1518 (1999), where the Court breathed new life into the largely dormant privileges and immunities clause of the Fourteenth Amendment. The introduction discussed the new judicial activism.

43. *E.g.*, Bradford Elec. Light Co. v. Clapper, 286 U.S. 145, 154–59 (1932).

44. Professor Weinberg writes that "[t]his neutralization of the full faith and credit clause was an inevitable consequence of Chief Justice Stone's perception that more than one state might have legitimate regulatory interests in a given matter, and his conclusion . . . that each such state ought to be allowed to vindicate its own laws and policies in its own courts." Weinberg, *supra* note 5, at 457.

45. For example, it would be difficult to apply the strict scrutiny standard that for a state's law to be constitutional the law must serve a compelling interest and be narrowly drawn to express only that compelling state interest to choice of law. *E.g.*, Reno v. Flores, 507 U.S. 292, 302 (1993); Roe v. Wade, 410 U.S. 113, 115 (1973).

46. JOHN E. NOWAK and RONALD D. ROTUNDA, CONSTITUTIONAL LAW 346 (5th ed. 1995).

47. *Id.*

48. *Id.*

49. *Id.*

50. Hilliard, *supra* note 27, at 104.

51. *See also* Hay, *supra* note 6, at 712; Larry Kramer, *Choice of Law in Complex Litigation*, 71 N.Y.U. L. REV. 547, 569–72 (1996).

52. Hilliard, *supra* note 27, at 102.

53. *Id.* at 96.

54. *Id.* at 100–01.

55. *Id.* at 105.

56. *Id.*

57. Exxon Corp. v. Governor of Md., 437 U.S. 117, 125 (1978); *see also* Ferguson v. Skrupa, 372 U.S. 726, 730-32 (1963); Williamson v. Lee Optical of Okla., Inc., 348 U.S. 483, 486-88 (1955); United States v. Carolene Products Co., 304 U.S. 144, 152 (1938).

58. *348* U.S. at 488.

59. *Id.*, *citing*, Munn v. Illinois, 94 U.S. 113, 134 (1877).

60. 372 U.S. at 729 (citations omitted).

61. *Id.* at 730, *citing*, Adkins v. Children's Hospital, 261 U.S. 525, 567, 570 (1923) (Holmes, J., dissenting).

62. 437 U.S. at 117.

63. *Id.* at 124, *citing*, *Ferguson*, 372 U.S. at 731.

64. *E.g.*, *Reno*, 507 U.S. at 302; *Roe*, 410 U.S. at 155.

65. NAACP v. Alabama *ex. rel.* Patterson, 357 U.S. 449, 460–61 (1958).

66. Harper v. Virginia State Bd. of Elections, 383 U.S. 663, 667 (1966).

67. Shapiro v. Thompson, 394 U.S. 618, 624–31 (1969).

68. Mayer v. City of Chicago, 404 U.S. 189, 193–94 (1971) (right to free trial transcript for indigent persons); Bounds v. Smith, 430 U.S. 817, 821–32 (1977) (access to the courts by providing law libraries or comparable alternatives); Douglas v. California, 372 U.S. 353, 358 (1963) (right to counsel for appeal by indigent defendant).

69. Santosky v. Kramer, 455 U.S. 745, 747–48, 753–57 (1982) (clear and convincing evidence required before a state can sever a parental relationship).

70. *Roe*, 410 U.S. at 113.

71. 517 U.S. 559 (1996).

72. *Id.* at 568–72.

73. *Id.* at 563–68.

74. *Id.* at 568.

75. *Id.*

76. *Id.*

77. *Id.* at 571. This, of course, is more relevant to full faith and credit than due process. The Court seems to be confusing these concepts in *Gore* like it did in *Allstate*.

78. *Id.*

79. *Id.* at 572.

80. *Id.* at 574.

81. *Id.* at 575–86.

82. Professor Sedler is one of the few scholars who advocates looking at due process limitations on choice of law in the same manner as other due process problems. *See* Sedler, *supra* note 5, at 76–92. However, he comes to the opposite conclusion from me, contending that courts should apply the rational basis test to all choice of law. *Id.* at 78. He asserts that "[w]hen a state has some factual connections with the underlying transaction, the choice of that state's law to govern rights and liabilities arising from that transaction would seem to be reasonable, notwithstanding that another state may have even more factual connections with that transaction." *Id.* I disagree with using the rational basis test for true conflicts for the reasons given in the text.

83. Southern Pacific Co. v. Arizona *ex. rel.* Sullivan, 325 U.S. 761, 770 (1945); *see also* Bibb v. Navajo Freight Lines *Inc.*, 359 U.S. 520, 523 (1959).

84. *Southern Pacific*, 305 U.S. at 779–80; *Bibb*, 359 U.S. at 529–30.

85. *Southern Pacific*, 325 U.S. at 761.

86. *Id.* at 788, 790.

87. *Id.* at 792.

88. Other cases that have struck down laws on due process grounds when a fundamental right was not involved include Moore v. East Cleveland, 431 U.S. 494 (1977) (struck down ordinance that limited dwellings to a single, narrowly-defined family); Vlandis v. Kline, 412 U.S. 441 (1973) (irrebuttable presumption that students are not residents for in-state college tuition unconstitutional); *see also* DeWeese v. Town of Palm Beach, 812 F.2d 1365 (11th Cir. 1987) (town ordinance that prevented men from jogging shirtless violated the rational basis test); Lansdale v. Tyler Junior College, 470 F.2d 659 (5th Cir. 1972) (struck down college hair length regulations).

89. The introduction discussed the structural lines of horizontal federalism.

90. U.S. Constitution, art. 4, § 1.

91. Laycock, *supra* note 6, at 290–95.

92. I have borrowed the term *quasi-sovereign* from Judge Posner. *See Thomas v. Indiana*, 910 F.2d 1413, 1415–16 (7th Cir. 1990); *Wood v. Mid-Valley, Inc.*, 942 F.2d 425, 427 (7th Cir. 1991).

93. Roberts v. Roberts, 185 P.2d 381, 385 (Cal. 1947), *overruled on other grounds*, Spellens v. Spellens, 317 P.2d 613, 618 (Cal. 1957); McFarland v. McFarland, 19 S.E.2d 77, 82 (Va. 1942).

94. Wisconsin v. Michigan, 295 U.S. 455, 462 (1935).

95. Skiriotes v. Florida, 313 U.S. 69, 77 (1941).

96. Dickie v. City of Tomah, 782 F. Supp. 370, 374–75 (N.D. Ill. 1991).

97. Smith v. Firemens Ins. Co. of Newark, 590 A.2d 24, 27 (Pa. Super. 1991).

98. Baker by Thomas v. General Motors Corp., 118 S.Ct. 657, 663 (1998), *citing*, Estin v. Estin, 334 U.S. 541, 546 (1948).

99. *Baker*, 118 S.Ct. at 663; *accord*, Milwaukee County v. M. E. White Co., 296 U.S. 268, 277 (1935); *see also* Roosevelt, *supra* note 6, at 2504 ("Questions that were political have been made legal—which is to say constitutional.").

100. Laycock, *supra* note 6, at 296.

101. *Cf.*, *Gore*, 517 U.S. at 571.

102. Jackson, *supra* note 7, at 33.

103. Roosevelt, *supra* note 6, at 2530–33; Laycock, *supra* note 6; John Hart Ely, *Choice of Law and the State's Interest in Protecting Its Own*, 23 WM. & MARY L. REV. 173 (1981).

104. Laycock, *supra* note 6. This section only discusses Professor Laycock's antidiscrimination theories.

105. *Id.* at 250.

106. *Id.* at 265, 269–70.

107. *Id.* at 274–75.

108. *Id.* at 276, *citing*, Lea Brilmayer, *Shaping and Sharing in Democratic Theory: Towards a Political Theory of Interstate Equality*, 15 FLA. ST. U.L. REV. 389, 412–13 (1987).

109. Laycock, *supra* note 6, at 277.

110. *See* CURRIE, *supra* note 16.

111. *See supra* notes 19–28 and accompanying text.

112. 475 F.2d 438 (2d Cir. 1973). Chapter 2 discussed this case from a normative viewpoint.

113. *Id.* at 443.

114. *Id.* at 444 (citations omitted).

115. *Id.* at 445.

116. *Id.* (citations omitted).

117. *Id.* at 446–47.

118. Other scholars have also criticized this decision. *See e.g.*, James A. Martin, *Constitutional Limitations on Choice of Law*, 61 CORNELL L. REV. 185, 225–27 (1976); Willis L. M. Reese, *Legislative Jurisdiction*, 78 Colum. L. Rev. 1587, 1605–6 (1978).

119. *Rosenthal*, 475 F.2d at 448 (Judge Lumbard, dissenting).

120. *Id.* The Massachusetts premium was $192, whereas a surgeon's premium in New York was $1,139.

121. *Id.*

122. *Gore*, 517 U.S. at 574.

123. *Cf.*, *id* at 571–72.

124. Hay, *supra* note 6, at 727.

125. See my discussion in Chapter 1 of the variations on governmental interest analysis.

126. Currie, *Symposium*, *supra* note 1, at 700–714.
127. *Id.* at 701.
128. *Id.*
129. *Id.*
130. William F. Baxter, *Choice of Law and the Federal System*, 16 STAN. L. REV. 1, 18 (1963). Chapter 1 discussed Professor Baxter's method.
131. *Rosenthal*, 475 F.2d at 444–45.
132. Currie, *Symposium, supra* note 1, at 702–04.
133. Hague v. Allstate Ins. Co., 289 N.W.2d 43 (Minn. 1978), *aff'd*, 449 U.S. 302 (1981).
134. *Id.*
135. *Id. at* 49. The court failed to show how Minnesota's rule spreads the costs more broadly than Wisconsin's rule.
136. *See Gore*, 517 U.S. at 585 ("The fact that BMW is a large corporation rather than an impecunious individual does not diminish its entitlement to fair notice of the demands that the several States impose on the conduct of business.").
137. *Id.* at 571.
138. As Professor Kramer has written, "it is axiomatic that there is no perspective from which to judge one version [of the just result] 'better' or more just." Kramer, *supra* note 6, at 339.
139. Kogan, *supra* note 6, at 692. Later he asserts that "[t]hrough its adoption of a body of regulatory policies, a state in effect chooses a vision of the Good." *Id.* at 697.
140. David Currie, *Full Faith and Credit to Marriages*, 1 GREEN BAG 7, 12 (1997).
141. Laycock, *supra* note 6, at 312.
142. If the law chosen under such an approach happens to be the law of the most closely connected state, the choice of law is not by design but by happenstance constitutional.
143. Chapter 1 discussed the SECOND RESTATEMENT. There are disagreements as to what should be emphasized under the SECOND RESTATEMENT (such as what factors should be stressed in § 6), and these differences could affect the constitutionality of the most significant relationship test under some circumstances. See the discussion of the SECOND RESTATEMENT in Chapter 4.
144. 423 N.E.2d 278 (Ill. App. 1981).
145. *Id.* at 279–81.
146. *Id.* at 280.
147. *Id.*
148. *Id.*
149. *Id.*
150. *Id.*
151. *Id.*
152. *Id.* at 281.
153. Another case where a court could constitutionally choose the law of either state is *Levy v. Daniels U-Drive Auto Renting Co*, 143 A. 163 (Conn. 1928). See the discussion of this case in Chapter 5.
154. Compare Bernhard v. Harrah's Club, 546 P.2d 719 (Cal. 1976) *with* Blamey v. Brown, 270 N.W.2d 884 (Minn. 1978).
155. See also the discussion of these criteria as the basis of choice of law methods above. Of course, if a court uses these criteria, but there is a separate constitutional basis for the choice of law, the choice of law would be constitutional.

156. *See also* Kogan, *supra* note 6, at 694 ("[T]he tension that arises between states due to conflicting laws, though real, is simply not as significant a constitutional concern, given the private nature of most litigation.").

157. Laycock, *supra* note 6, at 311; *see also*, Roosevelt, *supra* note 6, at 2511–12 ("The Full Faith and Credit Clause means that a state may not refuse to recognize rights created by the law of a sister state *simply because* those rights are foreign.").

158. Kogan, *supra* note 6, at 698.

159. As Professor Roosevelt has noted, constitutional principles can "constrain the states' resolutions in ways that produce a coherent jurisprudence of conflicts." Roosevelt, *supra* note 6, at 2454.

Chapter 4

Other Choice of Law Methods

Chapters 2 and 3 rejected several modern choice of law methods for use by American states, including Beale's method, governmental interest analysis, and the better rule approach, on normative and constitutional grounds. This chapter examines other possible methods for choice of law, including the *Second Restatement*, Professor Kramer's rights-based approach, and Professor Brilmayer's political-rights model.

A. THE *SECOND RESTATEMENT*

As Chapters Two and Three demonstrated, the *Second Restatement*'s most significant relationship test meets this study's normative and constitutional criteria, at least when isolated from other portions of the *Second Restatement*. However, the *Second Restatement* is unsatisfactory as a choice of law method because as a whole it is a hybrid of conflicting choice of law philosophies that gives little guidance to a court on how to apply its criteria.

The *Second Restatement* was originally to contain black letter rules written from the viewpoint of a neutral forum.[1] However, several scholars harshly criticized drafts of the *Second Restatement* for their failure to consider modern developments in choice of law, particularly governmental interest analysis.[2] Subsequently, the drafters added section 6 in response to these critics.[3] As Professor Patrick J. Borchers has pointed out, "the *Second Restatement* began as one kind of project and ended as another."[4]

However, this attempt to please everyone produced a hybrid approach that pleased almost no one. Professor Borchers has called the *Second Restatement* schizophrenic,[5] and Professor Kay has written, "[t]he Restatement Second was thus promulgated with two vastly different conceptions about how a choice of law problem should be addressed."[6] Professor Kay has added that "[i]n the drafters' attempt to mollify their critics, they have created an umbrella for traditionalist and modern theorist alike: a fragile shelter that may prove itself unable to survive any but the most gentle of showers."[7] Or, as Professor Brilmayer has stated more strongly, "[t]he overall picture reminds one of the famous humorous definition of a camel: namely a horse drafted by a committee."[8]

As Chapter 1 observed, the *Second Restatement* contains three layers of choice of law considerations: (1) the policies in section 6, (2) general rules like the most significant relationship test, and (3) more specific rules for particular situations. A major problem in the *Second Restatement* is that it provides no guidance on how these layers interact, except for section 145's vague comment that the most significant relationship should be determined "under the principles stated in § 6." How does a judge relate territorial rules like the most significant relationship test or the *Second Restatement*'s specific rules to general choice of law policies that often conflict with each other?

The *Second Restatement* also fails to give any direction on how to use the section 6 policies or how they interact. How does one reconcile "the relevant policies of the forum" with "the needs of interstate and international systems?" More fundamentally, as Professor Borchers has observed, "[s]ection 6 gives almost unlimited discretion to a court in choosing the applicable law."[9]

Even the specific black letter rules often provide judges "escape hatches." For example, section 146 of the *Second Restatement* states, "In an action for personal injury, the local law of the state where the injury occurred determines the rights and the liabilities of the parties *unless*, with respect to the particular issue, some other state has a more significant relationship under the principles stated in § 6 to the occurrence and the parties, in which event the local law of the other state will be applied."[10] The "unless" clause in section 146 allows judges to involve policy considerations and thus ignore the general rule. Other sections provide the "usual" rule. For instance, section 198 (2) states that "[t]he capacity of a party to contract will *usually* be upheld if he has such capacity under the local law of the state of his domicile."[11] As Professor Symeonides has declared, "the fact that these rules are almost never confining explains the judges' willingness to use them."[12] The "elasticity" in these rules allows judges to consider the content of the laws, which limits their multilateralist character.[13]

This lack of instruction has caused the courts to apply the *Second Restatement* approach in numerous ways, with some courts concentrating on the rules, others on section 6 policies.[14] As Professor Kramer has noted, "[b]ut one needs to read a lot of opinions in a single sitting fully to appreciate just how badly the *Second Restatement* works in practice."[15] Moreover, Professor Borchers has written that the *Second Restatement* has attracted such a large following in the courts because of its open-ended provisions (section 6), which allow judges to hide their use of judicial intuition.[16] In other words, many courts are using the *Second Restatement* for its general choice of law criteria, instead of its most significant relationship test.[17]

In sum, these deficiencies in the *Second Restatement* make it unsuitable as a choice of law method for American courts. However, the most significant relationship test without the other layers of the *Second Restatement* is an antecedent of the second step of the method presented in Chapter Five.

B. PROFESSOR KRAMER'S METHOD

Larry Kramer's two-step method (first, determine whether there is a conflict by looking to see if more than one state creates a right that applies to the case, and, second, if there is a conflict, employ a "second order rule of interpretation to choose between these laws")[18] is a significant advance in choosing law. Courts should first determine whether a state has created a right (or other legal relation) that applies to the controversy. I have modified Professor Kramer's first step in my method by combining it with Hohfeldian analysis.[19]

On the other hand, Professor Kramer's use of canons of construction to resolve true conflicts is unsatisfactory.[20] Professor Kramer declared that "moving from wholly domestic cases to cases with multistate contacts does not change the essential nature of the interpretative problem."[21] He continued, "If there is a [true] conflict, the court should then employ some second-order rule of interpretation to choose between these laws."[22] He added that "[m]ultisate canons must reflect the kind of compromises co-equal sovereigns would be likely to make."[23] Kramer then asserted, "[T]he optimal strategy in devloping canons is to identify situations in which both states agree that one type of policy is more important than another."[24]

Choice of law, however, is not interpretative on this level. Courts cannot resolve a true conflict by interpreting how far the lawmakers intended their laws to reach or how two lawmakers hypothetically might have negotiated the conflict. As was noted earlier in a different context, it is difficult to find a "policy" on which all states agree. Moreover, allowing these hypothetical canons to determine true conflicts interferes with the sovereignty of those states that disagree with these canons. True conflicts exist because two independent lawmakers want their laws to encompass the controversy; canons of construction cannot solve this impasse. Rather, once a court has identified the applicable states' legal relations, it should choose the law of the state with the closest connection to the controversy.

In addition, Kramer's approach will not solve all choice of law problems because his canons do not cover all types of cases.[25] Moreover, some of his canons will be difficult for courts to use. For example, his first canon is "if there is a conflict between two states' laws, and a failure to apply one of the laws would render it practically ineffective, that law should be applied."[26] How does one determine "when a failure to apply one of the laws would render it practically ineffective?" Isn't this a policy decision that will be difficult for a judge to make?[27] Likewise, Kramer's canon that "where one of the two conflicting laws is obsolete (*i.e.*, inconsistent with prevailing legal and social norms in the state that enacted it), the other law should apply" is problematic.[28] My criticisms of this canon are similar to my criticisms of the better rule: how does a foreign judge decide a state's law is obsolete, and where does that judge obtain the power to do so?

C. PROFESSOR BRILMAYER'S METHOD

As noted in Chapter 1, Professor Brilmayer's political rights model approach to choice of law is not a full-fledged system, but a normative constraint on choice of law.[29] Her approach requires that before a court can apply a state's law to an individual that court must demonstrate an adequate connection between the state and party burdened by the application of that state's law.[30] In addition, a court should look to see whether the party who is favored by the application of a law has "the sort of connection that would allow application of local law if the tables were turned and he or she stood to lose?"[31]

Although Professor Brilmayer's constraints are important to choice of law theory because they reinject fairness into conflicts jurisprudence, they are inadequate as constraints on choice of law because they do not eliminate many of the problematic choice of law results.[32] Professor Brilmayer's approach does exclude some of the more extreme cases of conflicts localism. For example, the court's choice of law in *Rosenthal* should be invalid under her approach because there is no political connecting factor between New York and the Massachusetts defendants that would justify the burden of imposing New York law upon them.[33] On the other hand, Professor Brilmayer's approach would probably not invalidate the choice of law in *Allstate*.[34] Minnesota would be able to impose its law on Allstate because its extensive insurance operations in Minnesota is a political connection that justifies this imposition.[35] In addition, the decedent had a sufficient political connection to Minnesota for application of Minnesota law to him because he worked in Minnesota.

The first problem with Professor Brilmayer's political rights model of choice of law is that her constraints, like those of the current constitutional standard, are unilateralist. If a state has a sufficient political connection to a party, it can impose its law on that party, regardless of the strength of the individual's connections to other states. Moreover, it is questionable whether political connections are sufficient to justify the application of a state's law to an individual in many cases. For example, the fact that a business is incorporated in a state is enough to allow the application of that state's law to the business under Professor Brilmayer's analysis.[36] But what if the cause of action is unrelated to the fact that the business is incorporated in a state? Does this political connection justify the adoption of the incorporation state's law? As Professor Bleisener has noted, Brilmayer's "political approach tends to rely on the wrong contacts between the individual and the state, i.e., it is not sufficiently specific to the general ties to a state separated from relevant dispute-related contacts to that state."[37]

Professor Bliesener presents a vivid example of the problem with relying on political connections that are unconnected to the cause of action to justify imposition of a state's law.[38] A Connecticut resident goes into New York to buy a computer. The sales contract includes a waiver of liability. Both New York and Connecticut enforce waiver of liability clauses. However, Massachusetts, the seller's state of incorporation, does not enforce such clauses. Thus, under Brilmayer's constraints, if the case were brought in Massachusetts, Massachusetts could apply its law because there is a justification for imposing the burden since the seller is incorporated in Massachusetts.[39] As Professor Bliesener points out, "the impracticality of applying Massachusetts law to a sale between the seller's New York branch and a Connecticut buyer goes without saying. There are serious doubts about whether it meets the legitimate expectations of the either party to apply the Massachusetts sales law."[40]

In addition, Professor Bliesener notes that Brilmayer's approach creates a new type of unfairness. He thinks that her approach merely reverses Currie's method.[41] Currie looks at the relationship between the state and the individual; Brilmayer examines the relationship between the individual and the state. Bliesener criticizes both approaches because they favor one side over the other.[42] Interest analysis favors insiders; Brilmayer's proposal prefers outsiders.

In sum, Professor Brilmayer's political rights model is important for choice of law because it brings fairness back to the forefront of conflicts analysis. However, she emphasizes the wrong type of fairness and creates a new type of unfairness. Rather, choice of law fairness should involve substantive and forum neutrality, predictability, and respect for the parties' expectations. Moreover, it should not favor any group; it should treat insiders and outsiders, plaintiffs and defendants, and individuals and businesses the same.

NOTES

1. Willis L. M. Reese, *Conflict of Laws and the Restatement Second*, 28 LAW & CONTEMP. PROBS. 679, 681, 692 (1963); *see also* Herma Hill Kay, *Theory into Practice: Choice of Law in the Courts*, 34 MERCER L. REV. 521, 552–53 (1983).

2. *E.g.*, Albert A. Ehrenzweig, *The Second Conflicts Restatement: A Last Appeal for it Withdrawal*, 113 U. PA. L. REV. 1230 (1965) (Professor Ehrenzweig advocated the view that the only "relevant policy is that of the forum." *Id.* at 1236.); Albert A. Ehrenzweig, *The "Most Significant Relationship" in the Conflicts Law of Torts: Law and Reason Versus the Second Restatement*, 28 LAW & CONTEMP. PROBS. 700 (1963).

3. Kay, *supra* note 1, at 553–55. Professor Reppy called § 6 "a sop tossed . . . to members of the American Law Institute who were unhappy with a purely territorial methodology." William A. Reppy, Jr., *Eclecticism in Choice of Law: Hybrid Method or Mishmash?* 34 MERCER L. REV. 645, 662 (1983).

4. Patrick J. Borchers, *Courts and the Second Conflicts Restatement: Some Observations and an Empirical Note*, 56 MD. L. REV. 1232, 1235 (1997).

5. *Id.* at 1240.

6. Kay, *supra* note 1, at 555. As Professor Juenger has noted, "unilateralism and multilateralism are antithetical to each other and therefore do not mix well." Friedrich K. Juenger, *A Third Conflicts Restatement?* 75 IND. L.J. 403, 410 (2000).

7. Kay, *supra* note 1, at 562.

8. LEA BRILMAYER, CONFLICT OF LAWS 75 (1995).

9. Borchers, *supra* note 4, at 1238.

10. SECOND RESTATEMENT § 146 (emphasis added).

11. *Id.* at § 198 (2) (emphasis added).

12. Symeon C. Symeonides, *The Judicial Acceptance of the Second Conflicts Restatement: A Mixed Blessing*, 56 MD. L. REV. 1248, 1275 (1997).

13. *See* David F. Cavers, *Re-Restatement of the Conflict of Laws: The Chapter on Contracts, in* XXTH CENTURY COMPARATIVE AND CONFLICTS LAWS 350 (Kurt H. Nadlemann et. al. eds., 1961).

14. Kay, *supra* note 1, at 556–62.

15. Larry Kramer, *Choice of Law in American Courts in 1990: Trends and Developments*, 39 AM. J. COMP. L. 465, 486–87 (1991).

16. Borchers, *supra* note 4, at 1233, *passim*; *see also*, Juenger, *supra* note 6, at 404–6 ("It simply furnished courts with any number of plausible reasons to support whatever result they wished to reach." *Id.* at 406); Symeon C. Symeonides, *The Need for a Third Conflicts Restatement (And a Proposal for Torts Conflicts)*, 75 IND. L.J. 438, 445–46 (2000) ("[T]he *Second Restatement* has provided convenient cover for judicial subjectivism and loose impressionistic thinking of the type which might be acceptable in some of the social sciences but which should not be acceptable in law.").

17. See, for example, the discussion of *Pfizer* in Chapter 6.

18. *See* Chapter 1.

19. Chapter 2 discussed Hohfeld's analysis of legal relations.

20. Chapter 1 listed Professor Kramer's canons.

21. Larry Kramer, *Rethinking Choice of Law*, 90 COLUM. L. REV. 277, 290 (1990).

22. *Id.* at 291.

23. *Id.* at 319.

24. *Id.* at 322.

25. Professor Kramer states that his canons are not intended to be exhaustive. *Id.* at 322. He adds that "my goal in this paper is less to produce a final product than it is to illustrate how that final product ought to look." *Id.*

26. *Id.* at 323.

27. Compare my analysis of *Lilienthal v. Kaufman* with Professor Kramer's later in footnote 38 in Chapter 5.

28. *Id.* at 334.

29. BRILMAYER, *supra* note 8, at 219–63.

30. *Id.* at 240, 262.

31. *Id.* at 262.

32. Professor Brilmayer notes that "two distinct aspects make up a rights-based approach. The first is an argument that rights are important to choice of law analysis; the second is an argument about what rights are. These two aspects of the theory are separable." BRILMAYER, *supra* note 8, at 224.

33. See my discuss of this case in Chapters 2 and 3.

34. See my discussion of this case in Chapters 1, 2, and 3.

35. *See* BRILMAYER, *supra* note 8, at 240–253. Professor Bliesener comes to a similar conclusion concerning the application of Brilmayer's approach to *Allstate*. Dirk H. Bliesener, *Fairness and Choice of Law: A Critique of the Political Rights-Based Approach to the Conflict of Laws*, 42 AM. J. COMP. L. 687, 701–2 (1994).

36. BRILMAYER, *supra* note 8, at 240–53.

37. Bleisener, *supra* note 35, at 702.

38. *Id.* at 703–4.

39. Assume the buyer worked in Massachusetts, which would constitute a political connection between him and that state.

40. *Id.* at 704.

41. *Id.* at 705; *see also* Jeffrey Brand-Ballard, *Legitimacy, Consequentialism, and Conflict of Laws: Lea Brilmayer's Rights-Based Theory*, 30 N. ENG. L. REV. 39, 64 (1995).

42. Bliesener, *supra* note 35, at 706.

Chapter 5

A Multilateralist Method of Choice of Law

A. A MULTILATERALIST METHOD OF CHOICE OF LAW

Because I believe that the existing choice of law systems are flawed, I have developed a new choice of law method that combines a modified version of Kramer's first step with a closest connection test. Under my approach, a court should (1) identify the legal relations created by the states whose laws might apply to the facts, and (2) when two or more states create legal relations that apply to the facts, choose the state's law that has the closest connection to the controversy.[1]

As mentioned in Chapter 2, state law creates rights, duties, privileges, no rights, powers, liabilities, immunities, and disabilities. More than one of these jural relations may apply to a situation. For example, an automobile accident takes place in Virginia. Virginia provides a right to recover damages in persons who are injured by another's negligence.[2] P is injured by D's negligence. Thus, P has a right (or a potential right) to recover damages against D.

However, P's right to recover damages against D is not the only legal relation Virginia establishes in connection with the accident. Virginia furnishes an immunity for automobile drivers from lawsuits by passengers in their cars (a guest statute). P was a passenger in D's car. In this instance, the immunity trumps the right (or potential right), and P has no remedy against D.

A similar situation can arise in a multistate context. D and P, a passenger in D's car, are involved in an accident in Virginia. P is a North Carolina citizen, and D is a Virginia citizen. Virginia creates a right to recover damages in persons who are injured by another's negligence in Virginia. Since P was injured by D's negligence in Virginia, P has a potential right to receive compensation from D for his injuries. However, Virginia also provides an immunity that passengers may not recover damages from drivers. The statute's purpose is to prevent collusion between drivers and passengers that raise Virginia insurance rates. Clearly, P has no remedy under Virginia law.

Multistate interests are involved in this case because P is a North Carolina citizen. North Carolina furnishes a potential right for its citizens to recover when they are injured by another's negligence regardless of where they are injured. North Carolina does not place any limitations on this right, so P would have a remedy against D—if North Carolina law controls. However, a court must consider the Virginia immunity because D is a Virginia citizen. Considering the North Carolina right and the Virginia immunity, can P recover damages against D?

1. Step 1: The Identification of Legal Relations

The first step in choosing law is to identify the legal relations created by the relevant states that might control a case. When step one reveals that more than one states' law might apply to the facts, then a court must go on to step 2—deciding which state's law should govern such true conflicts by adopting the law of the state with the closest connection to the controversy.

In the first step, a court should identify every legal relation that might encompass the controversy, as the above examples did. However, the judge should not use just any state law that might be advocated by one of the litigants;[3] the judge must determine the law's scope—whether the lawmaker intended the law to govern the dispute. The judge must establish whether the law has only intrastate applicability or whether the lawmaker intend it to extend beyond the state's borders, and, if so, to what situations.

In determining a law's scope, the court should try to ascertain the legislature's actual intent. If this is not possible (which will often be the case), the judge should attempt to establish the legislature's constructive intent by examining the law's purpose, as illustrated by the examples below. Professor Kramer has asserted that "if—in the interests of comity and mutual accommodation—we presume that a state's law is intended to apply only in cases that are connected to the state in some important way, the significant contacts ought to be those that implicate the reason the law was created for wholly domestic cases."[4] However, the judge should not decide a law's scope based on his or her opinion of what the law's scope should be or predicated on some objective standard of what interests a state should have.[5]

For example, Virginia created a right in a person who is injured by another's negligence to recover damages from the negligent party. What is the scope of this right? It is reasonable to conclude that the lawmaker intended the law to encompass accidents that occur in Virginia. Virginia has an interest[6] in regulating accidents that take place in that state (conduct regulation).[7] Similarly, one can infer that Virginia wanted its negligence rule to apply to accidents occurring in other states when its citizens are injured because Virginia has an interest in ensuring that its citizens are compensated for negligent injuries (compensation).[8] However, it is unreasonable to think that Virginia lawmakers intended its negligence rule govern accidents that take place in California between California citizens. Virginia does not have an interest in regulating California highways, nor does it have an interest in compensating California tort victims.[9]

The above analysis resembles (and is influenced by) governmental interest analysis's identification of state policies and interests. However, the method identifies states' interests to determine whether the lawmaker intended the law to encompass the issue, whereas, as noted previously, governmental interest analysis often seems to be employing an objective standard that ignores legislative preferences. In addition, the method does not use state interests to help choose law in step 2.

Step 1 shows that many putative choice of law problems are not problems at all because only one state's law applies to a situation.[10] There can be no conflict of laws if only one state creates an applicable legal relation.[11]

Assume that Virginia provides a right to recover damages in persons who are injured by another's negligence on Virginia highways or who are Virginia citizens and that North Carolina furnishes a similar right. Also assume that Virginia has a guest statute that immunizes Virginia defendants from lawsuits by passengers in their cars to protect Virginia insurers from collusion between drivers and passengers, but that North Carolina places no limit on recovery for negligence. An accident occurs in North Carolina in which P, a passenger in D's car and a Virginia citizen, is injured by D, a North Carolina citizen.

There is no conflict of laws in this example, despite the fact that parties from more than one state are involved. The Virginia guest statute is irrelevant because Virginia lawmakers did not intend that it govern accidents in other states involving non-Virginia defendants—where Virginia insurers are not subject to collusion.

Similarly, a Rhode Island plaintiff is injured in Rhode Island by a defective product manufactured in New York and bought from a Rhode Island retailer. The plaintiff wants to sue both the manufacturer and retailer under strict liability. Under Rhode Island law, a person injured by a defective product may recover from both the product's manufacturer and retailer under strict liability because Rhode Island believes that any party in the product's chain of distribution is better able to absorb the costs of defective products than injured consumers. On the other hand, New York shields retailers from strict liability under products liability because retailers usually do not have the ability to inspect for defects.

Step 1 ends the choice of law inquiry because only the Rhode Island law encompasses the case. The Rhode Island law applies to the controversy because Rhode Island wants to protect Rhode Island consumers by providing them with a right of recovery against retailers, and a Rhode Island consumer is involved. However, the New York law is irrelevant because the lawmaker did not intend that it cover foreign retailers.

In some instances, no state will furnish a legal relation. For example, assume North Dakota provides a right of recovery for alienation of affections when the tort occurs in North Dakota or when a North Dakota spouse is harmed. South Dakota, however, has abolished the tort of alienation of affections. A North Dakota resident alienates a South Dakota spouse's affections in South Dakota. No legal relation is created because South Dakota—the location of the tort—does not have an action for alienation of affections, and North Dakota's right does not extend to the alienation of a South Dakota spouse's affections that occurs in South Dakota. Thus, the plaintiff has no claim.

Some cases involve true conflicts in which two states' laws encompass a situation. For instance, California creates a right to recover for breach of contract for contracts entered into in California or with a California resident, but Oregon has enacted an immunity against contractual liability for its residents who have been adjudged spendthrifts. Sam, an Oregon spendthrift, executes a contract in California with a California resident, and Sam breaches the contract. California has an interest in upholding contracts made in that state or by its residents; Oregon has an interest in protecting its spendthrifts. Consequently, this case involves a true conflict because both the California right to recover for breach of contract and the Oregon immunity for spendthrifts apply to the facts. Resolution of this conflict requires a second step, as set forth below.

Another true conflict results from a variation on the guest statute hypothetical above. Virginia furnishes a right to recover for negligence for accidents that happen in Virginia or involve its residents, and it has a guest statute. North Carolina has a right for its residents to recover for damages caused by another's negligence, and it has no guest statute. An accident occurs near Charlottesville, Virginia, involving a Virginia driver, who was negligent, and a North Carolina passenger, who was injured. Virginia does not provide a remedy because of the guest statute. North Carolina creates a (potential) right to recover in the passenger, but the Virginia immunity also applies because the Virginia guest statute encompasses Virginia defendants. Consequently, a true conflict exists.

A final aspect of the scope of laws is whether a court can employ different states' laws with the same transaction or occurrence. When a state's law creates a legal relation, a court must employ all other legal relations that the lawmaker *intended* to go with it.[12] In other words, when a state's law establishes a right, a court applying that law must also adopt any limitations on that right. A court should not be able to choose only what legal relations it wants to allow a remedy that would not exist in the state that created the legal relations. For example, a court should not adopt a state's negligence rule (a right), but ignore the statute of limitations that goes with that rule to permit a remedy, when that state's legislature intended that both the right and the limitation apply to the facts. Similarly, a state should not employ another state's wrongful death statute to provide a cause of action, but disregard damages limitations in that statute.

Consider, for example, a case involving a motion to dismiss based on the expiration of the statute of limitations. Under my approach to choice of law, a court must adopt the statute of limitations of the state that created the right. Otherwise, it has provided a remedy that does not exist under any state's law. On the other hand, governmental interest analysis might furnish a remedy where none existed.

For example, P is injured in Illinois by a product manufactured in Indiana. Illinois has a cause of action for products liability under both strict liability and negligence, with a one-year tort statute of limitations. Indiana has a cause of action for products liability only under negligence, with a two-year tort statute of limitations. P files suit in Indiana thirteen months after he is injured. P can satisfy the requirements for strict liability, but not negligence.

Under governmental interest analysis, P would probably recover. There would be no cause of action under Indiana law because P cannot prove negligence. However, P can satisfy strict liability, and Illinois has interest in having its law adopted because it wants to regulate sales in Illinois. On the other hand, Illinois has no interest in applying its statute of limitations to cases that are brought in Indiana, and Indiana has an interest in using its statute of limitations to a case brought in that state. Consequently, P can recover under the Illinois right and the Indiana statute of limitations; a cause of action exists in a multistate setting that does not exist under any state's law.

Under my analysis, however, P would not recover. Illinois creates no cause of action because the action is barred by Illinois's statute of limitations. Likewise, Indiana does not have strict liability.

Some might view the above result as being unfair; P was injured by the product. However, if there is unfairness, the unfairness is not in choice of law; it is in the states' tort rules. P would not have recovered under either states' laws, absent the multistate setting. As stated above, a court should not use choice of law for substantive justice; substantive justice must exist in the legal relations furnished by state law.

2. Step 2: Choosing Law When a True Conflict Exists

Step 1 will eliminate many choice of law problems; conflicts do not occur when only one state's law (or no state's law) provides legal relationships that encompass the facts. However, many situations arise where two states create legal relations that apply to the case—where a true conflict exists.[13]

When a true conflict exists a court should adopt the law of the state that has the closest connection to the controversy. This inquiry is both quantitative and qualitative; it is a rigorous approach that requires a court to *carefully* analyze connections. First, the court should use only those connections that are relevant to the issue being decided. For example, the fact that a North Dakota resident owns business property in California is irrelevant in a lawsuit involving a traffic accident that occurred in California that is unrelated to the property's ownership. Second, some connections are more significant than others. For instance, the fact that a family is domiciled in Oregon is a more important connection when the issue concerns whether interspousal tort immunity applies than the fact that an accident happened in Illinois. Similarly, in a breach of contract case, the place of the contract's performance is usually more significant than one of the parties' domiciles.

A typical breach of contract case involving multistate parties illustrates my approach to identifying the state with the closest connection. P, a Georgia resident, entered into an oral contract with D, a Florida resident. The parties negotiated and entered into the contract in Florida, and it was to be performed entirely in Florida.

D allegedly breached the contract. The contract is not enforceable under Florida's statute of frauds, but it is enforceable under Georgia's. One can assume that Florida's legislature intended its statute of frauds to invalidate contracts that do not conform to its statute to protect its residents and those who enter into contracts in Florida from fraud. On the other hand, Georgia wants to validate its residents' contracts. Thus, both states create legal relations that apply to the controversy, and a true conflict exists.

Under my approach, Florida law would govern because the legal relations created by Florida law have the closest connection to the controversy. The contract was entered into, negotiated, and to be performed in Florida, all of which are significant connections. The only connection Georgia has with the controversy is that one of the contracting parties is domiciled there—a relevant connection, but not strong enough to overcome the stronger links with Florida. In addition, the parties would probably expect that Florida law would govern a contract negotiated, entered into, and to be performed in Florida.

Consider a true conflict involving a guest statute. An accident occurs in Virginia involving D, a Virginia resident, and her passenger, P, a North Carolina resident. Virginia creates a right to recover for injuries caused by negligence, but it has a guest statute. North Carolina provides a cause of action when its residents are injured by negligence, and it has repealed its guest statute. Thus, North Carolina furnishes a cause of action for P, while Virginia establishes an immunity for D. Which state's law governs? In this case, the accident occurred in Virginia, and the defendant is a Virginia resident. The only contact with North Carolina is that P is a North Carolina resident, and D lacks any relevant connection with North Carolina.[14] Consequently, the closest connection is with Virginia. Note also that to the extent one assigns expectations to the parties, it is more likely that the parties would expect Virginia law to apply.

One connection that has no relevance in my approach is forum—that a case is brought in a jurisdiction should not count in the choice of law analysis. Thus, in the first example above, Florida law should govern regardless of the place of the trial, and, in the second example, any court that hears the case should apply Virginia law.

Although my second step is theoretically simpler than many choice of law methods, it leaves open the possibility that courts will differ on which state's law has the closest connection to a case. Of course, the possibility that courts will reach different conclusions on the same facts is an intrinsic part of our legal system.

The drunken driving example in Chapter 3 illustrates such a close case. P, an Indiana resident, was badly injured in a traffic accident in Indiana by a drunken driver, and P sued the Kentucky tavern owner who served the driver the alcohol. Indiana holds tavern owners liable for injuries drunk drivers cause if the tavern owner knew or should have known that the customer was inebriated. The law's purpose is to compensate injured parties and to regulate the service of alcohol to reduce the number and severity of accidents in Indiana. Kentucky has an immunity from liability for tavern owners from persons who are injured by drunk drivers. The Kentucky law's purpose is to engender responsibility in all drivers and to avoid placing the burden of drunk driving injuries on tavern owners who often cannot tell when a customer is legally drunk. Because both states meant for their laws to encompass this controversy, a true conflict exists.

It is difficult to predict which state's law a court will apply to the above facts—both states have close connections to the controversy. The accident occurred in Indiana, and P is a state resident. On the other hand, the tavern owner is a Kentucky resident, and he served the drinks in Kentucky. As I stated in Chapter 3, I would adopt Indiana law because the fact that the accident occurred in Indiana seems more significant than the fact that the drinks were sold in Kentucky. In addition, P has no connection to Kentucky and would not expect that Kentucky law would apply, but the tavern owner should have known that a drunk driver might drive into Indiana.

In the above example, it might be tempting for a court to fall back on traditional choice of law devices. For example, a Kentucky court might be tempted to apply Kentucky law, while an Indiana judge might be inclined to adopt her state's rule. Similarly, a judge's choice of law might be influenced by how he felt about a tavern owner's responsibility and personal responsibility. However, a judge should reject such temptations because they are not forum and substantively neutral. The only inquiry in the second step is which state's law has the closest connection to the controversy. That this decision might be difficult or that different judges might come to different conclusions is not a reason to ignore the requirements of the choice of law system, especially because such deviations would violate the method's normative and constitutional bases.

B. ANALYSIS OF EXTENDED EXAMPLES

I will illustrate my method further by applying it to well-known choice of law cases and contrasting my solutions with those of other approaches.

1. *Emery v. Emery*

Among the issues in *Emery v. Emery*[15] was whether family tort immunity nullified the plaintiffs' causes of action for reckless disregard. Two minor daughters, who were California domiciliaries, were injured in an automobile accident in Idaho caused by the alleged recklessness of their brother, the driver of the car in which they were passengers. Justice Traynor looked to Idaho law to determine whether there was a cause of action, as was required under the vested rights approach.[16] Notably, he applied the Idaho guest statute, which allowed suits by passengers against drivers only when the driver's conduct is intentional or is caused by his intoxication or his reckless disregard of other's rights.

The next question was whether family tort immunity negated the sisters' remedy. Although Idaho would have employed family tort immunity, there was no California law on whether minors can sue family members for malicious or willful torts. If California law applied, Justice Traynor could follow the modern trend and refuse to adopt family tort immunity.[17]

Justice Traynor used characterization combined with language that resembles governmental interest analysis to find that California law applied. Traynor stated that three jurisdictions' laws might govern this case: (1) the law of the place where the injury occurred, (2) forum law, or (3) the law of the family's domicile.[18] Although one case had adopted the law of the place where the injury occurred, which is the normal rule under Beale's approach, Traynor thought that the question was not one of tort, but rather of the capacity to sue and be sued. Traynor pointed out that in such a case "the place of injury is both fortuitous and irrelevant."[19] A Georgia case had held that forum law applied, and analogous cases concerning husband-wife immunity had ruled similarly. However, Justice Traynor declared that

> [w]e think that disabilities to sue and immunities from suit because of a family relationship are more properly determined by reference to the law of the state of the family domicile. That state has the primary responsibility for establishing and regulating the incidents of the family relationship and it is the only state in which the parties can, by participation in the legislative process, effect a change in those incidents. Moreover, it is undesirable that the rights, duties, disabilities, and immunities conferred or imposed by the family relationship should constantly change as members of the family cross state boundaries during temporary absences from their home.[20]

Thus, Traynor used characterization ostensibly to stay within the confines of Beale's approach, along with the notion that the domicile state has the responsibility (interest) in regulating family relationships, to find that California law governed and the daughters could recover.

My method produces a similar result. California provides a right for its citizens to recover when they are injured by another's negligence, regardless of the place of the negligence. California does not have family tort immunity, at least when reckless disregard is involved. Idaho creates a right for persons to recover for negligence that occurs in Idaho (in order to regulate conduct), but it has family tort immunity. However, the Idaho family tort immunity should only encompass Idaho families, not California families that are only temporarily in Idaho. Consequently, there is no conflict of laws (or there is a false conflict) because California establishes a right, and the Idaho immunity does not apply.[21]

The fact that my method rejects Idaho law because I believe that the Idaho lawmaker did not intend its law to encompass these facts helps distinguish my multilateralist method from Beale's. A judge using Beale's system would probably have adopted the Idaho family tort immunity because the last act occurred there, even though Idaho probably did not intend its family tort immunity to apply to California families.

My analysis of the above example is based on the assumption that Idaho intended to extend family tort immunity only to Idaho families. This is probably correct because Idaho has no reason to regulate California families. But assume that the Idaho legislature specifically stated that its family tort immunity applied to all accidents happening in Idaho, which it could do under the due process clause because there is a significant contact with Idaho, the accident having occurred there. In this case, there is a true conflict—both the California right to recover and the

Idaho immunity encompass the facts. Idaho's connection to the controversy is that the accident took place there; California's is that the family was domiciled in California. Although the relevant connections are even quantitatively, the California connection is more significant qualitatively. Where a family lives is more important in relation to family tort immunity than where an accident occurs, especially considering that the family was only temporarily in Idaho.

2. *Alabama Great Southern R.R. v. Carroll*

Alabama Great Southern Railroad v. Carroll[22] involved the issue of whether Mississippi's fellow servant rule barred the plaintiff's claim for negligence. The plaintiff, an Alabama resident and a railroad brakeman, was injured in Mississippi when a link between two railroad cars broke while a train was going from Alabama to Mississippi. The accident was caused by the failure of the Alabama railroad's employees to inspect the line between the cars properly before the train left Alabama.

The plaintiff's lawsuit would be barred if Mississippi law governed because Mississippi had retained the fellow servant rule (an employee cannot recover from his employer based on another employee's negligence). On the other hand, the brakeman would have a cause of action under Alabama law because Alabama had abrogated the fellow servant rule by statute. Using the vested rights rule that law of the place of the injury governs, the court found that the Mississippi fellow servant rule barred plaintiff's claim.

This result is unsatisfactory because the law of a state with a tenuous connection governed—the place of the accident was fortuitous. However, the fact that the law of a jurisdiction with a tenuous connection to the controversy controlled does not affect the multilateralist nature of the analysis. The method was still trying to find the law of the most appropriate legal system. What this example shows, however, is that the last act may not be the best criterion to find the most appropriate legal system. What is needed is a multilateralist method that looks at all connections and carefully evaluates the significance of those connections, as mine does.[23]

Under my multilateralist approach, no conflict exists (or there is a false conflict). Alabama establishes a right to recover for injuries caused by negligence when the injury occurs in Alabama, the negligence takes place in Alabama, or when Alabama citizens are involved. In this case, the negligence occurred in Alabama, and the plaintiff was an Alabama resident. Because there was no limitation on the plaintiff's right to recover under Alabama law, the brakeman had a claim under Alabama law.

The brakeman had no cause of action under Mississippi law because of the fellow servant rule. However, the fellow servant rule does not create an immunity for the railroad that produces a true conflict because the Mississippi rule is only meant to protect Mississippi employers and the employer was an Alabama domiciliary.

3. *Grant v. McAuliffe*

Although *Grant v. McAuliffe*[24] restates the place of the wrong rule for torts, one can see Justice Traynor grasping for another approach. In *Grant*, three plaintiffs were injured in an automobile accident in Arizona. The other car's driver died nineteen days after the accident. When the plaintiffs filed claims against the driver's estate, the administrator rejected them because Arizona law did not allow for survival of causes of action. All the relevant parties—the plaintiffs, the decedent, and the administrator—were California residents.

The plaintiffs sued the administrator in California state court. The administrator filed a general demur and a motion to abate the complaints, arguing that under Arizona law a cause of action does not survive the tortfessor's death. The trial court, using Beale's approach, granted the motions, and the plaintiffs appealed.

The California Supreme Court reversed. Justice Traynor restated the vested rights rule that the law of the place where the tortious act occurs governs substantive matters. However, he continued by declaring that the forum does not adopt the procedural rules of the place where the tortious act took place. Characterizing survival of causes of action as procedural, Traynor employed California law, which permitted victims to bring negligence suits against estates.

My analysis of *Grant* resembles my analysis of *Carroll* in that only one state's law created a legal relation that encompassed the dispute. Arizona created a right of recovery for persons injured in Arizona by another's negligence. This right, however, was predicated on the tortfessor's survival. If the tortfessor died, the injured party did not have a claim against the tortfessor's estate under Arizona law. Because the rule's purpose was to protect Arizona estates, the survival statute had no force outside Arizona—that is, the survival statute did not apply to California estates.[25]

The plaintiffs had a cause of action under California law. California provided a right to its citizens to recover damages when its citizens were injured by another's negligence, regardless of the place of injury, and it had no survival statute. Therefore, there was no conflict in this case, and the plaintiffs had a remedy.

4. *Lilienthal v. Kaufman*

Lilienthal v. Kaufman[26] involved whether an Oregon spendthrift statute voided promissory notes executed and delivered in California in a case brought in Oregon. D, an Oregon citizen, had been adjudged a spendthrift, and, under Oregon law, a spendthrift's guardian could void a spendthrift's contracts, except for necessaries. D had entered into a promissory note with a California resident to finance a joint venture to sell binoculars. P was unaware that D had been declared a spendthrift and placed under a guardianship.[27] The guardian declared the notes void.

The court would have held the notes void if only Oregon law had been involved. The court had declared the same spendthrift's obligation to repay the unpaid balance of a check void based on almost identical facts.[28] Consequently, the only issue in this case involved choice of law.

The court determined that there was a true conflict—the obligation was enforceable under California law, but not under Oregon law.[29] The court also stated that it could not decide the matter by characterization.[30] The defendant had urged that the Oregon court apply Oregon law, arguing that the validity of a contract is a matter of procedure, not substance. The court, however, found that the issue was one of substance under standard definitions of substance and procedure.

The plaintiff contended that a contract's validity is governed by the place of the contract's making—in this case, California.[31] This was the rule under Beale's approach, and Oregon had restated this rule many times. However, the rule had also been under attack for many years, mainly on the ground that the place of a contract's making is often fortuitous, and, in such a case, the state of the contract's making has no interest in the parties or the contract's performance. The court, however, refused to overrule the *lex loci contractus* principle because the contract had other connections to California—(1) the defendant had gone to California to obtain the loan, (2) the plaintiff was a California resident, (3) the money was loaned in California, and (4) the money was to be repaid in San Francisco. Based on the above, the court stated that "apart from *Lex loci contractus*, other accepted principles of conflict of laws leads to the conclusion that the law of California should be applied."[32]

The court also felt that California law should govern based on the "rule of validation"—if a contract is valid under the law of any jurisdiction having a significant connection to the contract, the court will adopt the jurisdiction's law that validates the contract.[33] This is because "[i]n the general law of contracts we constantly strive to hold the contract valid and enforceable."[34]

Despite the above, the Oregon court refused to enforce the contract because Oregon had a strong public policy against enforcing spendthrift's contracts.[35] The court conceded that both the California and Oregon interests were of substance, and that neither was more important than the other. Nevertheless, the court declared that "[w]e are of the opinion that in such a case that the public policy of Oregon should prevail and the law of Oregon should be applied; we should apply that choice-of-law rule which will 'advance the policies or interests of' Oregon."[36]

If the case had been filed in California and California employed interest analysis, the result would have been exactly the opposite. Since both states had interests in having their laws applied, California would have selected its law. Thus, as is true in many cases, choice of forum determined the outcome.

These facts also demonstrate the problem with using the better rule approach, as well as any method that is not substantively neutral. Which rule is the better one—that courts should uphold the validity of contracts to provide predictability in the commercial world or that they should protect a spendthrift and his family?

My method would produce a different result from the one the Oregon court reached—mainly, because it is jurisdiction neutral. Although Oregon upholds the validity of contracts, it provides an immunity from obligations made by Oregon spendthrifts to protect spendthrifts and their families, so there is no remedy under Oregon law. California upholds the validity of contracts and has no spendthrift immunity. However, the Oregon legislature intended that its spendthrift statute encompass contracts made by Oregon residents outside of Oregon, so a true conflict exists.

Under my method's second step, a court looks to the state that has the closest connection to the controversy. Oregon has only one relevant connection to the facts—the defendant is an Oregon resident, but this is a significant connection in relation to the spendthrift statute.[37] The majority of the relevant connections, however, are with California, and they are also significant—the defendant executed the notes in California, the plaintiff gave the money to the defendant in California, the plaintiff was a California resident, and the money was to be repaid in California. Based on a quantitative and qualitative analysis of these facts, a court should apply California law and enforce the contract.

The above result advances California's interest in upholding the validity of contracts connected with California, at the expense of Oregon's interest in protecting spendthrifts. However, Oregon's interest is not significantly impaired because the facts have a closer connection to California than Oregon.[38]

5. *Auten v. Auten*

Chapter 1 used *Auten v. Auten*[39] to illustrate the "center of gravity" approach. In *Auten*, a wife sued her husband in New York to recover support that the husband allegedly owed her under a separation agreement. The agreement provided that "neither should sue 'in any action relating to their separation' and that the wife should not 'cause any complaint to be lodged against . . . [the husband], in any jurisdiction, by reason of the said alleged divorce or marriage.'"[40] The husband defended on the ground that an English action brought by the wife had repudiated the separation agreement.

The New York Court of Appeals concluded that English law governed because England had all the significant contacts with the case, while New York's sole contacts with the dispute were that it was the place of the contract's making and the place where the trustee had his office.[41] The court also felt that the separation agreement concerned the marital responsibilities of an English family and that England had the greatest interest in those responsibilities and in the wife's and children's maintenance.[42]

Several of the factual determinations and conclusions in *Auten* are faulty. First, the court was wrong that the only contacts with New York were that the contract was made in New York and that the trustee was resident there; the court omitted the significant fact that the husband lived in New York at the time he executed the agreement. Second, the court focused on the wrong subject matter—the marriage rather than the subject matter actually involved in the case—the separation agreement. The wife was not suing for support because the husband had a duty to support her because they had been married; she was suing because he owed her money under the separation agreement. Moreover, the husband could have reasonably believed that New York law governed the separation agreement's performance, considering that he lived in New York at the time of its execution, the parties executed it in New York, and he was to pay the money to the trustee in New

York (who would then send it to England).

There are actually two issues concerning whether the wife's initiation of the lawsuit repudiated the separation agreement. First, what was the legal meaning of the lawsuit's institution in England? Because the lawsuit was an English lawsuit, only English law is relevant to this issue. Second, did the initiation of the lawsuit, considering its legal meaning under English law, repudiate the separation agreement? A court might answer this question using either English or New York law.

Under my method, a true conflict exists for the second issue. New York law could apply to the matter because the separation agreement was executed there, it was to be partly performed there, and one of the parties to the agreement lived there when it was entered into and at least part of the time when it was being performed. England also had connections to the case that would allow the use of English law because the wife and children lived in England and the separation agreement was to be partially performed there.

Concerning the second step of my analysis, because the connections with New York and England concerning domicile and contract performance are both significant, the fact that the parties executed the contract in New York tips the balance toward New York. Consequently, looking only at the separation agreement and the facts pertaining to it, and ignoring the husband's duty to support his family outside the separation agreement, which was not at issue in *Auten*, New York had the closest connection to the controversy. If the New York Court of Appeals were to agree with the lower courts that under New York law the wife's action repudiated the separation agreement, the wife had no cause of action.

The above result seems unfair. A wife and children were left destitute by a selfish father, and the only reason the wife executed the separation agreement in New York was because that was the only place that she could find her husband. But was the unfair result caused by choice of law? Consider the same facts except that the wife lived in Albany, New York, rather than England. Since there is only one jurisdiction involved, a New York court would have to adopt New York law and tell the wife to go home penniless. Thus, the problem was with substantive law, not choice of law. The New York Court of Appeals suggested that the lower courts' rulings may have been wrong concerning what is required under New York law on repudiation,[43] and analysis of the substantive law would have been a preferable method for exacting substantive justice.

6. *Levy v. Daniels U-Drive Auto Renting Co.*

Levy v. Daniels U-Drive Auto Renting Co. presents a case where judges using my system might differ concerning which state's law to apply.[44] In *Levy*, a person rented a car in Connecticut from the defendant, an automobile rental company. The renter drove it to Massachusetts, where he negligently injured the plaintiff. Under Massachusetts law, the plaintiff had no right to recover from a car rental company based a lessee's negligence. On the other hand, Connecticut had a statute that stated "[a]ny person renting or leasing to another any motor vehicle owned by him shall be liable to any person or property caused by such motor vehicle while so rented or leased."

The plaintiff filed suit in Connecticut, which used Beale's approach. Under a strict application of Beale's method, Massachusetts law would apply because the place of the injury was Massachusetts, and the rule for torts is that the law of the place of the injury governs. Consequently, since there was no right to recover against an automobile lessor in Massachusetts, the court should have found for the defendant.

The court avoided this result by characterizing the issue as one of contract rather than tort. Because the issue was now a contract issue, Connecticut law—the place of the making of the contract—governed. The leasing contract was made in Connecticut, and, according to the court, the Connecticut statute became part of the contract.[45] Under this interpretation, the plaintiff could recover from the lessor.

Professor Leflar was undoubtedly right that the court used characterization to avoid what it believed was an unfair result.[46] The court thought that it would be unfair to allow the plaintiff to go uncompensated, so it recharacterized the issue as contract so that the Connecticut statute controlled. However, as has been mentioned several times above, courts should not use choice of law to attain substantive fairness. If Massachusetts law is unfair, the Massachusetts legislature or courts should change it. A Connecticut court should not be able to alter it by manipulating choice of law, thus interfering with Massachusetts's sovereignty.

Under my method, Connecticut creates a statutory right for a party who is injured by an automobile lessee's negligence to recover from a Connecticut lessor, even if the lessor is not at fault. On the other hand, there is no right against an automobile lessor for a lessee's negligence under Massachusetts law. This is not a false conflict; the fact that there is no right to recover against a lessor under Massachusetts law is a legally protected interest.

Because there is a true conflict, the analyst must determine which state has the closest connection to the controversy. The car's driver and the defendant/lessor were from Connecticut, and the parties entered into the contract there and partially performed it there. However, the accident occurred in Massachusetts, and the plaintiff apparently was from Massachusetts.

Looking at the parties' expectations produces contrary results. The plaintiff (assuming he knew Massachusetts law) would not have expected that he could recover from an automobile lessor for the lessee's negligence. On the other hand, a Connecticut automobile rental agency would have expected to be liable for its lessee's negligence because of the Connecticut statute.

One might be tempted to apply Connecticut law on policy grounds. The rental company could have bought insurance to cover the cost of its lessee's negligence, or it could have charged higher rates to compensate for the possibility of a renter's accident. Nevertheless, one should reject this reasoning because such analysis is for substantive law, not choice of law. In addition, for every policy there is usually an opposite policy. One might argue that allowing the plaintiff to recover would discourage persons from buying uninsured motorists insurance.

Although I believe that the choice of law in *Levy* could go either way under my method, I would adopt Connecticut law because that was where the relationship between the lessor and the lessee was centered and this relationship was the most important connection to the lessor's liability.[47] However, I would not argue with someone who reached the opposite conclusion. Only a highly mechanical choice of law method can give a single answer in all cases.

C. EVALUATION OF CHOICE OF LAW METHOD

My method essentially satisfies the normative requirements in Chapter 2 and the constitutional requirements in Chapter 3. First, my approach is grounded in positive law. It first determines what legal relations are provided by the states that might have a connection with the case. It does not adopt a state's law unless that state has created a legal relation that applies to the facts—that is, unless that state lawmaker has intended its law to encompass the controversy.

My choice of law approach is substantively neutral. It examines the legal relations created by the states, and it examines the scope of those relations without judging the wisdom of the rules. Then, with true conflicts, it chooses law, not based on substantive criteria, but on which state has the closest connection to the case.

My method is also forum neutral; in my system, choice of law does not depend on where the suit is filed. With true conflicts, a judge must adopt the law of the state that has the closest connection to the controversy, even if his state's interest must yield.

My system is relatively predictable. Parties will know that when two states create legal relations that apply to a case that a court will use the law of the state with the closest connection to the controversy. The outcome will not depend on the fortuitous criteria of which forum the case is filed in or which state's law a judge believes is the better rule.

As noted above, I do not claim that my system will always produce the same result in all similar cases. For example, judges may differ on a statute's or rule's scope and disagree as to which state's law has the closest connection to the matter. Still, my method is more predictable than existing systems because it is substantive and forum neutral.

My method is fair to the individual. First, a state can apply its law to a situation only when that state has established a legal relation that encompasses that situation; an individual will not be subjected to a law that was not meant to cover the dispute. Second, a judge cannot use choice of law to produce a judge's notion of substantive fairness; instead, the judge must adopt the law that most closely matches the parties' reasonable expectations regarding the legal regime that governs their conduct. Third, because choice of law is forum neutral under my method, a case's outcome does not hinge on the place where the lawsuit is filed. Consequently, an individual is not subjected to inconsistent laws. Fourth, as stated above, choice of law under my method is generally more predictable than it is under existing systems. This predictability allows an individual to conduct his behavior and structure his business transactions to conform to the law.

A major element of fairness in my system is that it conforms to the individual's expectations. An individual will usually expect that a court will adopt the law of the state with the closest connection to the controversy.[48] An individual will not be surprised when a state's rule that she thought had little relevance to the lawsuit governs the outcome, as is too often true under existing systems.

Finally, my system reflects the relevant states' interests. It looks to the interests and policies of the relevant states when determining what the legal relations are and the scope of those relations. Although it does not directly consider the states' interests in the second step (choosing law in cases of true conflicts), my approach furthers the states' interests by selecting the law of the state with the closest connection to the controversy. Thus, under my system, a state's interest will be furthered when a state has the closest connection to a matter, and the state's interest will yield when another state has the closest connection. I believe that adopting a state's law when it has the closest connection to a case but requiring that state to yield its interest when another state has a closer connection is the best method of protecting state interests.

My method obviously satisfies the "significantly closer connection" standard proposed in Chapter 3 for constitutional constraints on state choice of law because it selects the law of the state with the closest connection to the controversy, is fair to individuals, and respects state sovereignty and the Constitution's horizontal structural lines.

A reexamination of *Rosenthal* will show how my choice of law method complies with the proposed constitutional standard.[49] As noted earlier, both Massachusetts and New York created legal relations that might apply to the dispute. Massachusetts's rule encompasses this situation because the malpractice occurred there and because its damages limitation protects defendants, and the defendants were domiciled in Massachusetts. New York's unlimited damages rule also covers the situation because the decedent was from New York, and New York has an interest in seeing that its domiciliaries receive full compensation for injuries. Accordingly, a true conflict exists.

My method would select Massachusetts law because Massachusetts has the closest connection to the matter. The defendants are Massachusetts residents, and, most significant, the malpractice took place there. Although the plaintiff and her decedent are from New York, the decedent voluntarily came to Massachusetts for the operation. In addition, there was no evidence that indicated that the defendants sought foreign patients.

The above analysis meets the significantly closer connection standard because it chooses the law of the state with the closest connection to the dispute. In addition, it fulfills the due process and liberty concerns underlying this standard. Neither party is subjected to a state's law that has a tenuous connection to the case. Similarly, party expectations are met. The defendants would have expected that Massachusetts law would apply to medical malpractice that occurred entirely within Massachusetts. Likewise, the decedent should not have expected that he could take New York law wherever he went, especially considering that he voluntarily went to Massachusetts to have an operation performed in a Massachusetts hospital by a Massachusetts doctor.

The above analysis also respects state sovereignty. Massachusetts has a significantly closer connection to the controversy. Although New York's policy of full compensation does not apply here, its sovereignty is not significantly hindered because of the weakness of its connection to the dispute. Its sovereign interest will trump another state's when it has the closest connection to a case.

One might criticize my system for not developing specific or patterned rules to help judges in deciding which state has the closest connection to a controversy, like both of the *Restatements* do. However, I do not want to repeat Beale's mistake of developing rigid, mechanical rules that may assist the courts in some cases, yet produce absurd results in others. A contextual method that carefully evaluates connections is preferable to a rule-based approach that employs rules that might not be suitable for some situations. Similarly, I do not want to develop rules that contain exceptions that might devour the rule, as the *Second Restatement* does.

Although I do not claim that my system is perfect, I believe that it does a better job of choosing law than existing approaches. There is no "perfect" rule or system in the choice of law field, owing to the varying and complex fact patterns and the vastness and multiplicity of the laws of the several states. In the final analysis, the key is fairness to the parties. One can evaluate fairness using a Rawlsian approach. Professor John Rawls wrote, "A practice is just if it is in accordance with the principles which all who participate in it might reasonably be expected to propose or acknowledge before one another when they are similarly circumstanced and required to make a firm commitment in advance without knowledge of what will be the particular condition."[50] If we look at choice of law *ex ante*, which system is fairer: (1) an approach that uses a single, factor that can produce fortuitous results in some cases (Beale); (2) a method whose outcome depends on the forum in which a case is filed (Currie); (3) a system that allows an idiosyncratic judge to choose the law that he or she thinks is the "better rule" (Leflar); or (4) a method that selects the law of the state with the closest connection to the controversy (my method)?

NOTES

1. My method satisfies Professor Roosevelt's observation that choice of law involves two quite different inquiries. Kermit Roosevelt III, *The Myth of Choice of Law: Rethinking Conflicts*, 97 MICH. L. REV. 2448, 2467 (1999). Professor Roosevelt writes, "The first [inquiry, which he calls 'rules of scope'] is the determination whether the plaintiff has a right at all." *Id.* My first step undertakes this inquiry. The second inquiry, which involves a "conflicts rule," "specifies which rule [which state's law] shall prevail" when both parties have conflicting rights. *Id.* at 2468. My second step performs this function.

2. As stated earlier, the hypotheticals in this study do not necessarily reflect actual state law.

3. As Professor Kramer has noted, "the mere fact that the parties disagree about the applicable law does not mean that there is a *conflict* of laws." Larry Kramer, *Rethinking Choice of Law*, 90 COLUM. L. REV. 277, 311 (1990).

4. *Id.* at 296.

5. As I noted in Chapter 2, governmental interest analysis sometimes employs hypothetical interests.

6. When I use the term *interest* in connection with my method, I mean subjective interest.

7. *See also* Kramer, *supra* note 3, at 297.

8. *See also id.*

9. Professor Kramer has written that "[c]ourts presume that a state's laws, even when written in language that is unqualified, should not apply in cases that are wholly domestic to another state." *Id.* at 294.

10. This is a false conflict under interest analysis terminology.

11. There is also no conflict if the states' laws are the same.

12. When the lawmaker did not intend that the legal relations belong together, a court can apply different states' laws to different issues in the same case. See, for example, the discussion of loss-distribution issues in Chapter 6, which concludes that different states' laws can govern conduct-regulation issues and loss-distribution issues, such as vicarious liability, in the same case.

13. My use of the term *true conflict* is somewhat different than Currie's. I use true conflict to indicate those cases in which the law of two or more states create *legal* relations that govern the controversy. Currie uses true conflict to mean that two or more states have *policy* interests in applying their states' laws to the facts.

14. Lack of relevant connections to a jurisdiction is also important in step two of my method. When a party has no relevant connection to a jurisdiction, he would not expect that state's law would apply to him.

15. 289 P.2d 218 (Cal. 1955).

16. *Id.* at 221.

17. This does not violate the requirement that choice of law should be substantively neutral. Justice Traynor changed the California substantive rule; he did not manipulate choice of law to obtain the result he felt was just.

18. *Id.* at 222.

19. *Id.*

20. *Id.* at 223.

21. Unlike some analyses of this problem, my approach does not sever tort immunity from the right to recover. Under my analysis, the right to recover comes from California law, which does not have family tort immunity.

22. 11 So. 803 (Ala. 1892).

23. Professor Twerski has observed, "Territorial thinking has suffered in the past from a heavy emphasis on isolated events rather than an evaluation of the overall factual pattern." Aaron D. Twerski, *Neumeier v. Kuehnen: Where are the Emperor's Clothes*, 1 HOFSTRA L. REV. 104, 120 (1973).

24. 264 P.2d 944 (Cal. 1953).

25. This case also illustrates the problem in Beale's mechanical approach that I noted in connection with *Emery*. Under Beale's approach, which was apparently used by the lower court, the Arizona survival statute bars the cause of action because the accident occurred in Arizona. However, Arizona has not created a legal relation that governs the controversy because Arizona probably did not intend its survival rule to apply to California estates. As noted above, my method does not adopt the law of a state that the lawmaker did not intended to encompass the dispute.

26. 395 P.2d 543 (Or. 1964).

27. The plaintiff apparently had no way of ascertaining that the defendant was a spendthrift. *See* R. CRAMTON, DAVID CURRIE, & HERMA KAY, CONFLICT OF LAWS 253 (1987).

28. Olshen v. Kaufman, 385 P.2d 161 (Or. 1963).

29. *Lilienthal*, 395 P.2d at 545–46.
30. *Id.* at 546.
31. *Id.*
32. *Id.*
33. *Id.*
34. *Id.*
35. *Id.* at 546–49.
36. *Id.* at 549.
37. As stated above, the fact that the lawsuit was filed in Oregon is irrelevant under my method.
38. Professor Kramer disagrees with this conclusion. Kramer, *supra* note 3, at 303. Using his comparative impairment canon, he thinks that the Oregon policy behind the spendthrift statute is more impaired than the California policy of establishing a secure commercial environment. On the other hand, I believe that determining which state's policy is more impaired is as difficult and as subjective as establishing which jurisdiction has the better rule.
39. 124 N.E.2d 99 (N.Y. 1954).
40. *Id.* at 100.
41. *Id.*
42. *Id.* at 103.
43. *Id.* at 101.
44. 143 A. 163 (Conn. 1928).
45. Of course, the contract was between the defendant lessor and the lessee, not between the plaintiff and defendant.
46. ROBERT A. LEFLAR, AMERICAN CONFLICTS LAW 176–80 (1977).
47. In an earlier article, I stated that I would apply Massachusetts law to this problem because I (then) thought that the place of the accident and the plaintiff's domicile were the most significant connections. *See* Scott Fruehwald, *A Multilateralist Method of Choice of Law*, 85 KY. L.J. 347, 399–401 (1996–97). I changed my analysis of this case after undertaking a study of loss-distribution issues, such as vicarious liability. *See* Chapter 6. However, my main conclusion remains the same—that is, that a court could properly adopt either states' law in this case because there are close connections to both states.
48. This is true even in torts cases. One of the purposes of torts is to cause people to conform their behavior to the law. Obviously, people try to conform their behavior to the law they think applies.
49. *See* Chapter 3.
50. John Rawls, *Justice as Fairness*, in JUSTICE AND SOCIAL POLICY 80, 98 (1961).

Chapter 6

Selected Problems in Choice of Law

This chapter examines three choice of law problems that American courts have frequently dealt with in recent years: (1) choice of law and choice of forum clauses in contracts, (2) loss-distribution issues, and (3) insurance for environmental pollution.

A. CHOICE OF LAW AND CHOICE OF FORUM CLAUSES IN CONTRACTS

Professor Beale thought that the parties lacked the power to choose what law governed their contracts.[1] He felt that allowing the parties to select the law that controlled their contracts was a legislative act that interfered with state sovereignty. Beale declared: "The meaning of the suggestion, in short, is that since the parties can adopt any foreign law at their pleasure to govern their act, that at their will they can free themselves from the power of the law which would otherwise apply to their acts."[2] Moreover, he thought the rule was theoretically indefensible in connection with vested rights: "But the contract cannot be assigned to a state until it has come into existence; it is still first necessary to meet the theoretical objection that the law of the place where parties act must attach legal obligation to their actions."[3]

Several authors have criticized Beale's position on contractual choice of law clauses.[4] For example, Professor Cook pointed out that "[t]he 'rules of law' of the foreign state in question take effect not as 'law of' that state but merely as terms of the agreement of the parties."[5] Professor Yntema recognized the practical problems with Beale's rule:

> The basic principle in the law of contracts is to afford the needed protection to the transactions of individuals in accordance with their intentions. The contracts of individuals are a social phenomenon, not creations of the territorial sovereign . . . . Accordingly, the basic premise of the law of foreign, as of domestic, contracts is that the agreement of the parties, including their intention respecting the law to govern the agreement, should be given legal sanction, except as there are good reasons to the contrary.[6]

Modern courts generally enforce choice of law clauses, as long as the state whose law is being chosen bears a reasonable relation to the transaction, the parties are not trying to evade the law, and the parties are acting in good faith.[7] However, some states require a stronger connection with the state whose law is being chosen. For example, Kentucky mandates that "some vital element of the contract must be associated with the law of the state whose laws are designated to control."[8] Most states even allow parties to choose whose law governs contractual validity.[9]

American courts also generally enforce contractual forum selection clauses, as long as they are reasonable.[10] In enforcing a forum selection clause, "a court not specified does not lose its jurisdiction as a result of the clause, but such a court declines to exercise its jurisdiction in recognition that the parties by their consent have designated the most convenient forum for their litigation."[11] As the Supreme Court has noted, "[m]anifestly much uncertainty and possibly great inconvenience to both parties could arise if a suit could be maintained in any jurisdiction in which an accident might occur or if jurisdiction were left to any place where [the parties] might happen to be found. The elimination of all such uncertainties by agreeing in advance on a forum acceptable to both parties is an indispensable element in internal trade, commerce, and contracting."[12]

Mere inconvenience or added expense, such as the witnesses being located in another state, does not constitute unreasonableness.[13] To render a forum selection clause unenforceable, there must generally be unconscionability or fraud in the inducement.[14]

Under my approach, courts would generally enforce choice of law and choice of forum clauses. A court should determine whether such a clause is enforceable under the law of the state with the closest connection to the contract. Making this decision by reference to forum law is not proper unless the forum has the closest connection. The forum might not have created a legal relation that applies to the contract, and, even if it has, it is unfair to the parties if forum law controls when another state is more closely connected to the contract.

Enforcing such clauses respects state sovereignty without violating the full faith and credit clause. A state is not being ousted of jurisdiction; rather, its jurisdiction is being used to enforce freely bargained for contractual terms. In other words, the state has decided to allow the contracting parties to adopt another state's law.

Similarly, respecting the parties contractual choices does not violate the due process clause. The parties have freely bargained for choice of law or choice of forum, and they have no expectation that another state's law might apply or that a different forum might adjudicate their case. In such an instance, they have waived their due process right to have the law of a state with the significantly closer connection to the controversy govern their rights.

In *Application Group, Inc. v. Hunter Group, Inc.*, a California court of appeals refused to enforce a Maryland choice of law clause because the Maryland rule upholding covenants not to compete contravened California public policy.[15] In this case, a Maryland computing consulting business had entered into a contract with Ms. Pike, a longtime Maryland citizen. Ms. Pike worked at the company's Baltimore office, as well as at customer sites in Arizona, Colorado, Massachusetts, and New York. Although her employer did a small amount of business in California, Ms. Pike, never went to California during her employment.

A competing consulting business incorporated in California hired Ms. Pike while she was still under contract with the Maryland firm. The facts are unclear as to whether Ms. Pike was to move to California or to work in Maryland. The Maryland firm sued her for breach of contract and the California firm for unlawful interference with contract. Although a Maryland court held that the covenant not to compete was enforceable, it granted summary judgment for the defendants based on a failure to produce evidence of damages. The California company and Ms. Pike then filed a declaratory action in California, claiming, among other things, that the covenant was invalid. The trial court found for the company and Ms. Pike on most of the issues.

The court recognized that the case's outcome hinged on choice of law: if Maryland law governed, the clause would be valid; if California law controlled, it would be void.[16] California generally enforces choice of law provisions unless (1) "the chosen state has no substantial relationship to the parties or the transaction" or (2) "application of the law of the chosen state would be contrary to the fundamental policy of the state."[17] Under the second condition, if "there is a fundamental conflict with California law, the court must then determine whether California has a 'materially greater interest than the chosen state in the determination of the particular issue.' "[18]

Although the court found that there was a substantial relationship to Maryland, it also felt that Maryland's law was contrary to California's fundamental policy of not enforcing covenants not to compete.[19] First, "California has a strong interest in protecting the freedom of movement of persons whom California-based employers . . . wish to employ to provide services in California, regardless of the person's state of residence or precise degree of involvement in California projects."[20] Second, California has a policy of ensuring "that California employers will be able to compete effectively for the most talented, skilled employees in their industries, wherever they may reside."[21] Finally, "California has a correlative interest in protecting its employers and their employees from anti-competitive conduct by out-of-state employers."[22]

On the other hand, the court thought Maryland's interest in protecting its businesses from "recruitment of employees who provide 'unique services' and [from] the misuse of trade secrets, routes, or lists of clients, or solicitation of customers" was weak.[23] The court felt that although computer consultants are a scarce resource, Ms. Pike did not perform unique services for the Maryland company, nor was the Maryland company's proprietary information endangered.[24]

Thus, the court concluded that California had a "materially greater interest" in the dispute than Maryland.[25] The court declared that to have enforced the covenant "would have been to allow an out-of-state employer/competitor to limit employment and business opportunities in California."[26]

Hunter's reasoning and outcome is an egregious example of "conflicts localism." First, the court manipulated its own standard—that the court must find that California has a materially greater interest than Maryland in order to void the choice of law clause. Although California may have an interest in the case, it is difficult to argue that California has a *materially* greater interest than Maryland—the state in which the contracting parties were domiciled, the contract was executed, and the contract was mainly performed, and where (using the language of interest analysis) any injury to the Maryland company would have been felt.[27] The court is confusing the strength of California's policy with the strength of its connections to the case.

More fundamentally, California is asserting its weak interest in the case at the expense of Maryland's stronger interest and fairness to the individual, which under my approach violates both the full faith and credit and the due process clauses. First, Maryland has a stronger interest in the case than California. California is saying that it can apply its law to a contract that has all its major connections with Maryland solely because it affects a California company's ability to recruit employees outside the state. Second, the outcome is unfair to the Maryland company. The California court has voided a contract freely entered into in Maryland between Maryland citizens[28] that involves performance mainly in Maryland because it thinks California law is more enlightened. This is yet another case where a state is attempting to impose its law on the world, a violation of due process under *Gore*.[29]

A detailed examination of the facts using my method will further illustrate the problems in the California court's analysis. First, the main issue in the case is whether the choice of law clause is valid, not whether the covenant not to compete is proper. Looking at just this issue, there is *no* conflict because California cannot extend its law to the agreement between the Maryland company and Ms. Pike. Maryland has the main connections with the case; California has no connection to the contract at all. The contract is between Maryland domiciliaries, was executed in Maryland, and was mainly intended to be performed in Maryland.[30] The California company is not a party to the contract, and it has no relation to the contract. Although enforcing the covenant against Ms. Pike may have an effect on a California company, this effect does not give California the power to regulate contracts that are mainly connected with another state in which none of its citizens have an interest.[31]

The outcome would be the same if the choice of law clause did not exist; the presence of the clause only makes the parties' expectations clearer. California law does not extend to this contractual covenant not to compete because there is no California citizen that is a real party in interest to the contract.

The analysis, but not the outcome, would change if the issue had been whether the California company had unlawfully interfered with the Maryland contract.

Then, the scope of California law would potentially apply to the case because California would want its law to protect companies incorporated in California. However, the case's outcome would not change because Maryland still has the closest connection. In addition to the connection discussed above, the injury is being felt in Maryland. A Maryland company has lost a key employee that mainly worked in Maryland.

This analysis is constitutional under the standard set forth in Chapter 3. First, it adopts the law of the state with the closest connection to the issues, as the above analysis demonstrates. Second, it is fair to the individuals. The contracting parties voluntarily agreed that Maryland law govern their contract; they should not have been surprised that Maryland law could be used to validate the covenant not to compete. On the other hand, the Maryland company would not expect that a court would strike down a freely negotiated covenant not to compete, contained in a contract with a freely negotiated choice of law clause, where the contract's major contacts were with Maryland. Choice of Maryland law was not unfair to the California company concerning the noncompetition clause because it had no relation to the contract. If an unlawful interference with contract claim against the California company had been involved in this suit, adoption of Maryland law would still not have been unfair to the California company because the contract was a Maryland contract and the injury was caused to a company in Maryland.

Finally, my analysis does not violate the full faith and credit clause because the choice of Maryland law does not interfere with California's sovereignty. California has no power to apply its statutes or policy to a Maryland contract involving Maryland domiciliaries, even if it indirectly affects a California company. On the potential unlawful interference with contract claim, California should not be able to protect its resident company by extending its laws to wherever its corporate citizen might operate to protect that company. A state (in this case Maryland) must be able to regulate conduct within its borders.

The argument against the above analysis is that California should be able to enforce its policy in its courts.[32] I would agree if California and Maryland were independent sovereigns.[33] However, they are not; as stated earlier, they are part of a federal union subject to the full faith and credit and due process clauses. The interests of the federal union and the constitutional provisions make the use of the public policy exception both unwise and unconstitutional.[34]

First, in a federal union where citizens are supposed to be able to travel freely from state to state, allowing one state to ignore the law of another state when the other state is more closely connected to a controversy is unwise. It encourages forum shopping and fosters interstate hostility. Under such a system, it would not be surprising for a state to say, "You treated my citizen unfairly, so now I will treat your citizen unfairly."

Second, as was explained in detail in Chapter 3, the full faith and credit clause prevents a state from furthering its interests at the expense of another state's interests when the other state has a significantly closer connection to the case. Thus, the public policy exception is unnecessary and unconstitutional. When a state has the closest connection to case, it can and should apply its law; it does not have to worry about public policy. When another state has the closest connection, the first state should enforce the other state's law even if that law is against the first state's policy because the full faith and credit clause mandates that it do so, especially when the refusal to recognize the law is content based.[35]

California may justifiably feel that its policy is better, but that does not allow California to force its judgment on Maryland and its citizens. As Chapter 3 noted, each sovereign has the power to make value judgments for those within its authority, even if other sovereigns believe those value judgements are wrong. The full faith and credit clause allocates the authority among the states, and when Maryland, rather than California, has the authority to govern a transaction, California should not be able to usurp Maryland's sovereignty under the guise of the public policy exception.

Lastly, permitting California to enforce its policy to invalidate the choice of law clause and the covenant not to compete is grossly unfair to the Maryland company and should violate the due process clause. It had the very reasonable expectation that Maryland law would apply for the reasons given above, and it fully complied with the applicable law. To adopt California law is to destroy those reasonable expectations and to subject the Maryland corporation to inconsistent laws.

Finally, one might argue that the covenant not to compete was intended to restrict competition with a California company.[36] Such an argument is irrelevant; the Maryland company's actions were legal in the jurisdiction with the closest connection to the situation. The outcome would clearly have been different if the company had put covenants not to compete in contracts involving its California employees.[37]

B. LOSS-DISTRIBUTION ISSUES

Loss-distribution and similar issues,[38] such as vicarious liability, recovery for loss of parental consortium, and the availability of indemnity or contribution, often present complex choice of law problems when multistate elements are involved. In particular, in some of these cases, one state's law may control loss-distribution issues while another state's law governs conduct-regulation issues because the significance of connections often differs with the type of issue.

Vicarious liability[39] illustrates the effect of whether the tort issue involves conduct regulation or loss distribution on choice of law. Vicarious liability involves loss distribution because, under vicarious liability, the defendant is liable for someone else's conduct regardless of his or her own fault.

The traditional choice of law rule for vicarious liability was to adopt the law of the place of the wrong.[40] Some commentators and cases qualified this rule by requiring that the defendant have some material connection to the state whose law was to be applied. For example, the *First Restatement* stated, "In order that the law of the state of the wrong may apply to create liability against the absentee defendant, he must have submitted himself to the law of that state."[41]

Adopting the law of the place of the wrong for vicarious liability is a simplistic solution. The place of the accident in many cases will not be the most important choice of law connection for vicarious liability. Rather, three connections will usually be more important: (1) the place where the relationship between the tortfessor and the person who may be held vicariously liable is centered, (2) the connection between the plaintiff and the state whose law may be applied, and (3) the connection between the defendant and the state whose law may govern. The first connection is usually the most important one for vicarious liability because it relates to the relationship upon which vicarious liability is premised. However, the second connection is also important because a plaintiff should generally not be able to recover when that plaintiff has no connection to the state whose law is being applied, at least when that law is different from his or her state's.[42] Finally, as the variation on the traditional rule requires, there should be some connection between the defendant and the state whose law controls, unless the law of the defendant's domicile is the same.

Matson by Kehoe v. Anctil involved the issue of whether there was an agency or independent contractor relationship between the driver of a truck ("Anctil") and the truck's registered owner ("MBI") in connection with a truck accident.[43] If Anctil was MBI's agent at the time of the accident, MBI would be liable for the accident based on vicarious liability. If Anctil was an independent contractor, MBI would not be liable. Although Anctil owned the truck, MBI was the truck's registered owner, the insurance was in MBI's name, and MBI had obtained Canadian and U.S. permits for the vehicle. The accident occurred in Vermont, the injured party was from Rhode Island, and Anctil and MBI were Quebec domiciliaries. At the time of the accident, Anctil was transporting crushed cars to Quebec for a company unknown to MBI; and MBI claimed that Anctil was not acting on its behalf.

The court held that Quebec law, which favored MBI, controlled based on the most significant relationship test.[44] The court declared that the place where the defendant's relationship is centered is more important than the place of the accident or any other connections to the case, so Quebec law governed.[45] However, because there were factual issues in dispute, the court refused to enter summary judgment for MBI.[46]

I agree with the court's analysis. Quebec could apply its law to the dispute because the defendants were Quebec domiciliaries and their relationship was centered there. Vermont could also employ its law because the accident occurred there. However, the issue of whether the driver was an agent or independent contractor was more closely connected to Quebec because that was where the relationship was centered and the place of the accident was fortuitous. Although the plaintiff was from Rhode Island, Rhode Island's connection to a Vermont accident was not strong enough to overcome Quebec's stronger connections.

This case also illustrates that different states' laws may apply to different issues in the same case when one issue concerns conduct regulation and the other involves loss distribution.[47] In a related case, *Matson by Kehoe v. Anctil*, the Vermont court had applied Vermont law to the issue of whether the parents of an injured child were contributorily negligent when the mother was holding the child in her lap at the time of the accident.[48] Because contributory negligence regulates conduct, and the accident happened in Vermont, Vermont had the closest connection to the issue. On the other hand, as the later *Matson* case demonstrated, Vermont had little interest in who paid the damages caused by the conduct.

Some states have statutes or case law that make the owner of a motor vehicle liable for the negligence of anyone driving his or her vehicle. A choice of law question concerning the extraterritorial application of these laws arises when multistate elements are implicated, particularly when an owner who is not a citizen of the state that has the pro-liability law is involved.

In *Fu v. Fu*, several friends rented a car in New Jersey, intending to drive to Ithaca, New York, and later to Wisconsin.[49] While in New York, the automobile was involved in a single-car accident. Although the renters had insurance through their personal vehicles, the insurance policy limits did not compensate all the injured parties, in particular, one passenger who had medical expenses of almost $400,000. Consequently, the injured parties sued the rental company. The rental company did business in New Jersey and Pennsylvania, and the car was registered in Pennsylvania. All the plaintiffs were New Jersey residents.

The car rental company asserted that New Jersey law governed the case and that under New Jersey law a car owner is not liable for a driver's negligence unless the driver is the owner's agent or employee.[50] On the other hand, the plaintiffs argued that New York law controlled and that a New York statute allowed recovery from a car owner under the facts of the case. The New York statute stated that "[e]very owner of a vehicle used or operated in this state shall be liable and responsible for death or injuries to person or property resulting from negligence in the use or operation of such vehicle, in the business of such owner or otherwise, by any person using or operating the same with the permission, express or implied, of such owner."[51] The trial court originally granted the car rental company's motion for summary judgment on the ground that New Jersey law applied, but it reversed its decision upon a motion for reconsideration, and it ordered that the matter proceed under New York law.[52]

Using interest analysis, the intermediate appellate court reversed, holding that New Jersey law controlled.[53] The court noted that there was a conflict between the New York statute and the New Jersey common law.[54] The court then examined the policies behind the two laws. The policy behind the New Jersey law was "to shield an owner from liability in cases in which the owner has not been negligent and in which the culpable driver is not related to the owner in a way that will justify the imposition of vicarious liability."[55] Thus, New Jersey required either fault on the part of the car's owner or some special relationship between the owner and the driver.[56] On the other hand, the policy behind the New York statute was "to protect those injured in automobiles accidents and to 'discourage owners from lending their vehicles to incompetent or irresponsible drivers.'"[57] The court thought that the main purpose of this statute was loss distribution, rather than conduct regulation.[58]

The court concluded that New York's contacts with the case did not implicate the policies behind its statute.[59] The only New York contact was that the accident occurred there.[60] The court declared that "there must be a connection between the vehicle and its owner on the one hand and the state of New York [on the other]."[61]

The court concluded that "New York has no interest in the application of § 388 to this matter, which does not involve New York residents, New York vehicles, New York owners or a New York rental agreement. Nor does the statute implicate a standard of care for drivers [conduct regulation] using New York roadways."[62]

The New Jersey Supreme Court reversed because it decided New York's interests outweighed New Jersey's.[63] First, the court thought that the New York statute was intended to discourage "owners from lending their vehicles to incompetent or irresponsible drivers."[64] Second, the court believed that New Jersey's public policy of compensating tort victims had sapped New Jersey's common law rule protecting car owners of much of its vitality.[65] Finally, the court downplayed New Jersey's connections with the case.[66]

I agree with the intermediate appellate court's outcome and generally with its reasoning. Although New York could have applied its statute to the case under the first step of my due process standard[67] because the accident happened there, the important connections were with New Jersey. Most important, New Jersey was where the relationship between the owner and operator was centered; they entered into the rental agreement there. Moreover, the plaintiffs had no connections to New York; they were all New Jersey residents, and they rented the car in New Jersey. In addition, the place of the accident was fortuitous. Both the plaintiffs and defendant would expect that when New Jersey citizens rent a car in New Jersey from a New Jersey rental company that New Jersey law would govern the relationship between the owner and the driver. Similarly, New Jersey had an interest in protecting New Jersey car owners, whereas New York had no stake in compensating New Jersey plaintiffs by holding a New Jersey car rental company vicariously liable.

Even if the New Jersey Supreme Court's observations were valid, this would not change my analysis of the case. First, the Supreme Court's statement that the statute has a conduct-regulation basis is probably incorrect. As the dissent pointed out, "New York courts have consistently described Section 388 as a rule that allocates loss, not one that regulates conduct."[68] Even if the statute did have a conduct-regulation basis, the most important connections are still with New Jersey, as described above. Second, the fact New Jersey law has generally become pro-compensation is irrelevant. If New Jersey's rule is anachronistic, New Jersey should change the rule substantively; its courts should not manipulate choice of law. Finally, the court downplayed New Jersey's connections because it obviously wanted to compensate the plaintiff. Again, if this was the court's objective, it should have done it through substantive law, not choice of law.

Although the state that is the center of the relationship between the tortfessor and the party who may be liable for that tortfessor's actions is usually the decisive factor in determining choice of law for vicarious liability, other connections may require the use of another state's law. In *Brown v. National Car Rental, Sys.*, a Florida resident was injured in an accident in Florida by a car that was rented in Georgia by a New Jersey resident who lent it to a Georgia resident.[69] The car rental company was a Minnesota citizen doing business nationally. Significantly, the car was registered in Florida, and it had Florida license plates. Florida had created owner liability by case law, while Georgia did not hold an owner liable under the facts of the case. Using the *Second Restatement*'s most significant relationship test, the court held that Florida law applied.[70]

In *Brown*, unlike *Fu*, there are important connections to both states, and both states probably intended that their laws extend to the controversy. The owner-driver relationship was entered into in Georgia, but the accident happened in Florida, a Florida resident was injured, and the car was registered and licensed in Florida. Accordingly, the strong connections with Florida require that Florida law govern the case. A Florida resident would have expected that the Florida owner liability law would have applied to an accident that took place in Florida involving a car registered there. A Minnesota rental company, which registered its car in Florida, would probably not expect Georgia law to protect it from liability concerning an accident that occurred in Florida and injured a Florida resident, even though the parties entered into the rental agreement in Georgia.

Finally, *Ryder Truck Rental, Inc. v. Rosenberger* presents a case where a state owner liability law does not apply when the only connection to that state is that the defendant is a state citizen.[71] In *Ryder*, a minor was injured when a rental truck her father was driving struck a concrete bridge abutment on a Montana highway. The family had rented the truck from Ryder, a Florida corporation, in Seattle, Washington, to move the family from Seattle to Nebraska. As mentioned above, Florida has case law that permits recovery from a vehicle owner based on the driver's negligence. Montana does not have such a law.

In granting a motion to dismiss based on *forum non conviens*, the Florida court held that Florida law was not applicable to the accident.[72] The court noted that "[w]hile Florida has an interest in protecting its citizens and visitors from persons who put dangerous instrumentalities in another's hands, we are not here dealing with Florida plaintiffs, either residents or visitors."[73] The court added that "[t]he plaintiff, having no connection with Florida, would not be justified in expecting Florida law to apply."[74]

This analysis is correct. The fact that a company is a state domiciliary does not by itself give that state the power to regulate that company for all purposes throughout the country. In addition, Florida has no interest in compensating nondomiciliaries who are injured in other states; consequently, it is unlikely that Florida intended its law to encompass the facts of this case.

However, the majority's conclusion that the law of Montana—the place of the injury—controls is wrong.[75] The only connection that Montana had to the accident was that the accident occurred there; Montana had no connection to the relationship between the owner and the driver or to the injured party. As the dissent pointed out, "Montana is merely the fortuitous location of a one-vehicle accident which occurred during a trip from Washington to Nebraska and does not involve any Montana residents."[76]

The state with the closest connection to the dispute was Washington. The plaintiff and her family were domiciled in Washington and that was where they entered into the relationship with Ryder. No other state had a stronger connection to the issue.

Similar issues, such as recovery for loss of parental consortium and indemnity/contribution, should use similar choice of law principles. In *Sheldon v. PHH Corp.*, minors were trying to recover for the loss of parental consortium,[77] occasioned when their mother was seriously injured in a traffic accident.[78] The plaintiffs and their mother were New York residents, who at the time of the accident were riding in a car registered in New York. The accident occurred in Michigan; the other car's driver was a Michigan citizen. The other car was leased from a Delaware corporation whose principal place of business was New York. The rental company had leased the car through its New York office to the driver's husband's employer for use in Michigan. Michigan law allowed damages for loss of parental consortium, while New York law did not. Based on Michigan and New York choice of law rules, the court held that New York law governed because New York was the only state that had a substantial interest in applying its law.

Both states could apply their laws to the matter. New York was the plaintiffs' domicile and the place where the parent-child relationship was centered, while Michigan was the place of the accident. A court should adopt New York law because the place where the parent-child relationship was centered was the most important connection to the case—this relationship is the basis of parental consortium. Although Michigan had an interest in regulating the drivers' conduct since the accident occurred on its roads, it had little interest in whether New York children can recover for loss of parental consortium. The fact that the other car's driver was a Michigan domiciliary was irrelevant because the issue did not involve seeking damages from her. The driver-owner relationship was partially centered in Michigan, but this relationship also did not relate to the issue of recovery for loss of parental consortium.

What law governs the issue of whether indemnity[79] or contribution[80] is allowed is simple if both the defendant who paid the judgement and the person from whom indemnity or contribution is sought are from the same state. Consider, for example, an accident that occurs in California with a California citizen being injured by a Nevada citizen who works for a Nevada company. The California citizen sues the Nevada company under vicarious liability based on its employee's negligence and recovers. When a party has to pay damages because he is vicariously liable, the party can often recover from the person who is primarily liable. Accordingly, the company sues its employee for indemnity. Nevada permits indemnity under these conditions, while California does not. The court should adopt Nevada law because that is where the parties relationship is centered. California lacks any interest in who pays the damages, as long as its citizen is paid.

Glunt v. ABC Paving, Inc. presents a more complex situation.[81] The plaintiff's husband in *Glunt* was an Ohio trucker who was killed in a traffic accident in New York when he rear-ended another truck that had slowed down at a construction site. The wife sued a New York paving company, which was working at the construction site, along with two of its New York employees. The defendants then sued the husband's Ohio employer for contribution on the ground that the employer had negligently allowed the husband to drive its trucks when it knew he had a sleeping disorder. The employer moved for summary judgment on the contribution claim because it had already paid worker's compensation benefits to the widow, and Ohio law did not permit an action for contribution against an employer who had paid worker's compensation benefits.

The court ruled New York law, which allowed contribution, governed.[82] The court concluded that "[b]ecause Ohio and New York have irreconcilable interests in the enforcement of their workers' compensation laws, the place of the injury governs."[83]

Unlike the previous example, the right of contribution in this case does not depend on a preexisting relationship, and the parties are from different states. Both states have strong reasons to have their laws applied. Under Ohio's worker's compensation law, once an employer pays worker's compensation benefits to the proper party, it is no longer liable for the occurrence. The Ohio company had paid full worker's compensation benefits to an Ohio employee's widow. On the other hand, New York does not want a party to have to pay the full amount of damages when another party is also partially liable. A New York company was being forced to pay the entire damages in this case.

Although this controversy is another example of a close case, New York law seems to have the closest connection to the issue. The New York company would expect New York law to govern contribution when a New York company is seeking contribution for an accident that took place in New York. In addition, the New York company has no relevant connection to Ohio. Although the Ohio company might expect the Ohio rule to apply, this expectation is weakened because the driver was in New York on company business. Thus, it is not unfair to the company that New York law controls.

In sum, loss-distribution and similar issues illustrate that choice of law is a complex process that requires courts to consider carefully the significance of all connections. A court should not automatically apply the law of the state where the accident happened to such issues because that state may have a fortuitous connection to the issue and other states may have more significant connections. Even adopting a rule that a court should employ the law of the state where the relationship relating to the loss-distribution issue is centered is not proper because, in some cases, another state may be more closely connected to the controversy, as we saw in *Brown*, or the relationship may be multistate, as we saw in *Glunt*.

C. INSURANCE FOR ENVIRONMENTAL POLLUTION

Which state's law to apply to the interpretation of insurance contracts for environmental pollution has frequently occupied courts in recent years. Two issues, in particular, have taken center stage: (1) which state's law should govern pollution-exclusion clauses and (2) which state's law should control late-notice defenses?

At least four states' laws might apply to these questions: (1) the law of the insured's domicile, (2) the law of the insurer's domicile, (3) the law of the state where the insurer and the insured entered into the insurance contract, and (4) the law of the state where the insured risk is located. Many problems pose additional complications because corporations can be citizens of more than one state and may do business in several states, a contract may insure risks in several states, and hazardous waste may be generated in one state and stored in another.

According to Professor Symeon C. Symeonides, courts have generally adopted two approaches to determine the law to be applied to the interpretation of insurance contracts for environmental pollution: (1) the "uniform contract interpretation" approach and (2) the "site-specific" approach.[84] The uniform contract interpretation approach "aspires to apply the law of a single state even when the contract covers multiple risks situated in different states. This approach usually leads to the application of the law of a state which is either the law of the place of the making of the contract or has other significant connections with the contract and the parties."[85] On the other hand, the site-specific approach "abandons the goal of applying a single law to the whole contract and focuses instead on the interests of the state or states where the insured risks are located. The applicable law is usually the law of that state or states (the site-states), unless another state has a more significant relationship with regard to the particular issue."[86]

Pfizer, Inc. v. Employers Ins. of Wausau adopted the site-specific approach in a multisite, multistate, environmental insurance coverage case.[87] In *Pfizer*, a declaratory judgment action, an insured sought coverage for environmental contamination liability claims involving approximately ninety sites in nineteen states and Puerto Rico. Twenty-four of the sites were in New Jersey, the forum state. Pfizer's headquarters was in New York, and that was where the parties had executed the insurance contracts.

There were two issues in the case: (1) what law governs the interpretation of the pollution-exclusion clause in the policies and (2) what law controls the late-notice defense.[88] The insurance companies contended that New York law, the location of Pfizer's headquarters, or the law of the states where the sites were located should govern the non-New Jersey site claims. Pfizer asserted that the court should apply New Jersey to all claims.

The trial court concluded that New Jersey law should control all issues. Using section 6 of the *Second Restatement*, the trial court asserted that "the governing law should be the law of the state with the dominant significant relationship to the disputed issue."[89] The court thought that New Jersey had a commitment to protect its insureds through liberal insurance coverage.[90] Pfizer had done business in New Jersey since 1900, and it had employed 2,200 New Jersey residents in New Jersey and an additional 500 New Jersey residents in New York.[91] Moreover, it had shipped approximately $375 million dollars in products and services from New Jersey in 1993, and it had expended $31 million for research and development in New Jersey in that year.[92] The trial court concluded that "New Jersey has an interest in protecting its businesses through the application of its laws" and that "failure to apply New Jersey law to the pollution exclusion and the notice issues would frustrate significant New Jersey policies."[93]

The New Jersey Supreme Court noted that "there is no choice-of-law issue where the policyholder is located in one state, the environmental liability arises out of the same state, and the policies are issued by a state-based insurer for that one site."[94] However, when a policy insures sites in several states, multiple states' laws may govern coverage questions because different states "by statute require specific forms of insurance clauses."[95] Thus, "[i]n such a case, the single policy insuring multiple risks will usually incorporate the statutorily-mandated forms of the state involved, and the courts will, presumably, treat the policy as involving separate policies, each insuring an individual risk."[96]

The court used four different categories of interests derived from section 6 of the *Second Restatement* to analyze the two issues before it: (1) the competing interests of the relevant states, (2) the national interests of commerce among the several states, (3) the interests of the parties and the interests underlying the contract law, and (4) the interests of judicial administration.[97]

The first issue was what law governed the "sudden and accidental" exception to the pollution-exclusion clause.[98] This exclusion barred claims, "unless the discharge of contaminants was both sudden and accidental."[99] Under New York law "sudden" did not cover gradual discharges, but under New Jersey law it could.[100] The court assumed that the other involved states had the same rules as either New York or New Jersey.[101]

Concerning the first factor, the purpose of the New Jersey law was "in securing financial resources, both to remediate New Jersey toxic waste sites and to compensate victims of pollution in New Jersey."[102] The court concluded that these New Jersey interests were not implicated with out of state waste sites.[103] The court thought that New York or the waste site states had a closer relationship to the goals behind their laws.[104] The court declared, "New York is the principal place of business of Pfizer. The insurance contracts were negotiated there. Because the purpose of the New York rule was in part to discourage the provision of insurance against pollution, the rule's purpose would be served by its application. In addition, the states in which the waste has come to rest would have their laws rather than New Jersey's more fully advanced if applied to the matter in issue."[105]

Regarding the second factor, the court stated that "application of New Jersey's conflicting view of the pollution-exclusion clause would hinder the interests of commerce among the several states if that law were to be applied to determine a dispute with which New Jersey did not have a dominant and significant relationship."[106] Concerning the third factor, the court thought that the interests of fair expectation and predictability of results disfavored the adoption of New Jersey law because the policies were purchased, paid for, and maintained at Pfizer's New York office, and it would not be predictable that New Jersey law would govern coverage issues when the sites were outside New Jersey.[107] The court asserted, "The policies contain sweeping declarations of coverage that should be given effect where the risks arise."[108] Next, the court addressed the concerns of judicial administration, which it decided did not require the adoption of New Jersey law.[109]

The court concluded,

> [T]he policies to be advanced by the application of each state's law, the interest of commerce among the states, and the interest of predictability and ease of administration all point toward application in a New Jersey forum of the laws of New York or the specific waste sites concerning pollution exclusion. In the event

> of a conflict between the law of New York and the law of the waste site, the law of the waste site should be applied because under the site-specific approach it would have the dominant significant relationship to the issue.[110]

The second issue concerned the interpretation of the late-notice defense. Under New Jersey law, which followed traditional principles, breach of this provision would allow the insurance company's performance to be excused only if the insurer were actually prejudiced.[111] However, under New York law, the insurer does not have to show prejudice.[112] The court stated that "[t]he reason for the New York rule is to protect insurance companies so that they may make prompt investigation of claims . . . . The reason for the New Jersey rule is to protect the interests of policyholders because insurance contracts are contracts of adhesion and policyholders should not lose the benefits of coverage unless the delay has prejudiced the insurance company."[113]

Using the four-factor analysis, the court concluded that the waste site states had the strongest interests in having their laws applied.[114] First, because the purpose of New Jersey's late-notice rule was to protect New Jersey policyholders, the fact that Pfizer did some business in New Jersey was not enough to apply New Jersey law at the expense of the laws of the other interested states.[115] Second, using New Jersey law would unduly interfere with the interests of commerce among the states.[116] Third, the interests of predictability and fair expectation did not favor application of New Jersey law because the waste was not located there.[117] Finally, adoption of the New Jersey rule would not materially advance judicial administration because there was no genuine administrative benefit from using New Jersey law.[118] The court concluded that the law of the waste site should govern if it differed from New York law.[119]

As the court noted, a single-law approach to all issues in a multistate, multisite, environmental insurance coverage case will usually be unsatisfactory. An approach that focuses on the place of the making of the contract or the parties' domiciles does not work when the issue concerns the extent of coverage for a particular site. However, a site-specific approach will not work in all cases. Rather, a court should carefully examine all connections, and adopt the law of the state with the closest connection to the issue.

Consider first the issue of a pollution-exclusion clause. Assume New Mexico is the place of the making of the contract and the domiciles and principal places of business of both the insurer and the insured, but that the hazardous waste site is in Arizona. Also assume that New Mexico allows recovery when the pollution is gradual, but that Arizona requires that the pollution be sudden. In this case, a court should adopt Arizona law because it has the closest connection to the issue. Although New Mexico may have the most connections to the case quantitatively, the fact that the waste site is in Arizona is more significant qualitatively because the state where the waste site is located has the greatest stake in what is excepted in a pollution-exclusion clause. That state should have the right to decide whether it will require broad coverage to make sure that there are funds for clean up, or whether it wants to limit insurance coverage for pollution so that the polluter has to pay for its actions. The only change from the analyses above when waste sites in more than one state are involved is that the law of the particular waste site state will apply to that part of the case.

Although the law of the state where the waste site is located should control most coverage issues, the same is not always true concerning contract conditions, such as whether prejudice to the insurer is required for the enforcement of a late-notice clause. First, consider the issue of whether the contract is valid—that is, whether the requirements of offer and acceptance have been satisfied. Are not the connections of the state (or states) where the contract was made and the place where the parties relationship was centered more important than the location of the insured risk for this issue? Because in the above hypothetical all the important factors are connected with New Mexico, its law should govern the validity of the insurance contract. Next, consider the late-notice provision. This issue seems more closely connected to the state (or states) where the notice was to be given and the notice was to be received than to the location of the insured risk, so New Mexican law should also control.

A variation of this illustration demonstrates that a case by case consideration of connections is better than a rigid rule. Assume that the insurance contract was executed in New Mexico between a New Mexico insurance company and an Arizona insured that has no other connection to New Mexico. In that case, a court should adopt Arizona law because an Arizona insured would expect that Arizona law would govern contract conditions concerning a hazardous waste site located in Arizona that was operated by an Arizona insured. Surely, a New Mexican insurance company would not expect that New Mexican law would control its contracts in all other states. The additional fact that the parties entered into the contract in New Mexico should not alter this fact in most cases; if it did, insurance companies would always force their insureds to sign the insurance contracts in the insurer's domicile.

Two companion cases to *Pfizer* provide further variations on its facts.[120] Both cases involved the same issues as *Pfizer*: (1) the sudden and accidental exception to the pollution-exclusion clause and (2) the late-notice defense.

In *Unisys v. Insurance Co. of North America*, 43 percent of the total damages was from New Jersey sites, with the rest of the damages coming from sites in other states.[121] Unisys was a Delaware corporation with headquarters in Pennsylvania; a connected company for which coverage was sought had done substantial business in New Jersey. The parties executed the contracts in New York, which required pollution-exclusion clauses in liability policies. The insured argued that New Jersey law should apply on the grounds that the insured risk was foreseeably multistate, that the policies did not include a choice of law provision, and that 43 percent of the total damages were in New Jersey. The court, however, followed its analysis in *Pfizer*, and it held that the law of the waste site states would govern.[122]

The court was correct in rejecting the insured's argument that New Jersey law should control all claims. The fact that more of the damages were connected with New Jersey did not mean that New Jersey law should apply to non-New Jersey sites. In other words, the New Jersey lawmaker did not intend its law to extend to sites outside of New Jersey when there was no important connection to New Jersey. Of course, in such a case, New Jersey also could not constitutionally apply its law.

In *H.M. Holdings v. Aetna Casualty and Surety Co.*, the insured had its headquarters in New York at the time of the pollution, but it became a subsidiary of a New Jersey company after the coverage period at issue.[123] It had bought most of its insurance policies through a New York broker, and the waste sites were located outside of New Jersey and had no connection to New Jersey.

The trial court applied New Jersey law to all issues and sites on the ground that the insured was now a New Jersey company.[124] The trial court reasoned that "when operations are multistate, the location of the risk diminishes and the governing law is that of the state with the dominant significant relationship, according to Restatement (Second) of Conflict of Laws section 6."[125] The trial court observed that "[t]he states in which the sites are located have a policy interest in securing financial resources to compensate victims of pollution and to remediate its toxic-waste sites. The identification of these states' environmental interests makes clear that the application of New Jersey law would promote the states' environmental concerns by permitting coverage that might otherwise be defeated by the application of the laws of the states where the sites are located."[126]

The trial judge thought that the failure to adopt New Jersey law would frustrate New Jersey's public policy. He thus went on to hold that "[t]he defendants' failure to include a choice of law clause in any of the policies is evidence that they had no reasonable expectation that any particular state's law would apply to litigation under these policies. As New Jersey residents, plaintiffs are entitled to invoke this state['] s policies of liberal insurance coverage."[127]

The trial court's decision in this case represents choice of law analysis at its worst. In the first quoted passage, the trial court declares that it is going to ignore the laws of the site states and the policies behind those laws because adoption of New Jersey law would advance what the court thinks the policies of those states should be. In the second passage, the court demonstrates blatant "conflicts localism" and "foreigner bias." The court is asserting that a state resident can invoke state law whenever that law favors the state resident.

The New Jersey Supreme Court reversed the trial court using the same analysis as *Pfizer*. Concerning New Jersey's interest in protecting one of its own in connection with the pollution-exclusion clause, the court pointed out that "the policies were purchased by USI when it was a nonresident, negotiated outside of New Jersey, and were designed to cover risks not located in New Jersey . . . . That the policyholder has since moved to New Jersey does not deprive the policyholder of the protection of New Jersey law, but tempers the weight to be given to that factor."[128] On the other hand, the court thought that it should consider the move in connection with the late-notice issue: "Because the purpose to be served by New Jersey's late-notice rule is the protection of a New Jersey policyholder and the conduct about which we are concerned (the late notice) may have occurred at a time when the policyholder was a corporate resident of New Jersey, New Jersey's policies would be fostered by application of its late notice law."[129] The court concluded that the law of the waste-site states should again govern the pollution-exclusion issue and that the law of either New Jersey or the waste-site states should control the late-notice issue with the law of the waste-site states governing when these laws are different.[130]

The insured's move to New Jersey after the fact should have no affect on the choice of law analysis of the pollution-exclusion clause issue. As I stated in connection with my analysis of *Allstate* in Chapter 3, acquisition of a later-acquired domicile should not affect preexisting legal relations. As for the late-notice issue, the company's domicile in New Jersey would be a factor if the company were domiciled in New Jersey during at least part of the period in which it should have given notice because that is where the notice should have been given. However, the importance of the connections must be considered in light of the other material connections, especially that of the state in which the notice should have been received by the insured.

In sum, when hazardous waste sites are located in several states or other significant multistate elements are involved, it is improper to apply a single state's law to all issues involving insurance for environmental pollution. When a coverage issue is involved, such as the interpretation of a pollution-exclusion clause, the state of the waste site will usually have the most important connection to that issue because that state has the greatest stake in what is excluded under the clause. On the other hand, when the issue concerns the interpretation of a late-notice clause, the two most important connections will be the state where the notice is to be given and the state where the notice is to be received. If the state is the same for both connections, the relationship between the parties is centered there, and a court should adopt that state's law. If the states are different, the court should also consider other relevant connections.

NOTES

1. 2 JOSEPH BEALE, TREATISE ON THE CONFLICT OF LAWS § 332.2, at 1079–86 (1935). Professors Lorenzen and Goodrich expressed similar views. *See also* Ernest G. Lorenzen, *Validity and Effects of Contracts in the Conflict of Laws*, 30 YALE L.J. 655, 658 (1921); HERBERT F. GOODRICH, HANDBOOK ON THE CONFLICT OF LAWS 278–80 (1938).

2. BEALE, *supra* note 1, at 1080.

3. *Id.* at 1082–83.

4. Hessel E. Yntema, *Contract and Conflict of Laws: "Autonomy" in Choice of Law in the United States,* 1 N.Y.L.F. 46 (1955); Walter Wheeler Cook, *"Contracts" and the Conflict of Laws: "Intention" of the Parties*, 32 ILL. L. REV. 899 (1938); *see also* J. H. C. Morris, *The Proper Law of Tort*, 64 HARV. L. REV. 881, 882–83 (1951).

5. Cook, *supra* note 4, at 908.

6. Yntema, *supra* note 4, at 65.

7. *E.g.*, Seeman v. Philadelphia Warehouse Co., 274 U.S. 403 (1927); Medtronic Inc. v. Gibbons, 684 F.2d 565, 567-68 (8th Cir. 1982); Consolidated Jewelers, Inc. v. Standard Financial Corp., 325 F.2d 31, 34 (6th Cir. 1963); *see also* RESTATEMENT (SECOND) OF CONFLICT OF LAWS § 187 (2) (1971) [hereinafter, SECOND RESTATEMENT]; 17 C.J.S. Contracts § 15 (1999).

8. *Consolidated Jewelers*, 325 F.2d at 34; *see also* Kronovet v. Lipchin, 415 A.2d 1096, 1104 n.16 (1980).

9. *Kronovet*, 415 A.2d at 1104.

10. *E.g.*, Prudential Resources Corp. v. Plunkett, 583 S.W.2d 97, 99 (Ky. App. 1979); Smith, Valentino & Smith, Inc. v. Superior Ct. of L.A. Cty., 551 P.2d 1206, 1208–9 (Cal. 1976); *see also* SECOND RESTATEMENT § 80.

11. *Prudential*, 583 S.W.2d at 99, *citing*, SECOND RESTATEMENT § 80 comment a.

12. M/S Breman v. Zappatta Off-Shore Co., 407 U.S. 1, 13–14 (1972) (enforcing a forum selection clause in a contract between an American company and a German company that selected London as the forum to adjudicate all contractual disputes.).

13. *Id.* at 16–19; *Prudential*, 583 S.W.2d at 99–100; *Smith*, 551 P.2d at 1209.

14. *E.g.*, Colonial Leasing Co. v. Pugh Bros. Garage, 735 F.2d 380, 383 (9th Cir. 1984) (clause in form contract in fine print at the bottom of a page); Creditors Collection Bureau, Inc. v. Access Data Inc., 820 F. Supp. 311, 313 (W.D. Ky. 1993); M. G. J. Indus. Inc. v. Greyhound Financial Corp., 826 F. Supp. 430, 432 (M.D. Fla. 1993); *see also Breman*, 407 U.S. at 12–13.

15. 61 Cal. App. 4th 881 (1998).

16. *Id.* at 899–900.

17. *Id.* at 896.

18. *Id.* at 897.

19. *Id.* at 899–900. "In relevant part, section 16600 [of the Business and Professional Code] provides: '[E]very contract by which anyone is restrained from engaging in a lawful profession, trade, or business of any kind is to that extent void.' Section 17200 defines 'unfair competition.' It '. . . include[s] any unlawful, unfair or fraudulent business act or practice.'" *Id.* at 885 n.1.

20. *Id.* at 900–01.

21. *Id.* at 901.

22. *Id.*

23. *Id.*

24. *Id.* at 902–03.

25. *Id.* at 902.

26. *Id.*

27. The court also failed to discuss in any detail the policy behind Maryland's allowing contractual covenants not to compete as reflected in Maryland case law. This illustrates another example of the dangers of using hypothetical interests to make choice of law determinations.

28. There was no allegation of unconscionability.

29. *See* the discussion of *Gore* in Chapter 3.

30. Interestingly, there was no claim in *Hunter* that Ms. Pike lived in California at the time of the suit or moved to California to work for the California company. Based on this omission, one can conjecture that Ms. Pike worked for the California company in Maryland by telecommunicating. If this conjecture is correct, California's connection to the case was even weaker. Allowing California law to govern in such a situation would be like permitting Michigan law to control Ford Motor Company's relationships with its employees regardless of the state in which they worked.

31. To state the argument another way, a person who is not a party to a contract generally lacks standing to challenge that contract—the person is not a real party in interest.

32. Public policy exceptions are common in certain choice of law systems, particularly Beale's FIRST RESTATEMENT approach. *See* Scott Fruehwald, *Choice of Law and Same-Sex Marriage*, 51 Fla. L. Rev. 799, 821–25 (1999); Larry Kramer, *Same-Sex Marriage: Conflict of Laws, and the Unconstitutional Public Policy Exception*, 106 YALE L.J. 1965, 1971–72 (1997); see also the discussion of Beale's method in Chapter 1.

33. Professor Laycock declared that "[t]he public-policy exception is a relic carried over from international law without reflection on the change in interstate relations wrought by the Constitution." Douglas Laycock, *Equal Citizens of Equal and Territorial States: The Constitutional Foundations of Choice of Law*, 92 COLUM. L. REV. 249, 313 (1992).

34. Other scholars who have criticized the public policy exception include Fruehwald, *supra* note 32, at 821–25; Kramer, *supra* note 32, at 1980–92; Jennifer Gerarda Brown, *Competitive Federalism and the Legislative Incentives to Recognize Same-Sex Marriages*, 68 S. CAL. L. REV. 745, 791 (1995); Laycock, *supra* note 33, at 313; BRAINERD CURRIE, SELECTED ESSAYS ON CONFLICT OF LAWS 288–89 (1963); Robert H. Jackson, *Full Faith and Credit—The Lawyer's Clause of the Constitution*, 45 COLUM. L. REV. 1, 26–27 (1945).

35. Professor Kramer has asserted that "[a] case that has contacts with another state such that the forum deems it outside the forum's sphere of interest (as defined by forum choice-of-law rules) does not slip back into that sphere because of the content of the other state's law." Kramer, *supra* note 32, at 1987.

36. *Hunter*, 61 Cal. App. 4th at 887–88.

37. The company did not have restrictive covenants in its California contracts. *Id.* at 885–86.

38. "Loss allocating rules . . . are those which prohibit, assign, or limit liability after the tort occurs." *Sheldon v. PHH Corp.*, 135 F.3d 848, 853 (2d Cir. 1998).

39. Vicarious liability is "the imposition of liability on one person for the actionable conduct of another, based solely on a relationship between the two persons." BLACK'S LAW DICTIONARY 1566 (1990). Vicarious liability most often occurs with negligent torts, such as automobile accidents. As the discussion of *Levy v. Daniels U-Drive Auto Rental Co.* in Chapter 5 demonstrated, such cases often involve strong connections with two or more states.

40. ROBERT A. LEFLAR, AMERICAN CONFLICTS LAW 265 (3d ed. 1977); *see also* Young v. Masci, 289 U.S. 253, 258 (1933); Venuto v. Robinson, 118 F.2d 679, 681 (3d Cir. 1941).

41. RESTATEMENT OF THE LAW OF CONFLICT OF LAWS § 387 comment a (1934); *see also* Scheer v. Rockne Motors Corp., 68 F.2d 942, 943–44 (2d Cir. 1934).

42. In other words, both the person burdened by the application of a state's law and the person benefitting from that application should generally have a connection to the state whose law governs. I derived this principle from Professor Brilmayer's writings on choice of law. LEA BRILMAYER, CONFLICT OF LAWS 219–63 (2d ed. 1995). Also see my discussion of Professor Brilmayer's writings on choice of law in Chapter 1.

43. 7 F. Supp. 2d 423 (D. Vt. 1998).

44. *Id.* at 424–25.

45. *Id.* at 425.

46. *Id.*

47. As stated in the previous chapter, a court should not apply different states' laws to two different issues in the same case when they involve legal relations that the relevant lawmaker intended to belong together. However, liability and vicarious liability are separable.

48. 979 F. Supp. 1031 (D. Vt. 1997).

49. 707 A.2d 473 (N.J. Super. A.D. 1998), *rev'd*, 733 A.2d 1133 (1999).

50. *Id.* at 475.

51. *Id.*

52. *Id.*

53. *Id.* at 475–77.

54. *Id.* at 475.

55. *Id.* at 476, *citing*, Haggerty v. Cedeno, 653 A.2d 1166 (N.J. App. 1995).

56. *Id.*
57. *Id.*
58. *Id.*
59. *Id.*
60. *Id.*
61. *Id.*
62. *Id.* at 476–77.
63. Fu v. Fu, 733 A.2d 1133, 1147 (N.J. 1999).
64. *Id.* at 1139.
65. *Id.* at 1140.
66. *Id.* at 1145–47.
67. See the discussion of due process constraints on choice of law in Chapter 3.
68. *Id.* at 1154 (Pollock, J. dissenting).
69. 707 So. 2d 394 (Fla. App. 1998).
70. *Id.* at 396–97.
71. 699 So. 2d 713 (Fla. App. 1997).
72. *Id.* at 715–16.
73. *Id.* at 716.
74. *Id.*
75. *Id.* at 715–16.
76. *Id.* at 719 (Shevin, Judge, dissenting).
77. "In the parent-child relationship the term consortium refers to the loss of a parent's love, care, companionship and guidance." *Ueland v. Reynolds Metals Co.*, 691 P.2d 190, 191 n.1 (Wash. 1984) (citations omitted).
78. 135 F.3d at 848.
79. "A contractual or equitable right under which the entire loss is shifted from a tortfessor who is only technically or passively at fault to another who is primarily or actively responsible." BLACK'S LAW DICTIONARY 769 (1990).
80. "Under the principle of 'contribution,' a tort-fessor against whom a judgement is rendered is entitled to recover proportional shares of judgment from other joint tortfessors whose negligence contributed to the injury and who were also liable to the defendant." BLACK'S LAW DICTIONARY 328 (1990).
81. 668 N.Y.S.2d 846 (A.D. 1998).
82. *Id.* at 847.
83. *Id.*
84. Symeon C. Symeonides, *Choice of Law in American Courts in 1998*, 47 AM. J. COMP. L. 327, 362 (1998).
85. *Id.*
86. *Id.*
87. 712 A.2d 634 (1998).
88. *Id.* at 636.
89. *Id.*
90. *Id.*
91. *Id.*
92. *Id.*
93. *Id.*
94. *Id.* at 638.
95. *Id.*
96. *Id.*

97. *Id.* at 639. This is yet another example of where a court used the general policies of § 6 of the SECOND RESTATEMENT, rather than its most significant relationship test.

98. *Id.* at 640.

99. *Id.*

100. *Id.* at 641.

101. *Id.*

102. *Id.*

103. *Id.*

104. *Id.*

105. *Id.*

106. *Id.* at 641–42.

107. *Id.* at 642.

108. *Id.*

109. *Id.* at 642–43.

110. *Id.* at 643.

111. *Id.* at 643–44.

112. *Id.* at 644.

113. *Id.*

114. *Id.*

115. *Id.*

116. *Id.*

117. *Id.*

118. *Id.*

119. *Id.*

120. Unisys Corp. v. Insurance Co. of North America, 712 A.2d 649 (1998); HM Holdings, Inc. v. Aetna Cas. and Sur. Co., 712 A.2d 645 (1998).

121. 712 A.2d at 649.

122. *Id.*

123. *HM Holdings*, 712 A.2d at 645.

124. *Id.* at 647.

125. *Id.*

126. *Id.*

127. *Id.*

128. *Id.* at 648.

129. *Id.*

130. *Id.* at 648–49.

Chapter 7

Choice of Law in Mass Torts, Class Actions, and Multidistrict Litigation

One of the most difficult problems in choice of law concerns mass torts[1] where parties and laws from more than one state are involved. For example, a plane owned by a Texas corporation and manufactured by a Wyoming corporation takes off from Los Angeles, California, heading to New York City with passengers from ten states. After it makes an intermediate stop in St. Louis, Missouri, the plane crashes in Kentucky, killing all aboard. Assuming all claims are heard in a single action, should the court adopt a single state's law for all claims, or should the court apply different laws to different parties? Once this decision is made which state's or states' laws should govern?

This chapter deals with mass torts in class actions[2] and multidistrict litigation.[3] First, it examines how courts have generally dealt with choice of law problems in complex litigation—by employing a single jurisdiction's law in the case or, at least with each issue, and how scholars have praised or criticized this rule. Second, it discusses whether a court should adopt this single-law approach, using the normative and constitutional criteria set forth in earlier chapters. Based on these criteria, it rejects the single-law approach. Third, it analyzes problems involving mass torts and complex litigation, employing my choice of law method. Finally, it discusses whether certain choice of law problems involving mass torts require a federal solution—that is, whether Congress should pass statutes governing certain multistate torts.

A. THE SINGLE-LAW APPROACH TO CHOICE OF LAW WITH MASS TORTS

Courts have generally applied a single state's law to all claims in class actions and multidistrict litigation, often by using distorted reasoning or by ignoring significant differences between state choice of law rules.[4] For example, in the *Agent Orange* litigation, numerous claims by Vietnam War veterans for injuries allegedly caused by the defoliant Agent Orange with contacts with several jurisdictions had been transferred to the Eastern District of New York, and the court had certified a class under Federal Rule of Civil Procedure 23(b)(3).[5] The court had originally relied on federal question jurisdiction based on federal common law, but the Second Circuit had reversed, declaring that "there is [no] identifiable federal policy at stake in this litigation that warrants the creation of federal common law rules."[6] Consequently, the court was seemingly stuck with the usual rules that a federal court relying on diversity jurisdiction must adopt the choice of law rules of the state in which it sits[7] and that a transferee court must employ the law of the transferor court, including its choice of law rules, in a case transferred under 28 U.S.C. Section 1404 between federal courts.[8]

Judge Jack Weinstein circumvented these federal choice of law rules by the innovative, although inappropriate, notion of a national consensus law of manufacturer's liability.[9] Like most courts dealing with mass torts, Judge Weinstein wanted a single-law solution: "[T]he obviously sensible result of treating members of this nation's armed forces and their families in essentially the same way for any injuries suffered in a national war fought on foreign soil would, it is now provisionally found, be reached by each of the states."[10] Thus, he asked, "What would state courts do?"[11] In other words, he assumed the normal role of a federal judge and tried to predict what the various states would do if they faced the question before him.

First, Judge Weinstein looked at the states' interests in applying their laws to the suit, finding them "dwarfed by the national contacts in the case."[12] Next, he declared that using national consensus law was consistent with relevant state and federal decisions.[13] Finally, he asserted that "[a] state court would therefore have no rational choice but to apply federal or national consensus common law."[14]

Choice of law scholars have criticized Judge Weinstein's decision.[15] Judge Weinstein's decision is wrong because there is no reason to assume that any state would have adopted national consensus law instead of its own law,[16] as is supported by the numerous instances of state parochialism cited throughout this book and the lack of any clear consensus on choice of law. In addition, as Professor Twerski has pointed out, there was little substantive agreement among the states concerning the issues in *Agent Orange*, including enterprise liability, alternate liability, market share liability, and so on.[17] Similarly, Judge Weinstein's "relevant state and federal decisions" comprised only three federal cases, and he quickly rejected contradictory cases cited by the defendants.[18] Likewise, he ignored the Second Circuit's finding that no federal policy was at stake in the litigation. Simply put, there was no precedent and no rational basis for Judge Weinstein's decision.

One might, however, sympathize with Judge Weinstein's dilemma. He was trying to do the fair thing for American war veterans when there was little law on their side.[19] Although compensating injured parties is a major goal of our tort laws, developing unpredictable and insupportable choice of law rules is not a way to bring this about.[20]

In *In re Air Crash near Chicago, Illinois on May 25, 1979*, the court manipulated several states' choice of law rules to conclude that all the states' rules would have selected Illinois law, which did not allow the recovery of punitive damages against an airplane manufacturer.[21] Most interesting is the court's discussion of Michigan law, which permitted punitive damages against airplane manufacturers.[22] Michigan generally applies its law when it has any interest in the case.[23] However, the court ignored the clear mandate of Michigan law based on an ambiguous footnote citing an intermediate appellate case, and it concluded that Michigan would adopt the most significant relationship test, which in this case pointed to Illinois law.[24]

The *San Juan Hotel Fire* case used similar reasoning to determine that Puerto Rican law governed all punitive damages claims.[25] In that case, multidistrict mass tort litigation arose out of a deadly hotel fire in San Juan. Although some of the cases had been transferred from New York, and New York law would have allowed punitive damages under the facts, the court applied Puerto Rican law to these claims, by downplaying New York's interest. The court declared that "[o]nly a handful of parties are domiciled in New York. On the other hand, Puerto Rico is the 'locus' of the accident and has also revealed a strong policy concerning the application of punitive damages."[26] The court's analysis, however, is valid only under a single-law approach. If one balances Puerto Rico's interests against New York's on the New York claims and considers New York's usual strong interest in protecting its citizens, a New York court would probably find New York law applied.[27]

Most commentators agree that courts should adopt a single-jurisdiction's law in mass torts, at least for each issue.[28] The reasons for this include (1) unfairness in applying different states' laws to different parties when the injuries arise from the same tort; (2) inconsistent results occasioned by applying different states' rules to the same tort; (3) complexities, increased costs, and inefficiencies caused by using different states' laws with the same tort; and (4) forum shopping incentives created when multiple state laws apply.[29]

A few scholars, however, have rejected the single-law approach in favor of allowing different states' laws to be applied to different parties' claims in a mass tort.[30] For example, Professor Robert Sedler, an interest analysis advocate, has rejected the single-rule approach because it interferes with state sovereignty and probably would cause a return to the place of the wrong rule (Beale).[31] He has declared that "a federally-mandated 'law of a single jurisdiction' rule in mass tort cases is inconsistent with the constitutional concept of state sovereignty; among other things, it would require the states to sacrifice the strong policies underlying their substantive tort laws by foreclosing application of a state's law when the state has a real interest in implementing its policies."[32]

Moreover, Professor Sedler has asserted that "[i]n most mass tort cases, the only state's law that a federal court would be able to constitutionally apply to determine all the issues and claims of all the different parties in the case would be the law of the state in which the injury occurred, or the law of the state in which the allegedly tortious action took place."[33] Consequently, "[c]hoice of law in mass tort cases would almost always return to the long-discredited 'place of the wrong' rule,"[34] causing "a counter-revolution in these cases in the name of efficiency and consistency."[35]

Professor Kramer rejected the single-law approach for mass torts for positive law reasons: "What's striking is that the accepted wisdom seems so obviously wrong . . . . Because choice of law is part of the process of defining the parties' rights, it should not change simply because, as a matter of administrative convenience and efficiency, we have combined many claims in one proceeding; whatever choice-of-law rules we use to define substantive rights should be the same for ordinary and complex cases."[36]

B. MY ANALYSIS OF THE SINGLE-LAW APPROACH

The normative and constitutional criteria for choice of law set forth in earlier chapters mandate the rejection of the single-law approach for mass torts and class actions. First, the single-law approach is not grounded in positive law. A court might apply a state's rule to a controversy that under that rule's scope does not extend to some parties' claims.[37] For example, in *Phillips Petroleum Co. v. Shutts*, the Kansas trial court employed Kansas law for all claims in a class action concerning whether interest was due on suspended royalties on gas and oil leases, even for claims that had no connection to Kansas.[38] In fact, over 99 percent of the leases and 97 percent of the plaintiffs had no contacts with Kansas. Kansas obviously did not intend its rule to apply to leases and plaintiffs in other states; Kansas had no interest in regulating, or authority to regulate, property and persons outside of Kansas. That this was a class action did not alter this fact. As noted in Chapter 1, the United States Supreme Court ruled that the application of a single rule in a class action was constitutionally improper if there were significant variations among the laws of the connected states.

Agent Orange presents an even more egregious example of a court using law where there was no positive law basis.[39] There was *no* choice of law rule for adopting national consensus law, and, more importantly, there was *no* national consensus law. Law must emanate from a sovereign, and, except for Judge Weinstein's court, there was no sovereign to create national consensus law!

Second, the single-law approach is often not substantively neutral. Many class actions and multidistrict cases use the single-law approach to be pro-plaintiff, as we saw in *Agent Orange*.[40] Other courts adopt the rule that is the same as their state's rule, as we saw in *San Juan Hotel Fire*.[41]

Third, the single-law approach is not forum neutral because it applies a single jurisdiction's law to all claims and that law is usually forum law. For example, *In re Benedictin Litig.*[42] employed Ohio's rule that a plaintiff has the burden of proving fraudulent concealment in a products liability case, despite the fact that many of the claims had been transferred from other jurisdictions and those jurisdictions had a closer connection to the case. If the claims had been tried separately under the proper state law, some of the results might have been different.

Fourth, the single-law approach makes choice of law even more unpredictable. A case's outcome will hinge on whether a series of cases are heard individually or as a class action. The outcome will also depend on where the class action is filed or the cases are consolidated. Predictability is just as important as efficiency.

Fifth, as Professor Sedler has pointed out, the single-jurisdiction approach ignores the relevant states' interests in favor of judicial efficiency. A state should not have to sacrifice its sovereignty to apply its laws to parties and claims that are closely connected to that state just because finding the proper law takes time and resources. Courts rarely limit days of testimony and presentation of evidence in a trial; isn't the law to be applied to that trial just as important?

Finally, the single-law approach is unfair to the individual. It is unfair to a litigant that a different law is applied solely because the case involves complex litigation. As has been stated several times earlier, the fairest choice of law rule is the one that adopts the law of the jurisdiction that is most closely connected to the case. This allows the individual to conform his or her conduct to the law, and it prevents subjecting the individual to inconsistent laws.

Most important, the single-law approach violates the constitutional standard set forth in Chapter 3. Applying one state's law to all claims in a mass disaster will sometimes mean that a court will disregard the law of a state which has a significantly closer connection to a party's claim in favor of the law of a state with a tenuous connection to that claim.

Consider, for example, the hypothetical of a widget that allegedly caused cancer in persons who came into close contact with that widget over time. Injured parties file products liability claims against the widget's Ohio manufacturer in federal district court in all fifty states, and the cases are consolidated in the Southern District of Ohio. All of the states, except Ohio, would allow punitive damages. However, the court, using a single-rule approach, adopts Ohio law and grants partial summary judgment for the defendant based on reasoning similar to that found in the cases discussed earlier in this chapter.

Using Ohio law with the non-Ohio claims would violate my constitutional standard. Under this standard, the cases involving non-Ohio citizens would be more closely connected to the non-Ohio states. A non-Ohio state's connections to the controversy would be (1) the injured party was domiciled there, (2) the product was sold there, and (3) the injury occurred there. Thus, the non-Ohio state has strong quantitative and qualitative connections to the case. On the other hand, Ohio's only connection to the case is that an Ohio manufacturer made the widgets there. A non-Ohio state has a greater interest in applying its punitive damages law to products that were sold and caused injury to a citizen in that state than Ohio does in protecting a corporate domiciliary that does business in all fifty states. In other words, a state should not be able to insulate its domiciliaries for actions that occur in and are more closely connected to another jurisdiction.

Choice of Ohio law would interfere with the individual plaintiffs' due process rights. As stated above, their cases are more closely connected to their home states. Moreover, they would not have expected Ohio law to apply just because their cases had been consolidated with other cases in Ohio. Equally important, using the same law for all claims would interfere with the other states' sovereignty. Because a state has the primary power to regulate conduct within its territory, another state should be able to regulate conduct in that state only upon a showing that the other state has a strong interest in doing so. That a domestic company sells products throughout the United States is not such an interest.[43]

C. ANALYSIS OF EXTENDED EXAMPLES

1. A Hotel Fire Involving Parties from Several States

One can see the application of my method in a hypothetical loosely based on the *Puerto Rico Hotel Fire* case. Suppose a fire in a luxury hotel in Florida killed fifty guests from fifty states. Although a disgruntled employee started the fire, a California manufacturer's sprinkler system failed to stop the fire's spread. The case involves two issues: (1) whether the state of the art defense protects the manufacturer from strict liability and (2) whether the plaintiffs can sue the manufacturer for punitive damages.

Florida along with twenty-four of the other states have not adopted the state of the art defense,[44] while California and the other twenty-four states have. Consider two scenarios for this issue: (1) the state of the injury has not adopted the defense, but the decedent's domicile and the manufacturer's domicile have; and (2) neither the state of the injury nor the decedent's domicile has adopted the defense, but the state of the manufacturer's domicile has.

Under the first scenario, the law of three states are potentially involved: (1) the state of the injury, which does not allow a state of the art defense; (2) the decedent's domicile, which does; and (3) the manufacturer's domicile, which does. A court should adopt the law of the state of the injury because it has a significantly closer connection to the issue. The fact that an injury took place in a state is often the most important connection because a state has a very strong interest in regulating conduct that occurs within the state, regardless of whether the injured party is a state resident, when the place of the injury is not fortuitous.[45] The state where the decedent was domiciled has an interest in having its residents compensated, but not as strong an interest as the accident state has in regulating conduct within that state, particularly when the domiciliary voluntarily went to that state. Moreover, in this case, the rule would protect the manufacturer, not compensate a domiciliary. California does have an interest in protecting its manufacturers by adopting the state of the art defense, but again the interest of the state of the injury seems stronger because a state has to be able to regulate conduct within its territory. (Because under the second scenario the laws of Florida and the decedent's domicile are the same and I have already demonstrated that Florida has the closest connection, the result would be the same as under the first scenario.).

Consider two scenarios for the punitive damages issue: (1) where Florida does not allow punitive damages, but the decedent's domicile and the manufacturer' domicile do, and (2) where Florida and the decedent's domicile do not allow punitive damages, but the manufacturer's domicile does. In the first scenario, Florida's no punitive damages rule could apply to the case because the injury happened in Florida. Similarly, the law of the decedent's domicile could govern because a person's domicile has an interest in extending its pro-punitive damages rule to protect its citizens, while California might use its pro-punitive damages rule to regulate a state manufacturer. Florida, however, would have the closest connection because the accident occurred there; it has the greatest interest in using punitive damages to regulate conduct in Florida. Moreover, its no punitive damages rule probably makes products more available and cheaper in Florida. While the law of the decedent's domicile might constitutionally apply absent a conflict, its connection is not as strong as Florida's because the conduct occurred outside the state. Finally, California's connection is weaker than Florida's because its interest in applying its punitive damages rule to an action that took place in another state is relatively weak. (Again, the result under the second scenario is the same as under the first because Florida still has the closest connection.).

The above analysis would result in the same rules—the state of the art defense would not save the defendant from liability and punitive damages are not recoverable—being applied to all parties' claims. However, it does so by analyzing all potential claims, not by automatically applying a single-rule approach. Cases where different states' laws might apply to different parties' claims include the products liability/punitive damages example discussed earlier in this chapter and the two examples examined below.

2. A Bus Accident Involving Parties from Two States

Professor Sedler presents an example where a court should apply the laws of different states to a common disaster.[46] Twenty people charter a bus in Colorado to go to a convention in Phoenix, Arizona, from a Colorado bus company that operates mainly within that state. Thirty Arizona conventioneers join the others for a sightseeing tour around Phoenix. The bus overturns due to the drivers' negligence, and all the passengers are seriously injured. (Assume the existence of vicarious liability under both states' laws.) Colorado limits damages for noneconomic injuries to $250,000, but Arizona places no limits on such damages. Are there any limits on what the parties can recover for noneconomic damages?

Professor Sedler advocates a result that respects both states' interests: The Arizona plaintiffs should be able to recover unlimited damages under Arizona law, but the Colorado plaintiffs should be subject to the limitations contained in their law. First, a court should apply Colorado law to the Colorado plaintiffs "because the parties are residents of the same state, and the social and economic consequences of the accident, and of allowing or limiting recovery, will be felt by the parties in that state."[47] On the other hand, Professor Sedler believes the Arizona plaintiffs should obtain unlimited recovery under Arizona law because Arizona's policy of permitting such recovery is advanced when the victim is an Arizona resident and because it is not unfair to the Colorado defendant since the accident occurred in Arizona.[48]

Professor Sedler does not think that the difference in the damages recovered by the Arizona plaintiffs and the Colorado plaintiffs is unfair: "The 'mass' nature of the tort has nothing whatsoever to do with the consequences of that tort for the individual victims or the interests of the victims' home states in applying their respective laws to determine the victims' right to tort recovery. The consequences of this mass tort will be felt by the victims in their home states and it is the law of their respective home states that should apply to determine their right to recover."[49]

My method would reach the same result. I would examine each of the groups separately. Concerning the Arizona plaintiffs, Arizona law could apply because the plaintiffs are Arizona citizens and the accident happened there. The Colorado limitation on noneconomic damages could also govern because the Colorado legislature intended it to protect Colorado defendants and the bus company is a Colorado domiciliary. However, a court should adopt Arizona law because it has the closest connection to the case. The accident occurred there, the plaintiffs are from Arizona, and they contracted for the trip in Arizona. The plaintiffs would anticipate that Arizona law would control in such a situation, and the Colorado bus company would not expect that the Colorado limitations would protect it in another state when citizens of that other state are involved. Moreover, Arizona's sovereignty would be hindered if its law were ignored in a case involving an Arizona accident and Arizona citizens.

The situation is different for the Colorado plaintiffs. Although both states' laws could apply, Colorado has a closer connection to the case. The parties contracted for the bus trip in Colorado, the trip was to start and end there, and the parties are from Colorado. Now, the only connection to Arizona is the place of the accident, and, like most cases where common domiciliares are involved in an accident in another state, the place of the accident seems secondary. Moreover, it would impede Colorado's sovereignty if another state interfered with Colorado's ability to govern relationships between its domiciliaries.

3. An Airplane Crash

Airplane crashes present difficult choice of law problems because they usually involve plaintiffs from many jurisdictions, the defendants are often from several states, and, most important, the place of the accident is generally fortuitous because an airplane might crash anywhere along its route.[50] However, even in such a difficult situation, a court should examine each claim separately for the reasons given above.

Consider, for example, some hypotheticals in connection with the air disaster problem presented at the beginning of this chapter. All states allow unlimited damages for wrongful death, except for Kentucky, which caps wrongful death damages at $200,000. Bob is a California resident who bought his ticket in Los

Angeles and boarded the plane there. The place of the accident—Kentucky—is fortuitous so its law should not govern Bob's claim, which means that Bob's estate should recover unlimited damages.

Now assume that only Missouri has a wrongful death damages limitation. Missouri law should not control because it was merely a stopover; several states, including the decedent's domicile, have a closer connection to the case.

What if the only state with a damages limitation is Texas, the airline's domicile? A court should adopt California law to give the estate unlimited damages because California has the closest connection. Although the fact that the airline is incorporated in Texas is an important connection because Texas enacted the limitation to protect its citizens, the connections to California are more significant—the plaintiff is from there, he bought his ticket there, and the flight originated there. Under these circumstances, the plaintiff would probably have expected California law to govern an airplane crash; the airline certainly would not have expected the law of its state of incorporation to govern all accidents in which it might be involved.

What if the damages limitation is in California law? Was the California law intended to protect Texas domiciliaries? Governmental interest analysis would say no, but the analysis is more complex. The airline is operating in California, and the state may have wanted to encourage more airline flights to and from California by limiting the possible damages from airplane crashes.[51] Furthermore, the damages limitation may have lowered the cost of airplane tickets involving California connections. Consequently, this situation is within the scope of California's law. Moreover, California has the closest connection to the case considering the contacts discussed above. Again, Kentucky law should not govern because the place of the accident was fortuitous, and Missouri was merely a stopover. The defendants' domiciles—Texas and Wyoming—have stronger claims to have their laws applied, but California's connections are even stronger—as noted above, the plaintiff is from California, he bought his ticket there, and the flight originated there. When an accident occurs outside the defendant's domicile and parties from other jurisdictions are involved, a plaintiff should no more be able to get the benefit of the defendant's home state's law just because the defendant is domiciled there than a defendant should be able to claim the protections of those laws.[52]

The analysis would be similar if a Missouri resident had bought the ticket in Missouri and boarded the plane in St. Louis. Kentucky law would be irrelevant because the place of the accident is fortuitous. The fact that the flight started in California would also be irrelevant; the decedent probably did not know that the flight originated there. Of the remaining connections, the ones with Missouri seem most significant—the decedent was a Missouri resident, she bought the ticket there, and she boarded the plane there.

What if the decedent was returning from California to his home in New York where he had bought the round-trip ticket? A court should choose New York law because the trip originated there, the passenger bought the ticket there, and he was domiciled there. The fact that there was a longer stopover in Los Angeles than St. Louis is not enough to make California law apply.

Finally, what law should apply when the decedent is from a different state and bought the ticket in a different state than the one in which she started her plane trip. For example, assume that decedent was from Oregon and bought her ticket for Los Angeles to New York there, but took a bus from Portland to Los Angeles. In this case, a court should apply Oregon law because it has a stronger connection to the case than any other state since the plaintiff was domiciled there and she bought the ticket there. However, this conclusion seems a little troubling because Oregon law is being applied to an accident that occurred in Kentucky during a flight from California to New York involving a plane owned by a Texas corporation and manufactured by a Wyoming corporation. I suggest a statutory solution to this problem in the next section.

4. Choice of Law Principles for Mass Torts

One can extract a few principles from the above analyses of mass torts. When the tort occurs in a state where the place of the accident is not fortuitous (where the parties voluntarily and knowingly went to that jurisdiction and should have realized that that jurisdiction's laws could govern their rights and conduct), the place of the accident is usually the most important connection for choice of law, at least when the issue involves conduct regulation. An example of this is a hotel fire because the injured parties voluntarily went to that state. When the place of the injury is fortuitous, such as with an airplane crash, the place of the accident becomes less important, and other factors, such as the decedent's domicile, the state in which the decedent purchased an airplane ticket, and the state where the plane trip began, become more important. In either case, the analysis should not be mechanical; the court should consider each factor as it applies to the particular matter to determine which state has the closest connection.

D. A FEDERAL SOLUTION TO CERTAIN CHOICE OF LAW PROBLEMS CONCERNING MASS TORTS

I believe that a court must analyze choice of law separately for each party in a mass tort because combining claims through class action or consolidation should not change the choice of law analysis.[53] However, this solution is not totally satisfactory because it means that persons injured in the same accident might be compensated differently.

Some scholars are not bothered by this inconsistency.[54] For example, Professor Weintraub has written that two passengers from different states

> would be treated differently if there was no question that the law of their own state applied—each killed at home by a local tortfessor. This differential treatment is not arbitrary but, rather, the result of our federal system. It may well be that the state X limits on recovery are anachronistic, cruel, or any other pejorative that may leap to the outraged mind; however, that is the business of state X's residents and the X legislature. State X's law should not be displaced between parties from state X just because the plane had previously touched down in other states and

was destined to land in still other states.[55]

On the other hand, many scholars are bothered by this disparity for the reasons given earlier.[56]

Because, as mentioned above, choice of law cannot provide a solution to this disparity, the answer must come from substantive law. That answer, however, cannot come from federal common law because federal judges lack the power to make law for mass tort cases.[57] There is nothing in the Constitution that gives them such authority.

Congress, however, could provide remedies for injuries caused by mass torts with multistate connections under its interstate commerce power.[58] The question, then, is how far should Congress go? Congress should be careful in intruding into a state's power to regulate private, localized disputes, even when it has the power under the commerce clause to do so; Congress should pass laws regulating mass torts only when the tort is of a truly interstate character.

Mass torts where the tort is firmly centered in one state should not be governed by federal law, even if parties from several states are involved. The hotel fire in the above example is such a case because the place of the accident was not fortuitous since the parties had voluntarily gone to that state. In such a case, choice of law will generally not produce inconsistent results because the place of the accident will be the most important connection and the place of the accident is the same for all claims.

Mass torts that involve separate injuries to many defendants in several states, such as asbestos or silicone breast implant cases, should also not be subject to federal law. Because each injury is a separate injury involving products sold in a state to state residents, the state of the plaintiff's domicile should be able to decide the grounds for, defenses against, and amount of recovery; buying a product in a state localizes the transaction. I am not troubled by the fact that a plaintiff in State A might receive $100,000 in damages when injured by a product, while a defendant who is injured by the same product in State B receives nothing. Different states have different laws, and being part of a community is accepting that community's decisions.

Airplane accidents beginning and ending in different states and involving parties from several jurisdictions, however, are different. Justice seems to dictate that recovery be the same for all persons involved in the same accident who have similar injuries, unless there is a strong reason for different compensation. Moreover, in such a case, the controversy seems national rather than local.[59] First, the place of the accident is fortuitous; an airplane can crash anytime during a flight. Second, a flight starting in one state and ending in another is multistate by definition. Third, a flight starting in one state and ending in another brings together passengers from many jurisdictions. Finally, modern interstate travel normally involves defendants from many states.

Based on the above, Congress should pass a statute that gives uniform substantive law to mass disasters when the place of the injury is fortuitous, parties from different states are involved, and there are multistate elements involved other than the parties, such as when an airline flight begins and ends in different states. This rule should apply regardless of whether the claims are consolidated or heard in several jurisdictions.

Note that the above is a substantive solution, not a choice of law solution. I am not proposing that Congress develop choice of laws rule for certain mass disasters. Rather, I am advocating that Congress replace state substantive law with federal substantive law when a mass tort is truly multistate.

E. CONCLUSION

In sum, after examining whether the single-law approach should apply in mass disasters that involve class actions or multidistrict litigation, I have concluded that normative choice of law criteria and constitutional constraints on choice of law dictate that choice of law should be the same in complex litigation as it is in two-party litigation. The efficiency gained by the single-law approach simply does not overcome the losses to individual rights and state sovereignty. However, Congress should pass uniform federal substantive law for mass torts that are genuinely multistate.

NOTES

1. "A 'mass tort' is one in which many victims—dozens, hundreds, or, with increasing frequency, thousands—are injured by the same wrongful conduct." Russell J. Weintraub, *Methods for Resolving Conflict-of-Laws Problems in Mass Tort Litigation*, 1989 U. ILL. L. REV. 129 (1989).

2. "Unlike the typical two-party suit, a class action is a procedural device which allows a group of individuals with common interests to join together to pursue their collective claims through representatives." *Austin v. Pennsylvania Dep't of Corrections*, 876 F. Supp. 1437, 1454 (E.D. Pa. 1995). Class actions are most commonly brought under Fed. R. Civ. P. 23.

3. "When civil actions involving one or more common (and often complex) questions of fact are pending in several federal district courts, such actions may be transferred to one district for coordinated and consolidated management and trial under a single judge. 28 U.S.C.A. § 1407 . . . . Such cases are assigned and transferred by a Judicial Panel on Multidistrict Litigation, and are governed by the 'Manual for Complex Litigation' and 'Rules of Procedure on Multidistrict Litigation.'" BLACK'S LAW DICTIONARY 1015 (1990). Although transfer is intended for pretrial matters only, transferee courts have often retained cases for trial. Larry Kramer, *Choice of Law in Complex Litigation*, 71 N.Y.U. L. REV. 547, 552 (1996). However, the Supreme Court has recently eliminated this possibility. *Lexecon, Inc. v. Milberg Weiss Bershad Hynes & Lerach*, 118 S.Ct. 956, 962–64 (1998). Still, courts in consolidated cases must deal with choice of law problems in pretrial motions.

4. Larry Kramer has declared that "it is remarkable how often courts adjudicating mass actions nevertheless find that one law applies to all the claims or to each issue." Kramer, *supra* note 3, at 552.

5. In re "Agent Orange" Prod. Liab. Litig., 580 F. Supp. 690 (E.D.N.Y. 1984).

6. *Id.* at 693.

7. Klaxon Co. v. Stentor Elec. Mfg. Co., 313 U.S. 487, 496 (1941).

8. Van Dusen v. Barrack, 376 U.S. 612 (1964); *see also* In re Air Crash Disaster at Boston, Mass. on July 31, 1973, 399 F. Supp. 1106, 1119–22 (D. Mass. 1975).

9. *Agent Orange*, 580 F. Supp. 694, 696–97, 710–713.

10. *Id.* at 694.

11. *Id.* at 710.

12. *Id.* at 711.

13. *Id.*

14. *Id.* at 712.

15. Kramer, *supra* note 3, at 561–64; PETER H. SCHUCK, AGENT ORANGE ON TRIAL: MASS TOXIC DISASTERS IN COURTS 128–31 (1987); *see also* Aaron D. Twerski, *With Liberty and Justice for All: An Essay on Agent Orange and Choice of Law*, 52 BROOK. L. REV. 341 (1986) [hereinafter Twereski, *Agent Orange*].

16. There was no precedent for this.

17. Twerski, *Agent Orange*, *supra* note 15, at 353–67.

18. *Agent Orange,* 380 F. Supp. at 711–13.

19. Judge Weinstein has written, "Had it not been settled, the Agent Orange case would have had to be dismissed since there was insufficient evidence that the sprayings had caused illness to particular persons and because, under various Supreme Court cases, neither the government nor the companies from whom the herbicides had been purchashed could be sued for discretionary acts of the government in waging the Viet Nam War." JACK B. WEINSTEIN, INDIVIDUAL JUSTICE IN MASS TORT LITIGATION xii (1995). For a full discussion of the difficulties Judge Weinstein faced in the case, *see* SCHUCK, *supra* note 15.

20. Judge Weinstein's choice of law decision was never reviewed by an appellate court because the case was settled on the eve of trial. SCHUCK, *supra* note 15, at 143–67.

21. 644 F.2d 594 (7th Cir. 1981).

22. *Id.* at 629–30. Professor Kramer calls the court's analysis of Michigan law a "grotesque distortion." Kramer, *supra* note 3, at 559.

23. Sweeney v. Sweeney, 262 N.W.2d 625 (Mich. 1978); *see also* Herma Hill Kay, *Theory into Practice*, 34 MERCER L. REV. 521, 579–81 (1983); Gregory E. Smith, *Choice of Law in the United States*, 38 HASTINGS L.J. 1041, 1085–87 (1987).

24. *Sweeney*, 262 N.W.2d at 629–30.

25. In re San Juan Dupont Plaza Hotel Fire Litig., 745 F. Supp. 79 (D.P.R. 1990).

26. *Id.* at 86.

27. The court's conclusion is correct for a different reason, as set forth below. Nonetheless, a New York court would have adopted its law if the case had been heard in New York. *See* Rosenthal v. Warren, 475 F.2d 438 444–46 (2d Cir. 1973); Calla v. Shulsky, 543 N.Y.S.2d 666 (App. Div. 1989), *overruled by*, Huston v. Harden Bldg. Maintenance Corp., 617 N.Y.S.2d 335 (App. Div. 1994) (*Calla* is one of the cases cited by the court in support of its arguments).

28. WEINSTEIN, *supra* note 19, at 21, 25, 146; James A. R. Nafziger, *Choice of Law in Air Disaster Cases: Complex Litigation Rules and the Common Law*, 54 LA. L. REV. 1001 (1994); Friederich K. Juenger, *Mass Disasters and the Conflict of Laws*, 1989 U. ILL. L. REV. 105, 125–27 (1989); Briggs L. Tobin, Comment, *The 'Limited Generosity' Class Action and A Uniform Choice of Law Rule: An Approach to Fair and Effective Mass-Tort Punitive Damage Adjudication in the Federal Courts*, 38 EMORY L.J. 457 (1989); Paul S. Bird, Note, *Mass Tort Litigation: A Statutory Solution to the Choice of Law Impasse*, 96 YALE L.J. 1077 (1987).

29. Juenger, *supra* note 28, at 109; Tobin, *supra* note 28, at 480; Bird, *supra* note 28, at 1077; Willis L. M. Reese, *The Law Governing Airplane Accidents*, 39 WASH. & LEE L. REV. 1303, 1306–8 (1982); *see also* Kramer, *supra* note 3, at 566–67.

30. Kramer, *supra* note 3, at 547; Robert A. Sedler, *The Complex Litigation Project's Proposal for Federally-Mandated Choice of Law in Mass Tort Cases: Another Assault on State Sovereignty*, 54 LA. L. REV. 1085 (1994); Robert A. Sedler, *Interest Analysis, State Sovereignty, and Federally-Mandated Choice of Law in "Mass Tort" Cases, 56* ALB. L. REV. 855 (1993) [hereinafter Sedler, *Interest Analysis*]; Robert A. Sedler & Aaron D. Twerski, *State Choice of Law in Mass Tort Cases: A Response to "A View from the Legislature,"* 73 MARQ. L. REV. 625 (1989); Robert A. Sedler & Aaron D. Twerski, *The Case against All Encompassing Federal Mass Tort Litigation: Sacrifice without Gain*, 73 MARQ. L. REV. 76 (1989).

31. Sedler, *Interest Analysis*, *supra* note 30, at 861–64.

32. *Id.* at 870.

33. *Id.* at 863.

34. *Id.* at 862.

35. *Id.* at 869. For example, Professors Reavley and Wesevich advocate that Congress mandate a place of the wrong rule for single-accident mass torts. Thomas M. Reavley & Jerome W. Wesevich, *An Old Rule for New Reasons: Place of the Injury as a Federal Solution to Choice of Law in Single-Accident Mass-Tort Cases*, 71 TEXAS L. REV. 1, 43 (1992).

36. Kramer, *supra* note 3, at 549. Later he asserted that "because choice of law is substantive, the fact of consolidation alone is not enough to justify changing the otherwise applicable laws." *Id.* at 569.

37. Professor Kramer has written that "the extraterritorial reach of a law is still an element of a claim or defense based on that law, determined by a process of interpretation that is, because it directly defines the parties' rights, the very paradigm of what we mean by 'substantive.'" Kramer, *supra* note 3, at 571–72.

38. 472 U.S. 797 (1985). Chapter 3 discussed this case in detail.

39. *Agent Orange*, 580 F. Supp. at 690.

40. *See supra* notes 5–20 and accompanying text.

41. *See supra* notes 25–27 and accompanying text.

42. 857 F.2d 290 (6th Cir. 1988).

43. See the discussion of *Rosenthal* in Chapter 3, where I argued that a state does not have a strong interest in applying its law to all types of issues *solely* because a domicilliary is involved.

44. "In the context of products liability case means level of pertinent scientific and technical knowledge at time of manufacture." BLACK'S LAW DICTIONARY 1409 (1990).

45. The location of an accident would be fortuitous when the place of that accident is changeable. For example, an airplane crash can occur anywhere along the plane's route. A person would not expect that the law of such a jurisdiction would control the lawsuit. In the present case, the place of the accident is not fortuitous because the plaintiffs intentionally came to the jurisdiction, and they knew that that jurisdiction's laws might govern their rights and conduct.

46. Sedler, *Interest Analysis*, *supra* note 30, at 876–78.

47. *Id.* at 876.

48. *Id.*

49. *Id.* at 877.

50. This is mainly a problem with domestic air crashes. The Warsaw Convention has unified many aspects of international air transportation law. *See* P. John Kozyris, *The Conflicts Provisions of the ALI's Complex Litigation Project: A Glass Half Full?* 54 LA. L. REV. 953 (1994).

51. *C.f.*, Hall v. General Motors Corp., 582 N.W.2d 866, 869 (Mich. App. 1998).

52. As one court has stated, a state's interest in deterring a manufacturer from manufacturing defective products within a state's borders is adequately served by applying that state's laws to the claims filed by that state's plaintiffs. *Vestal v. Shiley, Inc.*, 1997 WL 910373, at *3 (C.D. Cal. 1997).

53. As Professor Kramer has pointed out, the *Asbestos School Litigation* effectively managed complex litigation involving the laws of several states without distorting those states' choice of law rules. Kramer, *supra* note 3, at 585–87, *citing*, *In re Asbestos School Litigation*, 104 F.R.D. 422, 434 (E.D. Pa. 1984) (other citations omitted).

54. *E.g.*, Weintraub, *supra* note 1, at 134; Sedler, *Interest Analysis, supra* note 30, at 876–78. Professor Sedler strongly opposes a federal statutory solution. *See* the Sedler articles, *supra* note 30.

55. Weintraub, *supra* note 1, at 134.

56. Reavley & Wesevich, *supra* note 35, at 23–24; Reese, *supra* note 29, at 1306–8; *see also supra* note 29.

57. Kramer, *supra* note 3, at 550; Larry Kramer, *The Law Making Power of Federal Courts*, 12 PACE L. REV. 263 (1992); Barbara Ann Atwood, *The Choice-of-Law Dilemma in Mass Tort Litigation: Kicking Around Erie, Klaxon, and Van Dusen*, 19 CONN. L. REV. 9, 19–27, 40–41 (1986); MARTIN H. REDISH, THE FEDERAL COURTS IN THE POLITICAL ORDER: JUDICIAL JURISDICTION AND AMERICAN POLITICAL THEORY 29–46 (1991); *but see* Linda S. Mullenix, *Federalizing Choice of Law for Mass Tort Litigation*, 70 TEXAS L. REV. 1623, 1631, 1660–62 (1992).

58. U.S. Const. art 1, § 8, cl. 3. *See, e.g.*, Reavley & Wesevich, *supra* note 35, at 37; Symeon C. Symeonides, *The ALI's Complex Litigation Project: Commencing the National Debate*, 54 LA. L. REV. 843, 852, 855 n.55 (1994). There have been several proposals for uniform federal law with certain mass torts. *E.g.*, THE AMERICAN LAW INSTITUTE, COMPLEX LITIGATION PROJECT PROPOSED FINAL DRAFT §§ 6.01–.07 (May 1993) (proposing a uniform federal choice of law rule); *The Multiparty, Multiform Jurisdiction Act of 1991*, H.R. 2450, 102d Cong., 1st Sess. (1991) (The House passed the bill, but it did not make it out of the Senate Judiciary Subcommittee on Courts and Administrative Practice. Sedler, *Interest Analysis, supra* note 30, at 860 n.20.).

59. Professor Kozyris has written that "at least in some fields, especially mass torts and certain standardized contracts, the assumption of localism is no longer true." Kozyris, *supra* note 50, at 953.

Bibliography

Amar, Akil Reed. *Of Sovereignty and Federalism*, 96 YALE L.J. 1425 (1987).

Atwood, Barbara Ann. *The Choice-of-Law Dilemma in Mass Tort Litigation: Kicking Around Erie, Klaxon, and Van Dusen*, 19 CONN. L. REV. 9 (1986).

Baxter, William F. *Choice of Law and the Federal System*, 16 STAN. L. REV. 1 (1963).

Beale, Joseph H. *Dicey's "Conflict of Laws,"* 10 HARV. L. REV. 168 (1896).

BEALE, JR., JOSEPH H. A SELECTION OF CASES ON THE CONFLICT OF LAWS (1900, 1902).

Beale, Joseph. *What Law Governs the Validity of a Contract*, 23 HARV. L. REV. 1 (1909).

BEALE, JOSEPH. A TREATISE ON THE CONFLICT OF LAWS (1935).

Bird, Paul S. Note, *Mass Tort Litigation: A Statutory Solution to the Choice of Law Impasse*, 96 YALE L.J. 1077 (1987).

Bliesener, Dirk H. *Fairness and Choice of Law: A Critique of the Political Rights-Based Approach to the Conflict of Laws*, 42 AM. J. COMP. L. 687 (1994).

Borchers, Patrick J. *The Origins of Diversity Jurisdiction, the Rise of Legal Positivism, and a Brave New World for Erie and Klaxon*, 72 TEX. L. REV. 79 (1993).

Borchers, Patrick J. *Courts and the Second Conflicts Restatement: Some Observations and an Empirical Note*, 56 MD. L. REV. 1232 (1997).

Brilmayer, Lea. *Interest Analysis and the Myth of Legislative Intent*, 78 MICH. L. REV. 392 (1980).

Brilmayer, Lea. *Methods and Objectives in the Conflict of Laws: A Challenge*, 35 MERCER L. REV. 555 (1984).

Brilmayer, Lea. *Shaping and Sharing in Democratic Theory: Towards a Political Theory of Interstate Equality*, 15 FLA. ST. U.L. REV. 389, 412-13 (1987).

Brilmayer, Lea. *The Role of Substantive and Choice of Law Policies in the Formation and Application of Choice of Law Rules*, 252 RECUIL DES COURS D'ACADEMIE DE DROIT

INTERNATIONAL (1989).

BRILMAYER, LEA. CONFLICT OF LAWS (2d ed. 1995).

Brown, Jennifer Gerarda. *Competitive Federalism and the Legislative Incentives to Recognize Same-Sex Marriages*, 68 S. CAL. L. REV. 745 (1995).

Cavers, David F. *A Critique of the Choice-of-Law Problem*, 47 HARV. L. REV. 173 (1933).

Cavers, David F. *Re-Restatement of the Conflict of Laws: The Chapter on Contracts, in* XXTH CENTURY COMPARATIVE AND CONFLICTS LAWS (Kurt H. Nadlemann et. al. eds., 1961).

CAVERS, DAVID. THE CHOICE-OF-PROCESS (1965).

CHEATHAM, ELLIOT E. ET. AL. CASES AND MATERIALS ON CONFLICT OF LAWS (1941).

Cheatham, Elliot E. & Willis L. M. Reese. *Choice of the Applicable Law*, 52 COLUM. L. REV. 959 (1952).

Cohen, Felix. *Transcendental Nonsense and the Functional Approach*, 35 COLUM. L. REV. 809 (1935).

Cook, Walter W. *The Logical and Legal Bases of the Conflict of Laws*, 33 YALE L.J. 457 (1924).

Cook, Walter W. *Scientific Method of the Law*, 13 A.B.A. J. 303 (1927).

Cook, Walter Wheeler. *"Contracts" and the Conflict of Laws: "Intention" of the Parties*, 32 ILL. L. REV. 899 (1938).

Corr, John Bernard. *Interest Analysis and Choice of Law: The Dubious Dominance of Domicile*, 1983 UTAH L. REV. 651 (1983).

CURRIE, BRAINERD. SELECTED ESSAYS ON THE CONFLICT OF LAWS (1963).

Currie, Brainerd. *The Disinterested Third State*, 28 LAW AND CONT. PROBLEMS 754 (1963).

Currie, David et al. *Choice-of-Law Symposium Transcript*, 48 MERCER L. REV. 639 (1997).

Currie, David. *Full Faith and Credit to Marriages*, 1 GREEN BAG 7 (1997).

Dane, Perry. *Vested Rights, 'Vestedness,' and Choice of Law*, 96 YALE L.J. 1191 (1987).

Dane, Perry. *Conflict of Laws,* in A COMPANION TO PHILOSOPHY OF LAW AND LEGAL THEORY (1996).

DICEY, A. V. A DIGEST OF THE LAW OF ENGLAND WITH REFERENCE TO THE CONFLICT OF LAWS (1896).

Dodge, William S. *Extraterritoriality and Conflicts of Law Theory: An Argument for Judicial Unilateralism*, 39 HARV. INT. L.J. 101 (1998).

DWORKIN, RONALD. TAKING RIGHTS SERIOUSLY (1978).

DWORKIN, RONALD. LAW'S EMPIRE (1986).

Ehrenzweig, Albert A. *The "Most Significant Relationship" in the Conflicts Law of Torts: Law and Reason Versus the Second Restatement*, 28 LAW & CONTEMP. PROBS. 700 (1963).

Ehrenzweig, Albert A. *The Second Conflicts Restatement: A Last Appeal for Its Withdrawal*, 113 U. PA. L. REV. 1230 (1965).

Ely, John Hart. *Choice of Law and the State's Interest in Protecting its Own*, 23 WM & MARY L. REV. 173 (1981).

FINNIS, JOHN. NATURAL LAW AND NATURAL RIGHTS (1980).

Fruehwald, Scott. *Choice of Law in Federal Courts: A Reevaluation*, 37 BRANDEIS L.J. 21 (1998–99).

Fruehwald, Scott. *Choice of Law and Same-Sex Marriage*, 51 FLA. L. REV. 799 (1999).

Fruehwald, Scott. *If Men Were Angels: The New Judicial Activism in Theory and Practice*, 83 MARQ. L. REV. 435 (1999).

Freund, Paul A. *Chief Justice Stone and the Conflict of Laws*, 59 HARV. L. REV. 1210 (1946).

FULLER, LON L. THE MORALITY OF LAW (1964).

GIERKE, O. VON. DEUTSCHES PRIVATRECHT (1895).

GILMORE, GRANT. THE AGES OF AMERICAN LAW (1977).

Grey, Thomas C. *Langdell's Orthodoxy*, 45 U. PITT. L. REV. 1 (1983).

GOODRICH, HERBERT F. HANDBOOK ON THE CONFLICT OF LAWS (1927).

Gottesman, Michael H. *Adrift on the Sea of Indeterminancy*, 75 IND. L.J. 527 (2000).

Hancock, Moffatt. *Choice-of-Law Policies in Multiple Contact Cases*, 5 U. TORONTO L.J. 133 (1943).

HARPER, FOWLER VINCENT & CHARLES W. TAINTOR II. CASES AND OTHER MATERIALS ON JUDICIAL TECHNIQUE IN CONFLICT OF LAWS (1937).

Harper, Fowler V. *Policy Bases of the Conflict of Laws: Reflections on Reading Professor Lorenzen's Essays*, 56 YALE L.J. 1155 (1947).

Hay, Peter. *Full Faith and Credit and Federalism in Choice of Law*, 34 MERCER L. REV. 709 (1983).

Hilliard, James W. *To Accomplish Fairness and Justice: Substantive Due Process*, 30 J. MARSHALL L. REV. 95 (1996).

Hohfeld, Wesley Newcomb. *Some Fundamental Legal Conceptions as Applied in Judicial Reasoning*, 23 YALE L.J. 16 (1913).

Hohfeld, Wesley Newcomb. *Fundamental Legal Conceptions as Applied in Judicial Reasoning*, 26 YALE L.J. 710 (1917).

HOLMES, OLIVER W. THE COMMON LAW (1881).

HORWITZ, MORTON J. THE TRANSFORMATION OF AMERICAN LAW, 1870–1960: THE CRISIS OF LEGAL ORTHODOXY (1992).

Jackson, Robert H. *Full Faith and Credit—The Lawyer's Clause of the Constitution*, 45 COLUM. L. REV. 1 (1945).

Juenger, Friederich K. *Mass Disasters and the Conflict of Laws*, 1989 U. ILL. L. REV. 105 (1989).

JUENGER,FRIEDRICH K. CHOICE OF LAW AND MULTISTATE JUSTICE (1993).

Juenger, Friedrich K. *A Third Conflicts Restatement*, 75 IND. L.J. 403 (2000).

Kay, Herma Hill. *Theory into Practice: Choice of Law in the Courts*, 34 MERCER L. REV. 521 (1983).

Kennedy, Duncan. *Towards an Historical Understanding of Legal Consciousness: The Case of Classical Legal Thought in America, 1850–1940*, 3 RES. LAW & SOC. 3 (1980).

Kirgis, Jr., Frederic L. *The Role of Due Process and Full Faith and Credit in Choice of Law*, 61 CORNELL L. REV. 185 (1976).

Kogan, Terry. *Toward a Jurisprudence of Choice of Law, the Priority of Fairness over Comity*, 62 N.Y.U. L. REV. 651 (1987).

Korn, Harold L. *The Choice of Law Revolution: A Critique*, 83 COLUM. L. REV. 772 (1983).

Kozyris, P. John. *Reflections on Allstate—The Lessening of Due Process on Choice of Law*, 14 U.C. DAVIS L. REV. 889 (1981).

Kozyris, P. John. *The Conflicts Provisions of the ALI's Complex Litigation Project: A Glass Half Full?* 54 LA. L. REV. 953 (1994).

Kramer, Larry. *Rethinking Choice of Law*, 90 COLUM. L. REV. 277 (1990).

Kramer, Larry. *Choice of Law in American Courts in 1990: Trends and Developments*, 39 AM. J. COMP. L. 465 (1991).

Kramer, Larry. *The Law Making Power of Federal Courts*, 12 PACE L. REV. 263 (1992).

Kramer, Larry. *Choice of Law in Complex Litigation*, 71 N.Y.U. L. REV. 547 (1996).

Kramer, Larry. *Same-Sex Marriage: Conflict of Laws and the Unconstitutional Public Policy Exception*, 106 YALE L.J. 1965 (1997).

Kreimer, Seth F. *Territoriality and Moral Dissensus: Thoughts on Abortion, Slavery, Gay Marriage and Family Values*, 16 QUINNIPIAC L. REV. 161 (1996).

Laycock, Douglas. *Equal Citizens of Equal and Territorial States: The Constitutional Foundations of Choice of Law*, 92 COLUM. L. REV. 249 (1992).
Leflar, Robert A. *Constitutional Limits on Free Choice of Law*, 28 LAW & CONTEMP. PROBS. 706 (1963).
LEFLAR, ROBERT A. AMERICAN CONFLICTS LAW (3d ed. 1977).
Lorenzen, Ernest G. *Validity and Effects of Contracts in the Conflict of Laws*, 30 YALE L.J. 655 (1921).
Lorenzen, Ernest G. *Territoriality, Public Policy and the Conflict of Laws*, 33 YALE L.J. 736 (1924).
Maier, Harold G. *Finding the Trees in Spite of the Metaphorist: The Problem of State Interests in Choice of Law*, 56 ALB. L. REV. 753 (1993).
Maltz, Earl M. *Visions of Fairness—The Relationship between Jurisdiction and Choice of Law*, 30 ARIZ. L. REV. 751 (1988).
Martin, James A. *Constitutional Limitations on Choice of Law*, 61 CORNELL L. REV. 185 (1976).
McDougal, III, Luther L. *Comprehensive Interest Analysis Versus Reformulated Governmental Interest Analysis: An Appraisal in the Context of Choice-of-Law Problems Concerning Contributory and Comparative Negligence*, 26 UCLA L. REV. 439 (1979).
Mensch, Elizabeth. *The History of Mainstream Legal Thought*, *in* THE POLITICS OF LAW (David Kairys ed., 1982).
MINOR, RALEIGH C. CONFLICT OF LAWS (1901).
Morris, J. H. C. *The Proper Law of a Tort*, 64 HARV. L. REV. 881 (1951).
Mullenix, Linda S. *Federalizing Choice of Law for Mass Tort Litigation*, 70 TEXAS L. REV. 1623 (1992).
MURPHY, JEFFRIE G. & JULES L. COLEMAN. PHILOSOPHY OF LAW: AN INTRODUCTION TO JURISPRUDENCE (1990).
Nafziger, James A. R. *Choice of Law in Air Disaster Cases: Complex Litigation Rules and the Common Law*, 54 LA. L. REV. 1001 (1994).
NEELY, RICHARD. THE PRODUCT LIABILITY MESS: HOW BUSINESS CAN BE RESCUED FROM THE POLITICS OF STATE COURTS (1988).
NOWAK, JOHN E. & RONALD D. ROTUNDA. CONSTITUTIONAL LAW (5th ed. 1995).
Pielemeier, James R. *Why We Should Worry about Full Faith and Credit to Laws*, 60 S. CAL. L. REV. 1299 (1987).
Posnak, Bruce. *The Court Doesn't Know Its Asahi from Its Wortman, A Critical View of the Constitutional Constraints of Jurisdiction on Choice of Law*, 41 SYRACUSE L. REV. 875 (1989).
Posnak, Bruce. *The Restatement (Second): Some Not So Fine Tuning for a Restatement (Third): A Very Well-Curried Leflar over Reese with Korn on the Side (Or Is It Cob)*, 75 IND. L.J. 561 (2000).
Pound, Roscoe. *Mechanical Jurisprudence*, 8 COLUM. L. REV. 605 (1908).
Pound, Roscoe. *The Theory of Judicial Decisions*, 36 HARV. L. REV. 641 (1923).
Prosser, William L. *Interstate Publication*, 51 MICH. L. REV. 959 (1952–53).
Rawls, John. *Justice as Fairness,* in JUSTICE AND SOCIAL POLICY (1961).
RAWLS, JOHN. A THEORY OF JUSTICE (1971).
Reavley Thomas M. & Jerome W. Wesevich. *An Old Rule for New Reasons: Place of the Injury as a Federal Solution to Choice of Law in Single-Accident Mass-Tort Cases*, 71 TEXAS L. REV. 1 (1992).
Redish, Martin. *Due Process, Federalism and Personal Jurisdiction: A Theoretical Evaluation*, 75 NW. U.L. REV. 1112 (1981).
REDISH, MARTIN H. THE FEDERAL COURTS IN THE POLITICAL ORDER: JUDICIAL JURISDICTION

AND AMERICAN POLITICAL THEORY (1991).
Redish, Martin H. *Procedural Due Process and Aggregation Devices in Mass Tort Litigation*, 63 DEF. COUNS. J. 18 (1996).
Reese, Willis L. M. *Conflict of Laws and the Restatement Second*, 28 LAW & CONTEMP. PROBS. 679 (1963).
Reese, Willis L. M. *Legislative Jurisdiction*, 78 COLUM. L. REV. 1587 (1978).
Reese, Willis L. M. *The Hague Case: An Opportunity Lost*, 10 HOFSTRA L. REV. 195 (1981).
Reese, Willis L. M. *The Law Governing Airplane Accidents*, 39 WASH. & LEE L. REV. 1303 (1982).
Reese, Willis L. M. *The Second Restatement of Conflicts Revisited*, 34 MERCER L. REV. 501 (1983).
Reiman, Mathias. Savigny's Triumph? Choice of Law in Contracts Cases at the Close of the Twentieth Century, 39 VA. J. INT. L. 571 (1999).
Reppy, Jr., William A. *Eclecticism in Choice of Law: Hybrid Method or Mishmash?* 34 MERCER L. REV. 645 (1983).
Reppy, Jr., William A. *Codifying Interest Analysis in the Torts Chapter of a New Conflicts Restatement*, 75 IND. L.J. 591 (2000).
RESTATEMENT OF THE LAW OF CONFLICT OF LAWS (1934).
RESTATEMENT (SECOND) OF CONFLICT OF LAWS (1971).
Roosevelt III, Kermit. *The Myth of Choice of Law: Rethinking Conflicts*, 97 MICH. L. REV. 2448 (1999).
SAVIGNY, FRIEDRICH CARL VON. PRIVATE INTERNATIONAL LAW (1869).
Scalia, Antonin. *The Rule of Law as a Law of Rules*, 56 U. CHI. L. REV. 1175 (1989).
SCHUCK, PETER H. AGENT ORANGE ON TRIAL: MASS TOXIC DISASTERS IN COURTS (1987).
Sedler, Robert A. *Constitutional Limitations on Choice of Law: The Perspective of Constitutional Generalism*, 10 HOFSTRA L. REV. 54 (1981).
Sedler Robert A. & Aaron D. Twerski. *The Case against All Encompassing Federal Mass Tort Litigation: Sacrifice without Gain*, 73 MARQ. L. REV. 76 (1989).
Sedler Robert A. & Aaron D. Twerski. *State Choice of Law in Mass Tort Cases: A Response to "A View from the Legislature,"* 73 MARQ. L. REV. 625 (1989).
Sedler, Robert A. *Interest Analysis, State Sovereignty, and Federally-Mandated Choice of Law in "Mass Tort" Cases, 56* ALB. L. REV. 855 (1993).
Sedler, Robert A. *The Complex Litigation Project's Proposal for Federally-Mandated Choice of Law in Mass Tort Cases: Another Assault on State Sovereignty*, 54 LA. L. REV. 1085 (1994).
Shreve, Gene R. *Choice of Law and the Forgiving Constitution*, 71 IND. L.J. 271 (1996).
Silberman, Linda. *Shaffer v. Heitner: The End of an Era*, 53 N.Y.U. L. REV. 33 (1978).
Silberman, Linda. *Can the State of Minnesota Bind the Nation? Federal Choice of Law Constraints after Allstate Insurance Co. v. Hague*, 10 HOFSTRA L. REV. 103 (1981).
Silberman, Linda J. *Can the Island of Hawaii Bind the World? A Comment on Same-Sex Marriage and Federalism Values*, 16 QUINNIPIAC L. REV. 191 (1996).
Simson, Gary J. *Resisting the Allure of Better Rule of Law*, 52 ARK. L. REV. 141 (1999).
Singer, Joseph William. *Real Conflicts*, 69 B.U. L. REV. 1 (1989).
Singer, Joseph William. *A Pragmatic Guide to Conflicts*, 70 B.U. L. REV. 731 (1990).
Singer, Joseph William. *Pay No Attention to the Man Behind the Curtain: The Place of Better Law in a Third Restatement of Conflicts*, 75 IND. L.J. 659 (2000).
Smart, J. J. C. & Bernard Williams. *An Outline of a System of Utilitarian Ethics* in UTILITARIANISM: FOR AND AGAINST (1973).
Smith, Gregory E. *Choice of Law in the United States*, 38 HASTINGS L.J. 1041 (1987).

Southerland, Harold P. *Sovereignty, Value Judgments, and Choice of Law*, 38 BRANDEIS L.J. 451 (2000).

Speziale, Marcia. *Langdell's Concept of Law as Science: The Beginning of Anti-Formalism in American Legal Thought*, 5 VT. L. REV 1 (1980).

STORY, JOSEPH. COMMENTARIES ON THE CONFLICT OF LAWS (1st ed. 1834).

Symeonides, Symeon C. *The ALI's Complex Litigation Project: Commencing the National Debate*, 54 LA. L. REV. 843 (1994).

Symeonides, Symeon C. *The Judicial Acceptance of the Second Conflicts Restatement: A Mixed Blessing*, 56 MD. L. REV. 1248 (1997).

Symeonides, Symeon C. *Choice of Law in American Courts in 1997*, 46 AM. J. COMP. L. 233 (1998).

Symeonides, Symeon C. *Choice of Law in American Courts in 1998*, 47 AM. J. COMP. L. 327 (1998).

Symeonides, Symeon C. *The Need for a Third Conflicts Restatement (and a Proposal for Torts Conflicts)*, 75 IND. L.J. 438 (2000).

Tobin, Briggs L. Comment, *The 'Limited Generosity' Class Action and A Uniform Choice of Law Rule: An Approach to Fair and Effective Mass-Tort Punitive Damage Adjudication in the Federal Courts*, 38 EMORY L.J. 457 (1989).

Twerski, Aaron D. *With Liberty and Justice for All: An Essay on Agent Orange and Choice of Law*, 52 BROOK. L. REV. 341 (1986).

Von Mehren Arthur T. & Donald T. Trautman. *Constitutional Control of Choice of Law: Some Reflections on* Hague, 10 HOFSTRA L. REV. 35 (1981).

Weinberg, Louise. *Choice of Law and Minimal Scrutiny*, 49 U. CHI. L. REV. 440 (1982).

Weinberg, Louise. *A Structural Revision of the Conflicts Restatement*, 75 IND. L.J. 473 (2000).

WEINSTEIN, JACK B. INDIVIDUAL JUSTICE IN MASS TORT LITIGATION (1995).

Weintraub, Russell J. *Methods for Resolving Conflict-of-Laws Problems in Mass Tort Litigation*, 1989 U. ILL. L. REV. 129 (1989).

WESTLAKE, JOHN. A TREATISE ON PRIVATE INTERNATIONAL LAW (1922).

White, G. Edward. *From Sociological Jurisprudence to Realism: Jurisprudence and Social Change in Early Twentieth-Century America*, in PATTERNS of AMERICAN LEGAL THOUGHT (1978).

WHITE, G. EDWARD. TORT LAW IN AMERICA: AN INTELLECTUAL HISTORY (1985).

WHITE, G. EDWARD. THE AMERICAN JUDICIAL TRADITION (1988).

Whitten, Ralph U. *The Constitutional Limitations on State Choice of Law: Full Faith and Credit*, 12 MEM. ST. U.L. REV. 1 (1981).

Whitten, Ralph U. *The Constitutional Limitations on State Choice of Law: Due Process*, 9 HASTINGS CONST. L.Q. 851 (1982).

Yntema, Hessel E. *The Hornbook Method and the Conflict of Laws*, 37 YALE L.J. 468 (1928).

Yntema, Hessel E. *Contract and Conflict of Laws: "Autonomy" in Choice of Law in the United States*, 1 N.Y.L.F. 46 (1955).

Index

About the Author

EDWIN SCOTT FRUEHWALD is a Legal Writing Instructor at Hofstra University School of Law. He has taught legal writing, appellate advocacy, legislation, advanced civil procedure, jurisprudence, and legal ethics at Hofstra, the University of Alabama, and Roger Williams University. He has published several articles in law reviews on choice of law, constitutional law, bankruptcy, statutory analysis, and copyright.